FEASTS

FEASTS

MENUS FOR HOME-COOKED CELEBRATIONS

LESLIE NEWMAN

HarperCollins*Publishers*

FIRST EDITION

DESIGNED BY JOEL AVIROM

Library of Congress Cataloging-in-Publication Data
Newman, Leslie.
    Feasts : menus for home-cooked celebrations / Leslie Newman. — 1st ed.
        p.   cm.
    ISBN 0-06-016467-0
    1. Quantity cookery.   2. Cookery, International.   3. Menus.
    I. Title.
    TX820.N48   1990
    641.5'7—dc20   89-46550

90 91 92 93 94   RRD   10 9 8 7 6 5 4 3 2 1

To David and Nathan and Catherine,
who have made my life a feast

▲

I never see any home cooking.
All I get is fancy stuff.

—DUKE OF EDINBURGH

C O N T E N T S

▲

ACKNOWLEDGMENTS

▲

At last, I get to say thank you:

To Paula Wolfert, whose talent is exceeded only by her generosity. Thank you for your friendship, your faith, and your help. Truly, you are the godmother of this book.

To Susan Friedland, who brought the parental principle of Tough Love to editing. Thank you for making me do the impossible, for making me laugh while I did it, and for making me feel—always, amazingly—like your only author.

To Arlene Donovan, my extraordinary agent. Thank you for boldly going where you had not gone before.

To Bette Publicker, who brought calm to the kitchen and baked cookies for two hundred. Thank you also for making soup just for me.

To my copy editor, Susan Derecskey, who valiantly dotted i's, crossed t's, and righted wrongs.

To Ruth Bronz, Craig Claiborne, Sam Cohn, Dacotah, Beulah England, Bert Greene, Suzanne Hamlin, Mary Nelson Kinloch, Maureen Lambray and Tom Carney, Anna Moore, Rose Newman, Nicholas Noyes, Maricel Presilla, Julie Sahni, Sayed Shah, Victoria Traube, and Punky. And they know why.

To the New York Knicks, who keep cooking with me.

To Warren Picower and the staff of Food & Wine.

To Lounge Lizard, the warmest reptile I ever knew.

To everyone who kept me company in the kitchen.

To everyone who ever ate at my table.

And to Bobby Drivas, who left the feast too soon.

INTRODUCTION

▲

I f you want to know how to feed a multitude, ask the people who've
been doing it for centuries—the vast families of peasants and farmers
and laborers who struggle to put bread on the table but serve up great
feasts to mark their harvests and holy days and births and marriages
and deaths.

The Hester Street *balabustah* who kept the carp swimming in the
bathtub while she got ready to make gefilte fish for tomorrow night's
seder, the Moroccan woman in the courtyard working the grains for
her couscous, the *fermière* lovingly tucking home-preserved goose into
her Sunday cassoulet—they didn't talk about entertaining. Or gourmet
cooking. And they—who raised four, five, six children in cramped quarters and scrubbed and cleaned and did the laundry by hand and then left
the dough to rise and the soup to simmer while they "helped out" in the
store or the fields—they, our grandmothers and great-grandmothers,
would surely be amused to hear that "we don't have time to cook like that
any more because we work now."

Time and money are valid concerns, of course, and will be dealt with.
But there is, I think, a simpler and more insidious reason why the last
decade has seen so many people spending so much time and money in
restaurants that seem like a party instead of giving the party themselves.
And the reason is fear—a fear that, ironically, grew out of what began as
a laudable demystification and simplification of haute cuisine.

The Gastronomic Revolution accomplished a great deal of good but,
like so many revolutions, finally went to extremes that intimidated the
very people it was supposed to liberate. It began—gloriously—in the
early sixties, as we cooked our first coq au vin and invited everyone over
to celebrate our love affair with the American woman who had begun "to
take a lot of the la-dee-dah out of French cooking because I think a lot of

it before was a sort of one-upmanship and We Happy Few and all that."
Alas, by the early eighties, one-upmanship was back with a vengeance as
home cooks anxiously "plated" pastiches of Guérard and Giradet and tried
to keep up with the trends set by the new Happy Few. We'd stopped
being terrified of using the wrong fork only to become terrified of serving
the wrong lettuce.

(True story, I swear: At the height of this Foodie Frenzy, a career-
minded friend of mine got married and suddenly realized she knew "nothing, but *nothing,* about cooking." She solved the problem by rushing to a
culinary academy and signing up for two courses—"How to Boil Water"
and "Pâtés and Terrines.")

Happily, basic human hungers reassert themselves. In two icons of
contemporary culture, *The Big Chill* and *thirtysomething,* large non-
nuclear "families" are constantly cooking together and eating together,
celebrating their small triumphs and fortifying themselves with food and
friendship against the "cold world out there."

Feasting.

It is the Biblical table set for us in the wilderness. It is M. F. K. Fisher's
"communion of more than our bodies when bread is broken and wine
drunk." (And when my cup runneth over, I don't worry about the vin-
tage.) We may be too busy to cook every day, but surely we can still find
time to feast, to make something special for the special moments in our
lives.

A feast is a grandmother's favorite dish, cooked for the family on her
eightieth birthday. A feast is loaves and fishes, enough for everyone.
Humble, hospitable Philemon's suddenly bottomless pitcher. The Cratch-
its' Christmas goose. Chicken every Sunday, and cowpeas and rice for
luck in the new year.

Anyone with money can call a caterer, and anyone with money and a
can opener can serve caviar. But money can't buy the plain cook's gift,
the patient and homely magic that turns bones into broth, and broth and
pork and cabbage and beans into great stews that even the rich and
famous—*especially* the rich and famous—never get enough of. Money
cannot buy the love that makes a feast.

Entertaining is what we do for others. Feasting is what we do for
ourselves. Every time a frugal family sets a lavish table, it celebrates its
own survival.

And the celebration begins in the kitchen.

FEASTS

1

The Nature of the Feast

I t is the best of times, it is the worst of times.

It's party time.

And at first glance, this seems to be the kind of party we all dread. Your husband's cousin's second wife invites you and twenty people you don't know to spend Christmas Eve together in front of a blazing Yule log tape loop on local TV. You burn your mouth on mulled wine. They blow a fuse. She lights some candles and goes on cooking, and everybody crowds into the kitchen, talking and tasting. It can't be two in the morning when you leave, and you can't remember when you laughed so much or swapped phone numbers with so many people. And you didn't even want to come to this party!

Christmas Day, on the other hand, is the kind of fête we all look forward to. You're sipping champagne with everyone you know at the annual Open House that pays off your best friend's social debts. No fuse will ever blow here. And, as everyone keeps assuring the host, everything is just delicious, it's delightful, it's de-lovely. So why are you looking at your watch? Why is this perfect party so . . . lifeless? And why was last night so lively? What's your husband's cousin's second wife's secret?

She's bemused by the question. There is no secret. "But I'm so glad you had a good time," she says, beaming. "I had a good time myself."

And that, of course, *is* the secret.

You, the host, are the life of the party. Your guests will have a good time only if you have a good time. And you can have a good time only if you know what you're doing. Here, then, is how to know what you're doing and have a good time doing it.

Plan a menu that suits your budget, your schedule, and your skills. For most of us this means not reproducing Paul Bocuse's dinner for the President of France. It doesn't mean you have to settle for Aunt Fanny's pot roast, although I'd rather eat a good pot roast than a bad pastiche any day.

The food for a special occasion should be special, but—no matter what the glossy magazines show and tell you—special is not a synonym for expensive or fancy. To me and Mr. Webster, *special* simply means "out of the ordinary."

Special is steak for poor poets and sausages for swells, a barbecue in a blizzard, a bride's chocolate cake, a taste of somewhere you have never traveled.

Homemade ice cream is special anytime, anywhere.

And oysters and caviar are special, of course. But so is the first local corn, which is always the reason for a feast at our house.

In fact, the only food I will never make for a party is Party Food—miniature quiches and médaillons of I-think-it's veal, fancy fare that's suitable for all occasions and special to none. Party Food is a gastronomic gift certificate. Worse still, Party Food is last-minute food, easy for professionals, difficult for you and me; a caterer's "no-fuss supper for twenty" becomes a home cook's nightmare when fillets of beef must be sliced while pans of snow peas are sautéed and both must be served at once.

Forget the fillets. Go for the gulyas.

Gulyas is typical of the food that tempts me both as cook and eater, the food that fills this book. Gulyas has a history and a geography, which is the history and geography of the ordinary people who make it a grand gulyas for special occasions. This grand gulyas has so much taste and texture that its frugality is hard to believe. Best of all, it can and should be completely prepared up to a month in advance and frozen; come party time, just reheat and serve with buttered noodles or plain steamed potatoes and a quick, cool cucumber salad that was also made in advance. Now, that's *my* idea of a "no-fuss supper for twenty!"

And it was terrific for 200 last New Year's Eve.

If you're wondering how you cook for 200, the answer is: you don't. You cook for 20 eight times. Yes, I know, 20 x 8 = 160, not 200. But I also know that at 12:00 A.M., 160 portions is enough for 200 people. Entertaining has its own equations:

Guests eat less when it's late than when it's early.

Guests eat less standing up than sitting down.

The larger the party, the less food is consumed per capita.

The larger the party, the more you should do in advance.

And cooking for a crowd—which I define as any number too large to fit around my table—has its own caveats:

Never serve food with bones. Even if it can be picked up, like spareribs or chicken, it's messy and hard to manage in a crowd.

Never serve food that needs cutting up, even if it's boneless.

Never serve food so soupy that sauces run into each other on the plate and flavors are blurred.

Avoid food that *must* be eaten ice cold or piping hot, because it may not be that way by the time everyone gets to it.

Provide at least one or two dishes that can be enjoyed by guests who have cut down on or given up meat.

Never serve shellfish to a large group. Too many people are allergic to some or all kinds of seafood; it doesn't hold up or reheat well; and —unless you're celebrating an inheritance—you can't afford it anyway.

Never serve anything in aspic. Nobody likes aspic except caterers who use it as edible plastic wrap.

Never serve a crowd frog's legs, kidneys, or blood sausage. These things are too good to be wasted on the masses.

So what (besides gulyas) *can* you serve to two hundred people?

Taramasalata with Fennel and Cucumbers

Lemon Veal Meatballs

▲

Pastitsio

Mixed Green Salad

Carrot, Orange, and Pomegranate Salad

▲

The New Year's Eve Fruit Compote

That was 1986. Other years have taken us to Russia for Siberian beef dumplings and kasha with toasted walnuts, to New Orleans for red beans and rice, to the Middle East for meat baked with cracked wheat and pine nuts, to South Africa for a cuisine created by Malay slaves, to China for stuffed flower mushrooms and long life noodles.

But no matter what the menu, the modus operandi for that midnight meal is always the same. On the fourth Friday of every November, the turkey platter and the gravy boat go back in the cupboard and the New Year's Eve recipes go up on the kitchen wall. For the next four weeks, I'll spend one day (or part thereof) a week preparing the feast.

Anything freezable is prepared in batches to serve twenty. Eight batches—two prepared on each weekly cooking day—are enough for two hundred. Each batch, when cool, is transferred to an aluminum foil roasting pan, which is then wrapped twice in heavy-duty aluminum foil and again, snugly, in a clear plastic dry-cleaning bag, and frozen. On New Year's Eve the just-thawed pans are reheated, the seasonings muted by freezing are perked up, and any finishing touches are added. Dessert is easy and unchanging: a huge Armagnac-laced compote of dried and fresh fruits (prepared two days earlier) and home-baked cookies.

Not everyone wants to cook for two hundred. God knows, I never did.

In fact, it only happened because I got lazy. As 1974 turned into 1975 and my husband waved wildly at another snow-covered, off-duty cab, I wearily vowed to spend next New Year's Eve at home. Our friends would just have to come to us.

And they did. Forty the first year, eighty-five the next. A hundred and thirty, a hundred and eighty, *it just kept growing.* . . . And I still have a few seconds of sheer animal terror when two hundred people storm the table at once. But the two hundred are our family and our old friends and our new friends and friends of friends and our friends' kids and our kids' friends, gathered again to watch the golden ball drop, kiss today goodbye, and eat the first meal of the new year together. And preparing the meal is a labor of love.

But there is no less love—just a lot less labor—in making a "little dinner" for eight. After all, such little dinners are where we renew and deepen the friendships that make us want to come together for grand celebrations. Without small parties, there would be no big parties.

For the cook, parties of any size are easier when preparations are staggered over several days. If possible, make any necessary stocks and seasoning mixtures conveniently in advance. And when you plan a menu of dishes that can be made ahead of time, make sure they don't have to be made ahead at the same time.

Before you begin to cook, clear time and space for the pleasure of cooking. Set aside a weekend afternoon, a weekday evening, or even a few of the wee small hours if that suits your schedule and your biorhythms. And then prepare your workplace as a professional would:

▲ Clear the decks. This means making your kitchen look totally unlike the magazine kitchens we *think* the professionals cook in. (I couldn't even make a peanut-butter sandwich with those herb pots all over the counter and those baskets hanging in my face.) Remove any appliances you will not be using—the espresso maker, the coffee grinder, the spice mill, even the state-of-the-art mixer, and, yes, the food processor. Clear your work surface of absolutely everything that does not pertain to your purpose today.

▲ Put your recipes where you can refer to them easily while you cook.

▲ Put your garbage can (preferably a large, open one) where you can reach it easily while you cook.

▲ Roll up your sleeves, sharpen your knives, and feel smug—without spending a cent, you have just streamlined your kitchen.

And you needn't spend a fortune preparing your table for a feast. Presentable dinner plates and wine glasses can often be had so cheaply at restaurant-supply houses and discount home-furnishings stores that a moderate budget might accommodate, say, twenty of each. Look for sales, and then look also for cotton napkins and simple stainless flatware. Or, if you'd rather mix than match, you can set a very festive table with flea-market finds.

For larger groups I rent rinse-and-return forks and dessert spoons and (plain white, please) china; good-quality paper napkins and plastic tumblers are, because they have to be, acceptable.

Paper plates are unthinkable.

Chafing dishes, too, seem to me to violate the spirit of home cooking, and for small- or medium-size feasts there are easy alternatives. Earthenware, for instance, brings the warmth of tradition to a table while retaining enough heat to keep a kibbeh or a gulyas or a pot of richly simple Midnight Pea Soup piping hot through second helpings. But at extra-large gatherings, a chafing dish may be a necessary evil. Try to find one that doesn't remind you of buffets in hotel dining rooms, and then serve your food from it yourself.

For food that doesn't need fuel underneath, I have an odd but attractive lot of serving pieces. I seem to find them wherever I go, and the keen pleasure I feel in their discovery (despite a tendency to find the largest when farthest from home) is evoked again every time I use them. The heavy blue-flowered basin that I bought for six dollars in a barn long ago has a crazed glaze and a fine crack running down one side, but it just wouldn't be New Year's Eve if we served The New Year's Eve Fruit Compote from any other bowl.

I like to serve, to fill my friends' plates with the good food I have prepared for them. At intimate gatherings, I feel the intimacy would be broken if strangers passed the bread and poured the wine. Even at a buffet, where there are servers or guests might serve themselves, I always serve one of the dishes.

It makes a connection. It makes a difference. It's one of the things that makes a guest write, "You may be cooking for hundreds of people, but we always take it personally." Which in turn makes me feel wonderful. And it's just this sharing—of good feelings and good food—that makes a feast.

I'm happy to share the work too. I mean, I love to cook, but when five pounds of onions have to be chopped I'm ready to spread my love around. Naturally, I turn first to my nearest and dearest. Who will help me chop my onions? Who will help me bake my bread? (The Little Red Hen had the right idea but the wrong friends.)

Even if your loved ones can't cook, do not think—and for heaven's sake, do not think out loud—that they are useless. Almost everybody can, as the saying goes, bring something to the party. A spouse who can't boil water can shuck two dozen ears of corn while you boil the water. A friend who comes over to chat while you're folding wontons will just naturally start folding wontons, too.

I once read that children could be sent out to pick vine leaves for the cheese tray, and I always wanted to pass that along.

Actually, there's quite a lot that children can do—setting the table, going to the store, taking phone messages, taking guests' coats. In addition, teenagers can handle invitations and RSVPs and occasionally dazzle their parents by computerizing the lists. Small children can shell peas, put rolls in a basket, keep Grandpa company, pass simple hors d'oeuvres, and go tell Daddy that Mommy needs him right away. Small children cannot peel carrots because they don't know when to stop.

The one "kitchen aid" I couldn't feast without is something borrowed from the pros—prep sheets. A prep sheet is to a kitchen what "Day-At-A-Glance" is to an office; it lists everything that has to be done. I write mine on a legal pad, labeling consecutive pages Monday, Tuesday, Wednesday, and so on through the day or night of the big (or small) event.

Prep sheets for a party should include not only kitchen details but all party-related tasks. Tuesday's sheet, for example, might tell you to "take dress to cleaner on way to work" and "get 1 pt. berries (for compote) on way home" as well as to "chop ¼ c. parsley (for soup and for kasha)."

Each task gets checked off as it's done; if, God forbid, Tuesday's parsley doesn't get minced, it's moved onto Wednesday's sheet, which gets hung up in the kitchen before you go to bed Tuesday night.

This isn't compulsive, it's just efficient. And in our busy lives, efficiency is everything. Efficiency means that nothing, including your sanity, gets lost in the shuffle, and you don't discover at dessert time that you forgot the berries. Prep sheets mean never having to say you're sorry.

Of course, even with prep sheets to organize the labor, there's still some labor I can live without. So I do. Believing that a penny not spent is a penny saved, I take all the pennies I saved by not hiring a caterer and hire someone to do the real dirty work: cleaning up. This makes me a great host because it not only stops me from scraping plates in the middle of the evening, it has me practically dancing on the table.

There are little things that make me happy while I'm cooking, too. Little things like two ounces of Russian Beluga. If somebody gives you caviar, eat it. Don't save it for a party and spread it thin on tiny canapés. Eat it all, all by yourself, while you cook kasha for the party. You will feel like a guest of honor in your own kitchen.

And you will make *wonderful* kasha.

The hardest time to be happy about your party is the day of the party. Leave as little as possible to be done then. Even finishing touches can be too much when they have to be applied to the hors d'oeuvres, the appetizer, the main course, the salad, the dessert, the house, and you.

If you're having a buffet, set up the bar and the table the night before. Try out the serving bowls and platters you plan to use, and decide how you will arrange them. Make sure that guests can move smoothly and swiftly around the table and that you and your food can move smoothly and swiftly between the table and the kitchen. The table for a sit-down dinner can also be set in advance; turn plates and glasses over to keep them spotless.

Before a grand gathering, take a slow, sharp-eyed stroll through your house, from the front door (*are there enough hangers?*) through the living room (*are there enough ashtrays?*), the bedrooms (*when did that light bulb go out?*), the bathrooms (*lots of pretty paper handtowels . . . but no wastebasket to toss them in?*), and the kitchen. Post a detailed menu on the refrigerator so you won't forget to serve the chutney. Stash a minimal makeup kit and pocket mirror in a kitchen drawer for emergency repairs. Put out clean potholders and clean kitchen towels (I always put out more than I think I'll need because I always end up needing them all). Put a big bottle of ice water right up front in the refrigerator; cooking for a crowd is thirsty work (and alcohol is best consumed afterwards, when you can safely drink to your success). Before a small party, ignore all of the above, but do decide who will sit where at dinner. Before any size party, hide your chenille bathrobe from college.

And try to think rationally about what you will wear at the party, because it takes planning to be glamorous in the living room and comfortable in the kitchen at the same time. Anything that floats, flows, billows, or swirls can be hazardous to your health. Ditto, dangling earrings and slippery slippers. Come party time, I step into a prized pair of pumps that I can step right out of when I have to move fast with heavy pots and pans. And I wear my breakaway jewelry—bangles and collars, no clasps, instant on and off—because even a thin chain will turn into a branding iron in seconds when you're bending over a hot oven. I've got my finery all figured out. But:

"Mom, do you realize there are people who've *never* seen you without an apron?"

Aprons. You can't party with them, you can't party without them. All you can do, I've decided, is to keep one nice one for special occasions and make sure it's pressed before you put it on. And try to remember to take it off once in a while. But if you forget, don't apologize; there are people who've never seen Julia Child without an apron either.

Having thought of everything, you now have nothing to be anxious about. True, you will probably feel a touch of stage fright, but that is nothing to be anxious about, either. There is no such thing as a carefree host, nor should there be. Hosts are *supposed* to care, and their heightened energy is what a good party runs on.

To sustain your energy, try to take a break before the party. Magazine articles always find a bubble bath relaxing, but I can't relax when I have to climb out and scrub the tub afterward. I don't nap either, not really, but I do get away from it all before a big evening by *telling* everybody I'm napping. Lie back, listen to silence, listen to music, listen to the sweet sound of somebody else answering the telephone.

And don't worry about losing track of time. There is one person in every household who, shortly before a party, always begins announcing the time, thus: "It's seven o'clock and the ice isn't here. It's seven-fifteen, where is everybody? It's seven-thirty, shouldn't we call about the ice?? It's quarter of eight, what if nobody comes???"

Firmly order this person to go into a closet and say these things where you cannot hear them.

And finally, briefly, let us speak of the unspeakable: disasters. The burnt and the raw. The cheeseless cheese soufflé. When Bad Things Happen To Good Cooks.

Most of them don't have to happen, of course. Pay attention, especially when measuring ingredients, combining ingredients, and setting oven temperatures. Get one of those little multi-channel timers and time everything; during the party, appoint someone in the kitchen to come and get you when it beeps, or, better yet, tuck it in a pocket so you'll hear it yourself. And avoid dishes that require split-second timing anyway.

Because food goes through a lot of changes as it heats and/or cools, always adjust seasonings cautiously, and then wait a few minutes and taste again before adding more of anything. Especially salt.

Remember that four pans of pastitsio in the oven will take longer to heat than the one pan you usually make. Remember that one very large pan will take longer to heat than two smaller pans. Remember to turn on the oven.

And when a disaster does happen, what then? Should you really "say nothing and they won't know the difference"? Well, yes and no. If you say nothing, they may just think *you* don't know the difference. On the other hand, you can't go from guest to guest with your tale of woe, like the Ancient Mariner. And you can't very well announce, "Dinner is served and I'm sorry about the roast."

When in doubt, think of Julia. When you must admit a defeat, do it briskly and cheerfully—and wryly, if you're good at that—and then *forget it*. If you can forget it and have a good time, everyone else will too. And then you can really forget it and have a great time.

You'll be the life of the party once again. And it just might be the best party of your life.

2

Feasts for All Seasons & Reasons

HOME COOKING

▲▲▲▲▲▲▲▲▲▲▲▲▲▲▲▲▲▲▲▲▲▲

Tarhonya

Chicken Paprikash

▲

Cream Cheese Pound Cake

*Small Glasses of Slivovitz or
Szilva Palinka
(Plum or Apricot Brandy)*

A LITTLE
NIGHT FOOD

▲▲▲▲▲▲▲▲▲▲▲▲▲▲▲▲▲▲▲▲▲▲▲▲▲▲

*Tartare of Salmon and
Norwegian Sardines*

▲

Midnight Pea Soup

▲

*Softly Frozen
Lingonberry Cream*

RED BEANS
AND RICELY
YOURS

▲▲▲▲▲▲▲▲▲▲▲▲▲▲▲▲▲▲▲▲▲▲▲▲

Oyster and Fennel Soup

▲

Royal Street Red Beans

Steamed Rice

Tangy Mixed Leaf Salad

French Bread

▲

Real Caramel Ice Cream

THE ROAD TO
HONG KONG

▲▲▲▲▲▲▲▲▲▲▲▲▲▲▲▲▲▲▲▲▲▲

Stuffed Flower Mushrooms

Wontons When You Want

▲

Congee

▲

Tea and Oranges

HUNGRILY
EVER AFTER

▲▲▲▲▲▲▲▲▲▲▲▲▲▲▲▲▲▲▲▲▲▲▲▲▲

Caesar Salad

▲

Meat Loaf

Mashed Baked Potatoes

▲

The Bride's Chocolate Cake

JUST PLAIN FANCY

▲▲▲▲▲▲▲▲▲▲▲▲▲▲▲▲▲▲▲▲▲▲▲▲▲▲▲▲▲▲

*Chicken Liver Mousse
with Currants*

▲

Chilled Minted Pea Soup

▲

Fricassee of Mussels

Steamed Rice

▲

Italian Wild Cherries Jubilee

PIGGING OUT IN THE DEEP SOUTH

▲▲▲▲▲▲▲▲▲▲▲▲▲▲▲▲▲▲▲▲▲▲▲▲▲▲▲▲

*Smothered Pork Chops from
Miss Ruby's Café*

Hoppin' John

*Whipped Sweet Potatoes with
Sweet Spices*

A Mess of Greens

Old-fashioned Corn Bread

▲

Lemon Buttermilk Ice

DINNER AT TABLE MOUNTAIN

The Cape Malay Cooking
of South Africa

▲▲▲▲▲▲▲▲▲▲▲▲▲▲▲▲▲▲▲▲▲▲▲▲▲▲▲▲

Coconut and Carrot Sambal

Bobotie

Geel Rys

▲

Mixed Red Salad

▲

Double Espresso Ice Cream

INDIAN WITHOUT TEARS

▲▲▲▲▲▲▲▲▲▲▲▲▲▲▲▲▲▲▲▲▲▲▲▲▲▲▲▲

*Chick-pea and
Roasted Cashew Puree
with Toasted Indian Bread*

*Calcutta Popcorn with
Julie Sahni's Fresh Coriander
and Mint Chutney*

▲

Tandoori Shrimp

*Cucumber, Walnut, and
Dill Raita*

Buttered Basmati Rice

▲

Preserved Ginger Ice Cream

A SPLENDID TIME

▲▲▲▲▲▲▲▲▲▲▲▲▲▲▲▲▲▲▲▲▲▲▲▲▲▲▲▲

*Couscous and Roasted
Pepper Salad*

▲

A Grand Ragout of Vegetables

*Bert Greene's Long-baked
Tomatoes*

▲

Frozen Peanut Butter Pie

FROM RUSSIA WITH LOVE

▲▲▲▲▲▲▲▲▲▲▲▲▲▲▲▲▲▲▲▲▲▲▲▲▲

Oysters and Caviar

▲

*Pelmeni with Mustard and
Sour Cream Sauce*

*Kasha with Wild Mushrooms
and Toasted Walnuts*

Endive and Beet Salad

▲

*The New Year's Eve
Fruit Compote*

AN ARABIAN NIGHT

▲▲▲▲▲▲▲▲▲▲▲▲▲▲▲▲▲▲▲▲▲▲▲▲▲▲

Bidon Lebna

▲

Kibbeh-Bil-Sanieh

Batinjan-Bil-Laban

Carrot and Orange Salad

▲

*Compote of Apricots with
Toasted Almonds
and Thick Yogurt Cream*

FED UP

▲▲▲▲▲▲▲▲▲▲▲▲▲▲▲▲▲▲▲▲▲▲▲▲▲▲

*Poached Chicken with
Mediterranean Tuna
Mayonnaise*

▲

*Escarole Soup with Eggs
and Cheese*

Crusty Bread

▲

Applesauce for Grown-ups

Grandma's Butter Cookies

LIGHT IN AUGUST

▲▲▲▲▲▲▲▲▲▲▲▲▲▲▲▲▲▲▲▲▲▲▲▲▲

Mojitos

▲

*Fresh Herb and
Cheese Custards*

▲

Mussels in Sorrel Sauce

Crusty Bread

▲

Red Fruits in Vanilla Cream

THE LAST CRAB OF SUMMER

▲▲▲▲▲▲▲▲▲▲▲▲▲▲▲▲▲▲▲▲▲▲▲▲▲▲

Buster Crabs Béarnaise

▲

Andouille and Oyster Gumbo

Steamed Rice

▲

Fresh Lime Ice Cream

AND THE DAYS GROW SHORT

▲▲▲▲▲▲▲▲▲▲▲▲▲▲▲▲▲▲▲▲▲▲▲

*Smoked Chicken, Celery Root,
and Tongue in
Horseradish Rémoulade*

▲

Alsatian Lentil Soup

▲

Mixed Leaf Salad

▲

*Warm Compote of
Autumn Fruits
with Armagnac Ice Cream*

BARBECUE IN A BLIZZARD

▲▲▲▲▲▲▲▲▲▲▲▲▲▲▲▲▲▲▲▲▲▲▲

North Carolina Chopped Barbecue

Sassy Slaw

Smallville Potato Salad

My Blue Heavenly Corn Bread

▲

Frozen Fruit Salad

GRECIAN HARMONIES

▲▲▲▲▲▲▲▲▲▲▲▲▲▲▲▲▲▲▲▲▲▲▲

*Taramasalata with Fennel
and Cucumbers*

Lemon Veal Meatballs

▲

Pastitsio

Mixed Green Salad

*Carrot, Orange, and
Pomegranate Salad*

▲

Paula's Black Grape Ice

COOK'S NIGHT OUT

▲▲▲▲▲▲▲▲▲▲▲▲▲▲▲▲▲▲▲▲▲▲▲

*Hearts of Romaine
with Buttermilk Bacon
Blue-Cheese Dressing*

▲

Steak by David

Roasted Potato Wedges

▲

*Peaches with the Last
of the Wine*

SUNDAY DUNCH

▲▲▲▲▲▲▲▲▲▲▲▲▲▲▲▲▲▲▲▲▲▲▲

Rillettes of Smoked Trout

*Creamed Herring with Oranges
and Lemons*

Smoked Fish

Hungarian Cucumber Salad

Three Onion Flan

▲

My Mother's Banana Bread

LES
BONS TEMPS

▲▲▲▲▲▲▲▲▲▲▲▲▲▲▲▲▲▲▲▲▲▲▲▲

Country Ham Balls with
Hot-and-Sweet Mustard

▲

Shrimp Étouffée

Steamed Rice

▲

French Bean and Tasso Salad

▲

Vanilla Lovers' Vanilla
Ice Cream with
Hot Buttered Rum Sauce

MY FAVORITE
CHINESE SIT-DOWN
DINNER

▲▲▲▲▲▲▲▲▲▲▲▲▲▲▲▲▲▲▲▲▲▲▲▲▲

Cantonese Poached Shrimp with
Chive and Ginger Dipping Sauce

▲

Velvet Corn and Crab Soup

▲

Szechuan Peppercorn Duck Breasts

Eggplant Coins with
Many Treasures

▲

Long Life Noodles with
Spicy Meat Sauce

▲

Bittersweet Chocolate Ice Cream

GUNS AND
BUTTER

A Feast of the Mujahedeen

▲▲▲▲▲▲▲▲▲▲▲▲▲▲▲▲▲▲▲▲▲▲▲▲

Aushe Keshida

▲

Skewers of Grilled Lamb

Basmati Rice Palow with
Leeks and Dill

Spinach Cooked with Sorrel

▲

Raspberries with
Thick Yogurt Cream and
Orange Blossom Honey

LIKE MOTHER
USED TO MAKE

A Pot-and-Pan-Asian Feast

▲▲▲▲▲▲▲▲▲▲▲▲▲▲▲▲▲▲▲▲▲▲▲▲

Ants Climbing a Tree

▲

Javanese Spareribs

Basmati Rice and
Sweet Corn Pilaf

Thai Cucumber Salad

▲

Toasted Coconut Ice Cream

O SAUERKRAUT,
CREATED IN
PARADISE

▲▲▲▲▲▲▲▲▲▲▲▲▲▲▲▲▲▲▲▲▲▲▲▲

Transylvania Gulyas of
Sauerkraut and Pork

Steamed or Boiled Potatoes

Marinated Cucumbers with
Sour Cream and Dill

Dark Bread or Rye Rolls

▲

Seckel Pears in Red Wine

HOME COOKING

▲▲▲▲▲▲▲▲▲▲▲▲▲▲▲▲▲▲▲▲▲▲▲▲▲▲▲▲▲

Tarhonya

Chicken Paprikash

▲

Cream Cheese Pound Cake

*Small Glasses of Slivovitz
or Szilva Palinka
(Plum or Apricot Brandy)*

▼

Chicken paprikash is not spectacular, just quick and easy and delicious and inexpensive—which, come to think of it, IS spectacular. You can make it as much as a day ahead but you don't have to. For me it's a family dinner, but it would also be great to dish out at eight to friends you invited at six.

I wrote that note fifteen years ago when I wrote this recipe down for my daughter—not for then, when she was seven, but for "someday." Now, suddenly, it's someday. She just came home with the keys to her first apartment, and as I hug her I realize: from now on she will be *going* home.

But she's not going far, and we like her new place and her pride in it. Her brother comes over to congratulate her, and then her father comes home and we drink champagne, and while I am making chicken paprikash, she sits in the kitchen telling me about *her* kitchen.

There are grander gifts I could give her tonight than this recipe, but it's the thought that counts, a thought I hope she will take from my kitchen into hers: it's in simple family dinners that we find our real sustenance and in sudden friendly feasts that we really feel the joy of cooking.

▲

Tarhonya

BUTTERED EGG BARLEY

*T*arhonya, barley-shaped egg pasta available at Hungarian markets, is made in two sizes. Fine tarhonya is usually served as a delicate garnish in soups. Coarse tarhonya is more like tiny dumplings, the perfect partner for a richly sauced gulyas or paprikash. SERVES 10 TO 12

4 tablespoons unsalted butter
1 cup finely chopped onions
2 cups coarse tarhonya
2 cups chicken stock
1/4 teaspoon Hungarian sweet paprika
1/8 teaspoon freshly ground black pepper
Salt

1 In a heavy 3-quart saucepan or flameproof casserole, melt the butter over moderately low heat. Stir in the onions, cover, and let steam in the butter until tender and translucent, about 5 minutes. Uncover, add the tarhonya, and stir for 1 or 2 minutes to coat with butter. Raise the heat to moderate and slowly pour in the chicken stock and 1½ cups water. Add the paprika, black pepper, and salt to taste.

2 When the liquid comes to a boil, cover the pot, reduce the heat to moderately low, and simmer until the tarhonya is cooked through but still slightly al dente, about 20 minutes. Uncover and fluff with a large fork. If the tarhonya is too moist, continue to lift and turn it lightly with your fork while cooking, uncovered, over low heat. When all the liquid has evaporated, the pieces of tarhonya should be separate, like grains of rice, and tender but pleasantly chewy. Tarhonya is probably best served immediately, but if allowed to cool completely before being covered and refrigerated, it reheats surprisingly well, especially in a microwave oven.

Chicken Paprikash

SERVES 10

8 pounds chicken breasts, legs, and/or thighs
4 tablespoons unsalted butter
2 tablespoons safflower or peanut oil
3 cups finely chopped onions
2 teaspoons finely chopped garlic
4 tablespoons Hungarian sweet paprika (see Note)
¼ teaspoon cayenne
3⅓ cups chicken stock
⅓ cup dry vermouth
2 tablespoons tomato paste
⅛ teaspoon sugar
Salt and freshly ground black pepper
1½ cups sour cream, at room temperature
3 tablespoons flour
2 tablespoons finely chopped flat-leaf parsley
2 tablespoons finely chopped fresh dill

1 Pat the chicken dry. In a heavy large skillet, heat the butter with the oil over moderate heat. Add as many pieces of chicken as will fit without crowding and sauté until lightly golden on both sides, 6 to 8 minutes; do not let brown. Remove the chicken to a large bowl and set aside. Repeat this process until all the chicken has been sautéed and transferred to the bowl. Add the onions and garlic to the skillet; lower the heat slightly and cook, stirring, until tender but not brown. Add the paprika and cayenne and cook, stirring, for 1 minute. Return the chicken to the skillet, reserving any juices that have accumulated in the bowl. Over moderately low heat, turn the chicken in the pan for 1 or 2 minutes to coat it lightly with the onion-paprika mixture. (Do this in 2 batches if necessary.) Transfer the chicken and onions to a large flameproof casserole, placing the dark meat on the bottom. Do not rinse the skillet.

2 In the skillet, combine the chicken stock, vermouth, tomato paste, sugar, and any reserved chicken juices. Season lightly with salt and pepper and simmer gently for 1 or 2 minutes, scraping and stirring to blend the flavors. Pour this sauce over the chicken in the casserole.

3 Cover the casserole and simmer over moderately low heat until the chicken is tender, 25 to 30 minutes. Remove the chicken with a slotted spoon, cover loosely, and set aside. Remove the casserole from the heat and skim most of the fat off sauce, leaving just a trace for flavor.

4 In a mixing bowl, stir the sour cream and flour until blended. Remove 2 cups of sauce from the casserole and slowly stir it into the sour cream, then gradually stir the sour cream back into the sauce in the casserole. Bring to a strong simmer, stirring constantly, and cook, uncovered, until the sauce is reduced and lightly thickened.

5 Return the chicken to the casserole. *(The recipe can be made up to a day ahead. Let cool completely, cover, and refrigerate. Return to room temperature, cover, and reheat to a simmer shortly before serving.)* Cook gently for a few minutes, just until piping hot throughout. Season with additional salt and pepper to taste and sprinkle with 1 tablespoon each of parsley and dill. Turn the chicken in the sauce, then sprinkle with the remaining parsley and dill. Serve with (but not on) Tarhonya, spätzle, or rice, and accompany with Hungarian Cucumber Salad (page 212).

NOTE For this or any other dish requiring paprika, buy only real imported Hungarian paprika and keep it in a tightly covered container in your refrigerator.

Cream Cheese Pound Cake

*E*ven at a grand family gathering where fine home-cooked food was abundant, this cake was a standout, moist and flavorful but still light enough to enjoy after a rich repast. Mary Nelson Kinloch of Virginia graciously gave me the recipe and the good news that this treasure can be made up to a month in advance. Small glasses of plum or apricot brandy are a perfect accompaniment. SERVES 12 TO 18

¾ pound (3 sticks) unsalted butter, at room temperature
8 ounces cream cheese, preferably preservative-free, at room temperature
3 cups sugar
Pinch of salt
1 teaspoon pure vanilla extract
2 teaspoons lemon extract
6 large eggs
3 cups sifted cake flour (not self-rising)

1 Preheat the oven to 325 degrees. Butter and flour a 10-inch tube pan or Bundt cake pan; invert the pan and tap it gently to knock out any excess flour.

2 In the large bowl of an electric mixer, cream the butter, cream cheese, and sugar until light and fluffy. Beat in the salt, vanilla extract, and lemon extract. Add the eggs one at a time, beating well after each addition. With the mixer on the lowest speed, gradually add the cake flour, scraping down the sides of the bowl with a rubber spatula and beating only until smooth and well blended.

3 Turn the batter into the prepared pan and level the surface. Bake for about 1½ hours or until a tester inserted in the center of the cake comes out clean. Remove from the oven and let rest in the pan for 10 minutes, then run a knife around the edges of the pan to loosen the cake. Turn it out onto a rack and let stand for an hour or more, until completely cool, before serving or wrapping for storage. *(Pound cake keeps well and so can be made well in advance; wrap snugly in aluminum foil or plastic wrap, seal in an airtight plastic bag, and refrigerate for up to 4 days, or freeze for up to 1 month. Let come to room temperature before serving.)*

A LITTLE NIGHT FOOD

▲▲▲▲▲▲▲▲▲▲▲▲▲▲▲▲▲▲▲▲▲▲▲▲▲▲▲▲▲▲▲▲▲▲▲▲▲▲▲

*Tartare of Salmon and
Norwegian Sardines*

▲

Midnight Pea Soup

▲

*Softly Frozen
Lingonberry Cream*

▼

College friends, returning to Norway, gave a farewell party I still remember thirty years later. There was punch and some frugal finger foods. They were young and poor, like us, and we were resigned to going home hungry. Then the campus clock struck twelve, and suddenly they came out bearing bowls and spoons and a great steaming tureen. "Night food," they said proudly, in Norwegian and in English, and we sat on the lantern-strung lawn at midnight eating pea soup, the best pea soup I have ever eaten.

▲

Tartare of Salmon and Norwegian Sardines

I have nothing against restaurants—without them, I'd never get a night off—but I seldom try to reproduce restaurant dishes at home. This recipe, from New York's Aquavit restaurant, is a rare exception. I make it because it requires no sous-chefs or sauce bases or salamanders, and because its elegance is easy and comfortable, and because it tastes so good that I don't want to wait for a night off to enjoy it. MAKES 8 SERVINGS

1½ pounds skinless salmon fillets
12 Norwegian canned sardines, drained, oil reserved
2 tablespoons mayonnaise, preferably homemade
½ teaspoon distilled white vinegar
8 cornichons, diced
2 tablespoons chopped capers
4 teaspoons chopped shallots
4 teaspoons chopped flat-leaf parsley
Salt and freshly ground white pepper
Lettuce leaves, for garnish
Lemon wedges, for garnish
Scandinavian crisp bread, for serving

1 To facilitate cutting, arrange the salmon fillets on a plate in a single layer, cover with plastic wrap, and place in the coldest part of the refrigerator (*not* the freezer) until cold and fairly firm. Arrange the sardines on a second plate. Cover with plastic wrap and refrigerate, like the salmon, until relatively firm.

2 With a very sharp knife, cut the salmon into ¼-inch dice. Dice the sardines and set aside separately.

(Continued)

3 In a large mixing bowl, stir the mayonnaise and vinegar to blend. Stir in the cornichons, capers, shallots, parsley, and 1 tablespoon of the oil from the sardines. Add the diced salmon and mix well. Add a little more mayonnaise, if necessary, to bind the mixture. Gently fold in the diced sardines. Season to taste with salt and pepper. *(The tartare can be prepared several hours ahead. Cover with plastic wrap and refrigerate until ready to serve.)*

4 With an ice cream scoop, form the mixture into 8 balls. Place on chilled salad plates and garnish with lettuce leaves and lemon wedges. Serve with Scandinavian crisp bread and small glasses of cold aquavit.

Midnight Pea Soup

1 pound green split peas, picked over and rinsed
1 ham bone with some meat on it or 2 smoked ham hocks
½ pound lean smoked bacon, in 1 piece
3 cups chopped onions
1½ cups sliced leeks, white part only
⅔ cup chopped celery (including some leaves)
½ cup peeled and diced carrots
¾ teaspoon finely chopped garlic
½ teaspoon crumbled dried marjoram
¼ teaspoon crumbled dried thyme
1 cup dry white wine
Salt and freshly ground pepper
Wholemeal bread and butter, for serving

1 In a heavy large saucepan or flameproof casserole, combine the split peas, ham bone, bacon, onions, leeks, celery, carrots, garlic, marjoram, thyme, wine, and 8 cups water. Bring to a boil, then reduce the heat to moderately low, skimming any foam that forms on the surface. Cover and simmer, stirring occasionally, until the peas are soft, 2 to 3 hours.

2 Remove the bacon and the ham bone. As soon as they are cool enough to handle, shred or dice any lean meat and add it to the soup; discard all fat, bones, and gristle. Simmer the soup until the peas are meltingly soft, usually about 15 minutes longer. Season with salt and pepper to taste, but remember to respect the soup's surprisingly delicate flavor. (*This soup can be prepared in advance. Let cool to room temperature, then cover and refrigerate for up to 2 days, or freeze for up to 2 months. Let return to room temperature before reheating.*) If the soup is too thick, thin it with a little water. Serve very hot with wholemeal bread and sweet butter.

Softly Frozen Lingonberry Cream

What a delicious mass of contradictions this dessert is—it's frozen but still soft, it's sweet but slightly tart, and it's Scandinavian but I made it up. SERVES 10 TO 12

4 ounces cream cheese, preferably preservative-free bulk cream cheese,
   at room temperature
Generous pinch of coarse (kosher) salt
⅔ cup sugar, preferably superfine
3½ cups Swedish wild lingonberries stirred in sugar, well chilled
1½ cups heavy cream, well chilled

1 In the bowl of an electric mixer, beat the cream cheese until fluffy. Beat in the salt. Then add the sugar a little at a time, beating until the mixture is soft and smooth. Remove the bowl from the mixer. Gradually stir the lingonberries into the cream cheese, blending well. Set aside.

2 In a chilled bowl with chilled beaters, whip the cream until it holds a soft but definite shape; do not let it become stiff. With a rubber spatula, casually fold about one-third of the whipped cream into the lingonberry/cream cheese mixture just to lighten it; the mixture will be streaky. Fold in the rest of the whipped cream, mixing gently but thoroughly until no streaks remain. Cover airtight and place in the freezer for at least 8 hours. (The recipe can be made 1 day in advance.)

3 At serving time, scoop the softly frozen berry cream into individual dessert dishes. Since ginger seems to enhance the flavor of lingonberries, I like to accompany this dessert with crisp, lightly sweet Swedish or English ginger snaps.

RED BEANS AND RICELY YOURS

▲▲▲▲▲▲▲▲▲▲▲▲▲▲▲▲▲▲▲▲▲▲▲▲▲▲▲▲▲▲▲

Oyster and Fennel Soup

▲

Royal Street Red Beans
Steamed Rice
Tangy Mixed Leaf Salad
French Bread

▲

Real Caramel Ice Cream

▼

Everybody who knows anything about food agrees that Cajun–Creole cuisine is no longer In. Everybody except the Cajuns and Creoles, for whom it was never In (or Cuisine), it was just what they ate every day.

I like to imagine a lot of Cajuns walking into the Carnegie Deli and telling everybody that pastrami is Out.

In New Orleans or New York or New Delhi for that matter, the only food that suddenly goes Out is food that suddenly came In—trendy restaurant dishes, clever creations quickly discredited by bad imitations. Truly popular cuisine—the cuisine, literally, "of the people"—stays popular. So-called Cajun popcorn may well be a flash in the pan, but in Louisiana red beans and rice is a way of life.

And this is real red beans and rice, the kind Louis Armstrong was thinking of when he signed his letters, "Red beans and ricely yours." This was the traditional Monday supper, slow-simmered with the bone of the Sunday ham until the weekly wash was all done and down off the line and the beans were melting in a thick natural gravy so rich with spicy sausage and ham bone marrow that all you wanted with them was some plain fresh-cooked rice and maybe a bit of salad.

Anything that tastes like this and is inexpensive and easy for a crowd and freezes beautifully is *never* going to be Out.

▲

Oyster and Fennel Soup

*T*his elegant soup can be prepared for a dozen guests in less than twenty minutes. Lighter and more complex than a traditional oyster stew, it is still quite rich. SERVES 10 TO 12

1 medium fennel bulb, feathery green tops reserved
5 cups chicken stock
1⅓ cups crème fraîche or heavy cream
⅔ cup milk
3 tablespoons glace de poisson (optional, see Note)
4 dozen freshly shucked oysters, liquor reserved
6 tablespoons unsalted butter
Pinch of cayenne
Salt and freshly ground white pepper

1 Slice the fennel bulb into strips about ⅛ inch thick and 1 inch long; measure out 1½ cups. Mince enough of the feathery fennel greens to measure 2 tablespoons; set aside separately to be used as a garnish.

2 In a heavy large saucepan, whisk the chicken stock into the crème fraîche. Stir in the milk, the glace de poisson (if using), and the oyster liquor. Bring to a simmer over moderate heat.

3 Meanwhile, in another large saucepan, melt the butter. Add the fennel strips and cook over low heat until barely translucent and still quite crunchy, 1 to 2 minutes. Quickly pour in the steaming cream-stock mixture and increase the heat to moderately high.

4 As soon as the soup comes to a boil, add the oysters. Reduce the heat to moderate and simmer just until their edges curl, 2 to 3 minutes. Stir in the cayenne and season with salt and white pepper to taste. Ladle the soup into small bowls, sprinkle each with a bit of the reserved minced fennel greens, and serve immediately.

NOTE Glace de poisson is fish stock that has been reduced to a thick glaze; it is used to enrich the flavor of sauces and soups. It can be mailordered from Maison Glass, 111 East 58th Street, New York, NY 10012. Stored in the freezer, it will keep indefinitely and can be thawed and refrozen whenever necessary. If unavailable, simply omit it.

Royal Street Red Beans

I live in New York, but I buy my red beans in the Royal Street A & P when I visit my folks in New Orleans. They're probably the same as red beans in New York, but those one-pound sacks cushion the corners of the cooler I fill with Creole cream cheese and crawfish and Barq's root beer. SERVES 8 TO 10

1 pound dried red kidney beans
½ pound lean salt pork with rind
3 tablespoons peanut or corn oil
1½ cups finely chopped onions
½ cup thinly sliced scallions, white and tender green
1 cup finely chopped green bell peppers
½ cup finely chopped red bell peppers (if unavailable, substitute another
    ½ cup chopped green peppers)
¾ cup finely chopped celery
1½ teaspoons finely chopped garlic
1 large bay leaf, broken in half
1 teaspoon finely chopped fresh thyme leaves or ⅓ teaspoon crumbled dried thyme
¾ teaspoon paprika
¼ teaspoon cayenne
¼ teaspoon freshly ground black pepper
1 large meaty ham bone, sawed into 3-inch pieces
Salt
¾ pound andouille sausage or other good-quality smoked sausage, such as kielbasa,
    cut into ¼-inch slices
3 tablespoons finely chopped flat-leaf parsley
Hot-pepper sauce
Steamed Rice (recipe follows), for serving

1 Rinse the beans and pick them over to remove any grit. Place in a large bowl, add cold water to cover by 3 inches, and let stand overnight. Or, if pressed for time, bring the beans and water to a boil in a large pot; boil for 2 minutes, then cover and set aside to soak for 1 hour.

2 Cut the rind off the salt pork. Cut the rind into ¼-inch strips, then cut the strips crosswise into ¼-inch squares. In a medium saucepan, cover the diced rind with 4 cups cold water; bring to a boil, reduce the heat to moderately low, and simmer slowly, uncovered, for 30 minutes. (This process softens the rind, so it will melt into the beans during their long cooking.) Drain, rinse under cool running water, and drain again. Pat dry with paper towels and set aside.

3 Cut the salt pork itself into ½-inch cubes and blanch for 5 minutes in 2 quarts of boiling water. Drain the cubes, rinse, and drain again. Pat dry, and reserve separately from the rind.

4 Drain the soaked beans, rinse under cool running water, and drain again. Place the beans in a heavy large flameproof casserole and add fresh water to cover by about 2 inches. Bring to a boil over moderate heat, skim foam that forms on the surface, then cover the pot and reduce the heat to maintain a gentle even simmer.

5 Meanwhile, in a heavy large skillet, heat 2 tablespoons of the oil. Add the blanched salt pork and sauté slowly until the cubes are lightly crisped and most of their fat is rendered, 8 to 10 minutes. Add the onions, scallions, green and red bell peppers, celery, garlic, bay leaf, thyme, paprika, cayenne, and black pepper. Raise the heat to moderately high and cook, stirring constantly and briskly, until the vegetables are softened and lightly browned, about 10 to 15 minutes. Scrape the pan, when necessary, to prevent sticking and burning, but do not lower the flame; high heat, which brings out the full flavor of spices while caramelizing the sweet juices of peppers and onions, is what gives so many Cajun and Creole dishes that special burnished edge.

6 Transfer the contents of the skillet to the simmering bean pot. Add 2 cups water to the empty skillet and set over moderately high heat, scraping the bottom of the pan to loosen and dissolve coagulated cooking juices; pour the resulting rich liquid into the bean pot. Stir in the blanched diced pork rind. Add the pieces of ham bone, burying them in the beans. If necessary, add additional water to cover the beans. Bring to a boil over moderate heat. Cover the pot and reduce the heat to maintain a slow simmer until the beans are very tender but not mushy, about 2 hours; stir from the bottom of the pot frequently to prevent sticking and add a little warm water if the beans seem dry.

(Continued)

7 When the beans are tender and a thick creamy gravy has formed, remove the pieces of ham bone. Strip off the meat and cut it into bite-size pieces. Scoop out the ham bone marrow. Stir the meat and marrow into the beans; discard the bones, fat, skin, and gristle. Season with salt to taste. (*The recipe can—and for maximum flavor should—be prepared ahead to this point. Let the beans cool to room temperature; cover and refrigerate for up to 2 days, or freeze for up to 2 months. Let return to room temperature before proceeding.*)

8 About 30 minutes before serving, return the beans, covered, to low heat; add a little warm water to loosen the gravy if necessary, and stir frequently while heating. Meanwhile, in a heavy skillet, heat the remaining tablespoon of oil and sauté the sliced andouille sausage over moderate heat until lightly browned on both sides, about 8 minutes. Stir the sausage into the bean pot and continue cooking the beans very slowly until heated through. Adjust the seasoning with more salt and pepper, if necessary. Add the parsley and stir in hot-pepper sauce to taste, mixing well.

9 To serve, spoon freshly cooked rice onto each plate and ladle the hot, creamy beans over the rice. A tartly dressed, crisp green salad is the traditional and perfect accompaniment.

▼▼

Steamed Rice

▲▲

MAKES 6 CUPS

2 cups long-grain white rice
1 tablespoon unsalted butter, cut into 3 or 4 pieces
1 teaspoon coarse (kosher) salt

1 Put the rice and butter in a heavy 3-quart saucepan or flameproof casserole with a tight-fitting lid. Add 3½ cups water. Sprinkle in the salt, stir, and bring to a boil over moderately high heat. Stir again, cover tightly, and reduce the heat to very low. Cook, without lifting the lid, for 15 minutes.

2 Turn off the heat under the pot. Lift the lid, quickly stretch a clean kitchen towel over the pot, and immediately replace the lid on the pot over the towel. Pull up the corners of the towel and fold them on top of the pot lid. Let stand for 10 minutes. During this time, the retained heat in the pot will complete the cooking process while the towel absorbs rising steam that would otherwise condense on the underside of the lid and drip back onto the rice, making it wet and sticky.

3 Remove the lid and the towel. With a large fork, lift and fluff the rice gently. Serve immediately or replace the lid on the pot and keep warm in a low oven for up to 20 minutes.

Tangy Mixed Leaf Salad

SERVES 8

8 large handfuls mixed greens: chicory (white part only), arugula,
* radicchio, mâche, et cetera*
½ teaspoon Creole mustard
2 tablespoons tarragon vinegar
Pinch of cayenne
½ teaspoon coarse (kosher) salt
Freshly ground black pepper
7 to 8 tablespoons olive oil

1 Wash the salad greens thoroughly, lifting them out of the water each time to leave any sand or grit behind. Drain well and spin dry. Discard all tough stems and tear large leaves into bite-size pieces. Layer the salad greens between paper towels or roll loosely in clean kitchen towels; refrigerate in plastic bags until serving time.

2 In a small bowl, combine the mustard, vinegar, cayenne, salt, and pepper; whisk to blend. Whisking constantly, gradually add the oil, by droplets at first and then in a thin stream, to make an emulsified vinaigrette. Cover and set aside.

3 When ready to serve, place the chilled greens in a large salad bowl. Add the dressing and toss to coat the leaves lightly and evenly. Season with additional salt and pepper, if necessary, and serve at once.

Real Caramel Ice Cream

This is butterscotch for grown-ups, a homey sweet turned rich and tantalizing with the burnished edge of real caramel. But though the taste is sophisticated, the procedure is simple. Just be sure to allow an extra ten or fifteen uninterrupted minutes to prepare the caramel immediately after making the custard base, so that you can combine them while they are both still warm. MAKES ABOUT 1¼ QUARTS

1 cup milk
2½ cups heavy cream
1¼ cups sugar
Pinch of salt
4 large egg yolks
1 teaspoon fresh lemon juice
1 teaspoon vanilla extract

1 In a heavy medium saucepan, combine the milk, 2 cups of the cream, ½ cup of the sugar, and the salt. Cook over moderate heat, stirring frequently, until the sugar dissolves and the mixture is hot, 6 to 8 minutes.

2 In a large bowl, beat the egg yolks lightly. Gradually whisk in the hot cream in a thin stream. Return the mixture to the saucepan and cook over moderately low heat, stirring constantly, until the custard thickens enough to coat the back of a spoon lightly, 5 to 7 minutes. (Do not let the temperature exceed 180 degrees.) Remove from the heat and set aside.

3 Proceed immediately to make the caramel. In a small heavy saucepan, combine the remaining ¾ cup sugar with the lemon juice and 2 tablespoons water. Melt the sugar over moderately low heat without stirring, brushing any sugar crystals from the sides of the pan with a wet brush. Let the sugar boil gently, undisturbed, until the syrup begins to color, about 15 minutes. Continue boiling, swirling the pan frequently, until the caramel is a deep, rich amber, about 5 minutes longer. (Do not let the syrup darken any further, or the caramel may develop a bitter, slightly burnt taste.) Remove from the heat and stir in the remaining ½ cup cream. Stir the caramel cream into the warm custard and mix thoroughly.

(Continued)

4 Pour the caramel custard through a fine-mesh sieve into a metal bowl. Set the bowl in a basin of cold water and ice and let stand, stirring occasionally, until the custard has cooled to room temperature. Stir in the vanilla extract. Cover and refrigerate for at least 4 hours, or until very cold.

5 Pour the chilled custard into an ice-cream maker and freeze according to the manufacturer's instructions. Let the ice cream soften slightly before serving.

THE ROAD TO HONG KONG

▲▲▲▲▲▲▲▲▲▲▲▲▲▲▲▲▲▲▲▲▲▲▲▲▲▲▲▲▲▲▲▲

Stuffed Flower Mushrooms

Wontons When You Want

▲

Congee

▲

Tea and Oranges

▼

I said to my wife, "Where do you want to go for your anniversary?"
She said, "I want to go somewhere I've never been before."
I said, "Try the kitchen."

—HENNY YOUNGMAN

Take his advice, please.

The road to Bali—or Morocco or Borneo or Zanzibar or Utopia or anywhere else you've never been and probably never will be—runs right through your kitchen. If you've finally realized that the only people who accumulate enough bonus mileage to fly to Hong Kong are the people who fly to Hong Kong all the time anyway, try gastronomic tripping instead.

When you eat what is eaten in another land, you ingest at least a little of its history and geography, enough to make you want more. When you cook what another people cooks, you learn what their markets smell like and what their kitchens look like, what they will not touch and what they hunger for, what we all have in common and what still keeps us a world apart.

Bon appetit. Bon voyage.

▲

Stuffed Flower Mushrooms

Varied grades of Chinese dried black mushrooms, also known as flower mushrooms, forest mushrooms, and winter mushrooms (and dried shiitakes), are available in Asian markets. For this special dish—on this otherwise economical menu—I splurge and buy the best, banquet-quality thick, dark caps with pale fissures. When soaked, they develop a plush, meaty texture and a heady, almost smoky aroma; their intense flavor makes them not a replacement for fresh shiitakes but a rare pleasure in their own right. MAKES 20 TO 30 STUFFED MUSHROOMS

20 to 30 medium-large finest-grade Chinese dried black mushrooms
6 ounces ground pork butt
6 ounces shrimp, peeled, deveined, and finely chopped
4 water chestnuts, preferably fresh, peeled and finely diced
2 tablespoons tiny scallion rounds, white and tender green
1 teaspoon minced fresh ginger
1½ tablespoons light soy sauce
1½ tablespoons dry sherry
1 tablespoon cornstarch
½ teaspoon plus ⅛ teaspoon superfine sugar
¼ teaspoon coarse (kosher) salt
⅛ teaspoon freshly ground black pepper
½ teaspoon Oriental sesame oil
3 tablespoons peanut or corn oil
¾ cup chicken stock
1 tablespoon oyster sauce

1 In a very large bowl (or 2 bowls, if necessary), cover the mushrooms with very hot water and soak until soft. Snip off the stems with scissors; rinse the mushroom caps under running water and pat dry.

2 In a medium bowl, break up the pork with your fingers. Add the shrimp, water chestnuts, scallions, ginger, soy sauce, and sherry. Sprinkle with the cornstarch, ½ teaspoon sugar, salt, and black pepper; drizzle the sesame oil over all. Using your hands, mix gently but thoroughly.

(Continued)

3 Mound a reasonably generous portion of the mixture in each mushroom cap. Round and smooth the tops with lightly oiled fingers; do not pack the stuffing down hard.

4 In a heavy large skillet (nonstick, if possible), heat the peanut or corn oil over moderate heat. Add the mushrooms, stuffing side down, and brown lightly. Carefully turn the mushrooms over, stuffing side up, and remove any oil that remains in the skillet.

5 In a small bowl, blend the chicken stock, oyster sauce, and remaining ⅛ teaspoon sugar. Add this braising liquid to the skillet. Bring to a simmer, cover tightly, and turn the heat low. Simmer very gently, basting the mushrooms once, for 10 to 15 minutes, until the stuffing is cooked through; if the liquid starts to evaporate, add a little water and continue cooking.

6 Remove the skillet from the heat and give the mushrooms one final basting. These mushrooms are best hot but very good even at room temperature. (*The recipe can be prepared in advance. Let the mushrooms cool completely. Measure the braising liquid in the skillet; if necessary, add enough water to make ½ cup. Pour this liquid into a shallow baking dish just large enough to hold the mushrooms in a single layer. Arrange the mushrooms in the dish, stuffing side down, and cover tightly with plastic wrap if refrigerating or with a double thickness of heavy-duty aluminum foil if freezing. Refrigerate for up to 2 days, or freeze for up to 1 month; if frozen, defrost before reheating. To reheat, bake the mushrooms in their cooking liquid in a tightly covered dish in a 300-degree oven for about 20 minutes. Turn stuffing side up before serving.*)

Wontons When You Want

*H*aving wontons in your freezer is the next best thing to having room service in your very own home.

Want a midnight snack? Light lunch? Hot stuff at half-time? Fast food for the kids, warm welcome for a weary traveler, sophisticated little-something-to-have-with-drinks? Heat water, drop in wontons, boil 5 minutes. Serve with (20 second) soy and balsamic vinegar dipping sauce.

Want a golden crispy teenage treat? Hors d'oeuvres for your cocktail party, star turn for your Sunday brunch? Heat oil, drop in wontons, fry 5 minutes. Serve as is, or with soy and balsamic vinegar dipping sauce.

Want a super soup for supper? Boil water, drop in wontons, cook 5 minutes. Drain and add to hot chicken broth. You could also add some slivers of cooked meat or poultry or take-out Chinese roast pork, and/or a handful of spinach leaves or leftover peas or a sliced mushroom, whatever you have. Simmer till hot. Stir in a frew drops of sesame oil and some scallion rounds and serve. MAKES 5 TO 6 DOZEN WONTONS

2 tablespoons cornstarch
2 teaspoons dry sherry
2 teaspoons light soy sauce
1 tablespoon oyster sauce
¾ teaspoon Oriental sesame oil
1 pound ground pork butt
3 tablespoons tiny scallion rounds, white and tender green
1 teaspoon minced garlic
1½ teaspoons minced fresh ginger
½ teaspoon coarse (kosher) salt
⅓ teaspoon freshly ground black pepper
1 teaspoon sugar, preferably superfine
1 large egg, lightly beaten
60 thin wonton wrappers

SOY AND BALSAMIC VINEGAR DIPPING SAUCE

½ cup light soy sauce
¼ cup balsamic vinegar
½ teaspoon coarsely ground black pepper

(Continued)

1 In a small bowl, combine the cornstarch, sherry, soy sauce, oyster sauce, and sesame oil. Stir until the cornstarch is dissolved.

2 In a large bowl, break up the ground pork with your fingers. Scatter the scallions, garlic, ginger, salt, pepper, and sugar over the pork. Restir the cornstarch mixture and add. Pour the beaten egg over all. Using your hands, mix lightly but thoroughly. Cover and refrigerate for at least 6 hours or overnight, if possible, to let the flavors meld and to facilitate handling.

3 When ready to fill the wontons, set up a simple assembly line, going from left to right. On the left, the wonton wrappers, loosely stacked in a plastic bag large enough to reach into easily. Then the filling, well-chilled. Next, a small bowl of water and a clean thin brush (I keep a small watercolor brush for dumpling-making). Finally, 1 or 2 large nonstick or lightly floured baking sheets or trays (having 2 makes it possible to continue making wontons by filling the second while the first is in the freezer), each covered with a clean kitchen towel. Before beginning, clear a flat space in your freezer for the baking sheet.

4 Lay a wonton wrapper on your work surface, positioning it to look like a diamond. Place a teaspoonful of filling in the center. Lightly moisten your brush and run it around the edges of the wrapper. Bring the south corner of the wrapper up over the filling to the north corner, but do not align the 2 upper points. Instead, fold the wrapper at a slight angle so the upper points lay side by side about ½ inch apart. Pinch/press the edges of the triangle tightly to seal, completely enclosing the filling. Now bring the 2 other corners together, drawing them forward and slightly downward until their tips overlap; moisten the tips and pinch them together. Place finished wontons slightly apart on the baking tray and keep them covered with the towel.

5 Place the filled tray in the freezer, uncovered, until the wontons are frozen hard. Rap the tray lightly on your work surface to loosen the frozen wontons and quickly pack them in plastic freezer bags; seal and return to the freezer immediately. *(Bagged airtight, the wontons can be frozen for up to 1 month. Do not thaw before cooking.)*

6 Shortly before cooking, prepare the soy and balsamic vinegar dipping sauce by combining the soy sauce, balsamic vinegar, and pepper. Stir to blend well and pour into small dishes for dipping.

7 To cook wontons, bring a large kettle of water to a rolling boil. Drop in a dozen frozen wontons and boil gently for 6 minutes. Transfer the cooked wontons to a bowl, along with a ladleful of cooking water; cover loosely and keep hot. Return water to a rolling boil at the start of each batch. Drain well and serve at once with dipping sauce.

Congee

CHINESE CREAMY RICE SOUP

Whoever said, "East is East and West is West and never the twain shall meet," must have been looking at a Chinese breakfast menu. The traditional eye-opener—and the eyes open awfully early over there—is congee, a thin rice gruel which the very young and the very old take straight and which everyone else punches up with pickled vegetables, hundred-year-old eggs, and fermented bean curd.

Westerners do not want to wake up and smell the fermented bean curd. And hundred-year-old eggs are what I'm always afraid of finding at the back of the refrigerator. But forget the fixin's—congee itself does have possibilities.

Start with medium-grain rice, which is creamier than the usual long-grain. Add flavor with leeks and ginger. Cook in a light stock instead of plain water. Serve at eleven P.M. instead of seven A.M. That's all it takes to turn a plain breakfast porridge into soup of the evening, beautiful soup.
SERVES 8

2 medium leeks, white parts only
2 quarter-size slices fresh ginger, peeled
1 cup medium-grain rice
8 cups chicken stock (see Note)
Salt and freshly ground white pepper

1 Slit the leeks, rinse under cool running water, and cut into shreds about ¼ inch wide. Rinse the shreds to remove any remaining dirt; pat dry and set aside. Bruise the ginger slices with the dull edge of a cleaver or heavy knife and set aside.

2 To rinse the rice, put it in a large bowl and add cold water to cover by several inches. Stir with your fingers until the water becomes milky. Drain the rice into a large strainer. Return the rice to the bowl, cover with water, and stir and drain again. Repeat this process several times, until the rinsing water is almost clear. Finally, drain the rice well and transfer it to a heavy 4-quart casserole or saucepan.

3 Add the leeks, ginger, chicken stock, and 4 cups water and bring to a boil over moderately high heat. Reduce the heat to moderate and let the liquid bubble for a minute or two. Stir well, then cover tightly and turn the heat as low as possible. Simmer very gently for 60 to 90 minutes, or until the rice has almost melted into the broth and the mixture is thick and porridge-like; stir occasionally to prevent sticking and scorching, especially during the last 30 minutes of cooking. Discard the ginger. Season with salt and freshly ground white pepper to taste. (*The congee can be prepared ahead. Let cool, then cover and refrigerate for up to 2 days. Let come to room temperature before reheating.*)

4 Congee, like many other rice dishes, is best reheated in a microwave oven, where scorching is unlikely. It can also be reheated over a low flame; stir frequently and add a little water if it becomes too thick. This congee is tasty enough to need no further embellishment, but if you're in the mood for mix-ins (and they are kind of fun), hold the fermented bean curd and try one or more of the following:

In the kitchen

Shredded young bok choy leaves, added to the congee shortly before serving and cooked just until tender

2 large eggs, lightly beaten with ½ teaspoon peanut oil and gently stirred into the pot during the final moment of simmering for an egg-drop soup effect

At the table

Slivers of raw fish, tossed with a few drops of sesame oil and sherry. Diners can place these in their bowls just before the steaming congee is ladled out; the heat of the soup is sufficient to cook the fish

Bite-size pieces of smoked fish for the diners to add to their hot soup

Thin slivers of take-out Chinese roast pork

Thinly sliced scallions, white and tender green

Chopped fresh coriander leaves

Oriental sesame oil

Chinese hot chili oil

NOTE Do not be tempted to improve your congee by making it entirely with chicken stock; it will be less delicate and less interesting than a congee made with stock and water.

Tea and Oranges

We might have lychees, too, if they're in season. Or fresh pomegranate seeds, heaped on a bed of crushed ice. And little bowls filled with honeyed walnuts and dried cherries and crystallized ginger.

I like this dessert. It isn't really served, it just happens, everyone leaning back and sipping and nibbling and talking quietly as the evening winds down and the nice smell of oranges fills the room.

HUNGRILY EVER AFTER

▲▲▲▲▲▲▲▲▲▲▲▲▲▲▲▲▲▲▲▲▲▲▲▲▲▲▲▲▲▲▲▲▲▲▲▲

Caesar Salad

▲

Meat Loaf
Mashed Baked Potatoes

▲

The Bride's Chocolate Cake

▼

Music may, as the poet said, be the food of love, but so is pizza. I know because we lived over a pizzeria when we were first in love. I was a freshman and he was a junior at the University of Michigan.

It was so long ago that when I came home one day after classes, there was this note on the door:

"The milkman was here and he had something called yogurt. I thought you might like it so I got some."

Something called yogurt. . . .

But I don't remember the yogurt of 1956 as well as I remember the pizza. Or as well as I remember the toasted pecan rolls we ate for breakfast across the street at Red's Rite Spot, where Red would just take out his scissors and cut off anybody's necktie if he didn't like it.

We had different schedules, went to or missed different classes all day long. Sometimes when I stopped in Michigan Drug for lunch, he was already sitting at the counter; somebody always moved over so we could be together. We ate ham salad sandwiches. He drank a Coke and I ordered a cherry phosphate, which was mystifying to a boy from New York.

Cherry phosphates were to be his undoing that year. "I got a part-time job as a soda jerk," he recalls, "and the fourth or fifth afternoon an adorable little girl came in and asked for a cherry phosphate. I pumped the cherry syrup plunger and nothing came out. Empty. I went in back and found a jug of cherry syrup. I neglected to read the label, which would have told me this was 'concentrate'—one part syrup to ten parts water. I just poured it in straight, vaguely wondering why it had the consistency of molasses in January. Then I put the paper cup under the spigot and nearly got a hernia forcing this stuff up the pump and out into the cup. When I added the soda water and tried to stir it, the spoon stood straight up. Gradually—it was hard labor—the concentrate diluted slightly and the paper cup turned cherry red. By then I knew I'd done something wrong, but the kid was waiting for her phosphate. So then I had the excruciating experience of watching an innocent child trying to suck this sludge up through a paper straw. Her cheeks caved in, her eyeballs popped out, and her mouth turned bright red when the first taste finally made it up the straw. I quit the next day."

We left our paradise over the pizzeria then and found a cheaper place to live. It had lovely old wallpaper, it had a swing on the porch downstairs, it had everything except a kitchen. We didn't care. We lived on love and Krazy Jim's Blimpee Burgers and barbecued beef on a bun at Woolworth's and cider and Spudnuts, wonderful potato-dough doughnuts which we bought warm on our way to football games. Once in a while we went to Leo Ping's for Yat Ca Mein, a deeply satisfying supper-in-a-big-bowl of noodles and roast pork and Chinese greens and half a hard-boiled egg in steaming broth.

We were eating Chicken in the Rough ("half a fried chicken served in a basket with french fries and hot rolls with honey") when he asked me to marry him. And in June 1958, I did. It was a good-size wedding and afterwards there were long tables of beautiful food. I don't remember any of it.

We moved into our first licit apartment. I unpacked my first shiny set of pots and pans. Krazy Jim's had been okay for crazy kids but we were grown-ups now. And as I stood there in my first very own kitchen, I realized two enormous truths.

We were going to eat dinner together for the rest of our lives.

And I didn't know how to cook.

▲

Caesar Salad

*E*ven before everybody loved salad, this was a salad everybody loved.
SERVES 8 TO 10 AS A FIRST COURSE, 4 TO 6 AS A MAIN COURSE

3 large cloves garlic, peeled
Coarse (kosher) salt
1½ cups extra-virgin olive oil
3 heads of romaine lettuce, about 1 pound each
½ cup freshly grated imported parmesan cheese, preferably Parmigiano-Reggiano
16 to 18 flat anchovy fillets
4 cups ½-inch bread cubes, cut from crustless day-old homestyle white bread and
*   then left out to become slightly stale*
1 teaspoon coarsely ground black pepper
3 teaspoons fresh lemon juice
2 large eggs

1 Twenty-four hours before serving, cut the garlic cloves in half length-wise and remove any green sprouts. With a large sharp knife, chop the garlic very fine, then sprinkle with a generous pinch of coarse salt and mince to a near-puree. Or crush the garlic cloves with the salt in a mortar. Do not crush the garlic through a press. In a small bowl, stir the garlic and the olive oil together; cover and let stand at room temperature for 24 hours.

2 The lettuce can—and for maximum crispness, should—be prepared 24 hours before serving. Discard the dark outer leaves. Strip the tender inner leaves from the stalks and break off the tough bottom end of each leaf. Rinse the leaves carefully, tear neatly into large bite-size pieces, and dry in 2 or 3 batches in a salad spinner. Roll each batch loosely in a clean kitchen towel. Refrigerate in plastic bags until serving time.

3 Anytime up to 24 hours before serving, grate the parmesan cheese into a small bowl. Cover and refrigerate.

4 About 4 hours before serving, dip the anchovy fillets in a bowl of cool water to rinse; dry gently on paper towels. Coarsely chop the fillets, put them in a small bowl, and strain over them ½ cup of the garlic-flavored oil you prepared in Step 1. Cover and set aside to steep until serving time.

5 Meanwhile, prepare the croutons. Strain ¼ cup of the garlic-flavored oil into a heavy large skillet. Heat the oil, add 2 cups bread cubes, and sauté over moderate heat until golden brown. Sprinkle with a generous pinch of coarse salt, toss, and immediately turn out of the skillet to cool on paper towels. Wipe out the skillet, add another ¼ cup strained garlic oil, and sauté the remaining 2 cups bread cubes.

6 Shortly before serving, grind the black pepper into a small dish; cover and set aside. Drain the anchovies and combine the oil you covered them with in Step 4 with the remaining ½ cup of garlic-flavored oil from Step 1. Strain into a small clean bowl and set aside to dress the salad; discard the crushed garlic. Set out your largest salad bowl; beside it, place the salad ingredients in the order of their use: oil, pepper, lemon juice, eggs, anchovies, grated parmesan, coarse salt, and croutons.

7 Assemble the salad as follows:

▲ Arrange the romaine leaves in the salad bowl.

▲ Drizzle on ¾ cup of the oil and toss to coat the leaves evenly.

▲ Sprinkle with the black pepper, pour on half the lemon juice, and toss again.

▲ Break the eggs in a small bowl, beat lightly, and add to the salad. Add the remaining lemon juice. Toss to blend, and add some or all of the remaining olive oil, as necessary.

▲ Scatter the chopped anchovies and grated parmesan over the greens. Mix well.

▲ Season with salt to taste and add more pepper and/or lemon juice, if desired. The salad should be very zesty. Sprinkle on the croutons, toss again, and serve at once.

Meat Loaf

If the way to a man's heart is through his stomach, surely the road is paved with slabs of meat loaf. This recipe yields juicy pink slices of lean ground beef, studded with still slightly crunchy onions and peppers, and topped with a thick baked-on tomato glaze (don't try to improve on ketchup here, because you can't).

Leftovers are delicious at room temperature or slightly cooler; meat loaf should never be served straight from the refrigerator (though it is wonderful to eat meat loaf straight from the refrigerator in the middle of the night, especially with someone you love). SERVES 8

3 pounds ground beef round
1¼ cups chopped onions
¾ cup chopped green and/or red bell peppers
2 tablespoons matzo meal or dried breadcrumbs
1 teaspoon crumbled dried marjoram
½ teaspoon coarse salt
¾ teaspoon freshly ground black pepper
3 large eggs, lightly beaten
1¼ cups tomato ketchup, at room temperature

1 In a large bowl, break up the meat, loosening it with your fingers. Set aside while you prepare and assemble the other ingredients. After about 20 minutes, when the meat has lost a little of its chill and become more malleable, scatter the chopped onions and bell peppers into the bowl and sprinkle on the matzo meal, marjoram, salt, and pepper. Toss briefly and gently, just to distribute the ingredients evenly. Pour on the beaten eggs and ¼ cup of the ketchup. Now roll up your sleeves, take off your rings, and get your hands in there; mix lightly and loosely, but well.

2 In one quick motion, scoop the loose mixture up in both hands and set it down in a large shallow baking pan. Pat—do not press—into a fairly symmetrical loaf about 10 x 7 x 2 inches. If there are any large cracks or fissures in the structure, smooth them shut with your fingers. Cover the pan airtight with plastic wrap or aluminum foil and refrigerate for 4 to 8 hours to let the flavors blend. Remove from the refrigerator, uncover, and let stand at room temperature for 30 minutes before proceeding.

3 Preheat the oven to 350 degrees. With the palm of your hand, spread the remaining cup of ketchup evenly over the top and sides of the meat loaf, as if frosting a cake. Bake in the middle of the oven for about 1¼ hours; an instant thermometer inserted in the center of the loaf will register 130 to 135 degrees when the beef is cooked through but still rosy pink and juicy inside. Remove the pan from the oven and let stand for 5 to 10 minutes, then slide two sturdy metal spatulas under the meat loaf and lift it onto a large warmed platter. Bring the platter to the table and listen to the oohs and aahs while you slice and serve.

Mashed Baked Potatoes

I don't know if mashed potatoes are my favorite food, but I do know the best thing about meat is the gravy and the best thing about gravy is how good it is on mashed potatoes.

Especially these mashed potatoes, which are the best because they begin with baking rather than boiling. Baking means never having to feel sorry for yourself; there's no peeling (the cooked pulp is simply scooped out of its crusty skin) and no pots to wash. Plus, there are no nutrients lost and all that lovely baked potato flavor gained. And the texture! No boiling or all-purpose potato soaks up milk and butter like a hot fluffy russet. Baking gives you all this and a bonus—the potato skins, which you can keep for days, if you want, and then crisp under the broiler and serve.

Technically, my mashed potatoes aren't mashed. They're actually riced potatoes, with the hot pulp put through an old-fashioned (but still widely available) gadget called a ricer, which looks and works like an overgrown garlic press. Ricing is a lot quicker and easier than the old up-and-down with a traditional masher, and it gives a smoother result. Which is how I like it. I figure you get your lumps often enough in this life, you don't need them in your potatoes.

Cream gives a special richness here, but for not-so-special occasions you could forego it and just moisten the potatoes with hot milk. You could use less butter. Or just leave out the butter sometime and put in rendered chicken fat instead. If you do that and put in the *gribenes* (cracklings) too and maybe some fried chopped onions, please invite me.

SERVES 8

6 medium-large baking potatoes, preferably russets, 3½ to 4 pounds
¾ cup heavy cream or crème fraîche
¾ cup milk
8 tablespoons (1 stick) unsalted butter, cut into 16 pieces, at room temperature
Salt and freshly ground black pepper

1 Preheat the oven to 425 degrees. Scrub and dry the potatoes and prick each in several places with a sharp fork to let steam escape. Bake for 1 to 1½ hours, or until the potatoes feel very soft when pierced with a skewer or a small sharp knife.

2 Meanwhile, a few minutes before the potatoes are done, heat the cream and milk together in a heavy small saucepan until steaming but not simmering. Set aside, partially covered.

3 Cut the baked potatoes in half crosswise. Using a large spoon, scoop the pulp out of each half and put it through a ricer into a warmed serving bowl.

4 Fold 12 pieces of the butter into the potatoes. As it melts, gradually add the hot cream and milk, whipping the puree with a big fork or a large whisk until thick and fluffy. Season with salt and pepper to taste. If not ready to serve immediately, cover the surface of the puree with a piece of plastic wrap or a circle of buttered wax paper and keep warm in a pan of hot water in a low oven for up to 20 minutes. Or cover and set aside at room temperature for up to 30 minutes and then reheat in a microwave oven; whip the reheated puree for a few seconds to loosen and lighten it again, adding 1 or 2 extra tablespoons of warm milk if necessary.

5 Dot with the remaining 4 pieces of butter. Rush the bowl to the table, swirl the little pools of gold into the hot potatoes, and serve at once.

NOTE Mashed potaotes are always at their best when freshly made, but leftovers—even leftovers that have been refrigerated for 2 or 3 days—are eminently edible when reheated in a covered bowl in a microwave oven.

The Bride's Chocolate Cake

When I was a young bride, my mother handed me a file card with a brief and rather vague version of this recipe typed on it. Where she got it in the late fifties, decades before chocolate became decadent and mousse became cake, I have no idea. But this recipe and a lot of enthusiasm were just about my whole gastronomic trousseau.

One *tablespoon* of flour? One *pound* of sweet chocolate?? Bake *fifteen* minutes??? This cake is as richly improbable as marriage and requires almost as much faith.   SERVES 12 TO 16

1 pound sweet, semisweet, or bittersweet chocolate, broken into squares or coarsely
   chopped (see Note)
10 tablespoons unsalted butter, at room temperature
1 tablespoon sugar
1 tablespoon all-purpose flour
4 large eggs, separated
Pinch of coarse (kosher) salt

1 Preheat the oven to 425 degrees. Butter the sides and bottom of an 8-inch springform pan. Line the bottom with a piece of wax paper cut to fit. Butter the paper and dust it lightly with flour; invert the pan and tap gently to knock out any excess flour. Set aside.

2 Place the chocolate in the top of a double boiler over (not in) hot (not simmering) water. Cover and let stand, stirring occasionally, until melted. Uncover and stir until the chocolate is completely smooth. Remove from the heat. Add the butter. Stir gently until the butter has melted and the chocolate is smooth and homogeneous again. Blend in the sugar and flour. Beat the egg yolks lightly and stir them into the chocolate.

3 In a large mixing bowl, beat the egg whites with the salt until they hold a definite shape but are not dry. Using a rubber spatula, fold about a third of the beaten whites into the chocolate just to lighten it; the mixture will be streaky. Add the remaining egg whites and gently fold them in until the batter is smoothly blended and no white streaks remain.

4 Pour the batter evenly into the prepared springform pan and smooth the surface with a spatula. Bake in the middle of the preheated oven for 15 minutes, *no longer*. The cake will still be soft, but it will become dense and fudgy as it cools. Remove the cake pan from the oven to a wire rack. Let cool completely, then carefully remove the sides of the springform pan. Cover the cake with plastic wrap and refrigerate until cold and firm.

5 Carefully invert the chilled cake onto a flat serving plate. Remove the bottom of the springform pan and discard the wax paper lining. The unmolded cake (or any portion thereof) can be wrapped airtight and kept in the refrigerator for up to a week, but is best served at room temperature or just a little cooler.

NOTE As Maida Heatter points out in her *Book of Great Chocolate Desserts,* "If a recipe calls for sweet or semisweet, you have an endless choice. . . . Chocolates that fit into the sweet-semisweet-bittersweet category . . . can be used interchangeably." Depending on the occasion and the state of my budget, I've made this cake with everything from supermarket Baker's German Sweet Chocolate to Krön Chocolatier's elegant bittersweet; there are some differences, but there are never any leftovers.

JUST
PLAIN
FANCY

▲▲▲▲▲▲▲▲▲▲▲▲▲▲▲▲▲▲▲▲▲▲▲▲▲▲▲▲▲▲▲

*Chicken Liver Mousse
with Currants*

▲

Chilled Minted Pea Soup

▲

*Fricassee of Mussels
Steamed Rice*

▲

Italian Wild Cherries Jubilee

▼

Why do we serve the least appealing food on the most important occasions? And why do cookbooks and magazines tell us to?

Pot roast with onion gravy, potato pancakes, and homemade applesauce is okay for the family, but company gets boned chicken breast with snowpeas.

I know which night I want to be invited.

And I know which meal I'd rather make. Most party food is not only less flavorful, it's also more expensive and requires more last-minute attention than what we eat for dinner every day. (Yes, filet mignon *is* tender, but how often do you give a party for people who've just had major dental work?)

Good plain home cooking is often good enough for guests these days, and ethnic and regional specialties can make an evening memorable. But there are nights when you just can't dazzle them with dumplings. And meat loaf may have a new reverse chic in certain circles but, believe me, it won't impress your mother. Sometimes you just have to serve something fancy.

But, please, not chicken breast with snowpeas. The best "fancy" is not an arbitrary assemblage of upscale ingredients. The best "fancy," it seems to me, comes out of "plain."

Take, for instance, a plain pot of mussels steamed in wine (which becomes a little fancier when you call it moules marinière, but all that actually means is mussels in the style of the sailor's wife because he brought them home and she threw them in the pot); this is fine family fare, quick, light, and inexpensive, a classic example of good "plain" cooking.

But just as simple Cinderella became the loveliest girl at the ball, this homey kettle of mussels in wine can, on a special evening, be enriched and enhanced and refined into a creamy Fricassee of Mussels that is fancy enough for a prince. No magic wand necessary; the techniques to accomplish this transformation are within the scope of most home cooks just as all the ingredients are within their budgets. And since most of the work can be done well in advance, everyone, even the cook, can have fun at the ball.

▲

Chicken Liver Mousse with Currants

I was making my chicken liver mousse one day and had no truffles (that happens to me a lot), so I used something that was also small and black but a lot cheaper. The result delighted me and my friends, including Wolfgang Puck, who sometimes has it on the menu at Spago now. This rich suave mousse, studded with Madeira-soaked currants, must be prepared at least thirty hours before serving and will keep in the refrigerator for up to five days. I like to serve it with thin dry toast and accompany it with champagne, or better yet, a chilled lightly sweet wine such as Beaumes-de-Venise. MAKES ABOUT 2 CUPS

1 pound chicken livers, trimmed
Milk
¼ cup dried currants
1½ tablespoons plus ¾ teaspoon Madeira
8 tablespoons (1 stick) unsalted butter, at room temperature
¼ cup Armagnac
1 small clove garlic, bruised
2 tablespoons crème fraîche or heavy cream
⅛ teaspoon Quatre-Épices (recipe follows)
1½ teaspoons fresh lemon juice
Salt and freshly ground black pepper
¼ cup clarified butter

1 Separate the 2 lobes of each chicken liver and place them in a bowl with milk to cover. (Soaking liver in milk makes it taste richer and sweeter.) Cover with plastic wrap and refrigerate at least 6 hours, or overnight.

2 In a small saucepan, combine the currants with 1½ tablespoons Madeira and ⅓ cup water. Bring to a boil. Remove from the heat immediately and set aside until the currants are soft and plump, 10 to 15 minutes.

(Continued)

3 Meanwhile, drain the chicken livers and pat dry with paper towels. In a heavy large skillet, melt 3 tablespoons of the softened butter. Add the chicken livers and cook over moderate heat, tossing, until firm but still pink inside, about 5 minutes. Remove from the heat. Using a slotted spoon, transfer the livers to a food processor. Add the Armagnac to the skillet and stir and scrape to blend it with the pan juices.

4 Pour the liquid from the skillet into the processor. Add the garlic, crème fraîche, Quatre-Épices, lemon juice, and the remaining ¾ teaspoon Madeira and 5 tablespoons softened butter. Puree, turning the machine on and off and scraping down the sides of the bowl occasionally, until the mixture is smooth. The mousse will be very soft and loose at this point but will firm up when cold.

5 Scrape the mixture into a bowl. Drain the currants and stir them into the mousse. Season with salt and pepper to taste. Spoon into a 2-cup crock or terrine and smooth the surface. Pour a thin layer of the clarified butter over the top to seal. Cover tightly and refrigerate for at least 24 hours to mellow and blend the flavors. Remove the mousse from the refrigerator about 30 minutes before serving.

Quatre-Épices

▲

Quatre-Épices is a French mixture of white pepper, nutmeg, cloves, ginger, and/or cinnamon; proportions vary, but the pepper almost always predominates. Sold in many specialty stores and easily made at home, this blend of ground spices flavors sausages and pâtés and enlivens soups, stews, and bean dishes. MAKES ABOUT 3½ TABLESPOONS

2 tablespoons white peppercorns
2 teaspoons freshly grated nutmeg
2 teaspoons ground ginger
½ teaspoon ground cloves
¼ teaspoon ground cinnamon

1 Grind the peppercorns to a fine powder.

2 In a small bowl, combine the pepper, nutmeg, ginger, cloves, and cinnamon and mix very thoroughly. Pass through a fine sieve. Store in a tightly covered container away from heat and sunlight.

Chilled Minted Pea Soup

SERVES 8

3 tablespoons unsalted butter
1 cup finely chopped onions
2 heads Bibb lettuce, coarsely torn or shredded
6 cups tiny tender peas, thawed if frozen
1 teaspoon sugar
⅓ teaspoon coarse (kosher) salt
3 cups chicken stock
1 cup heavy cream
2 tablespoons finely chopped fresh mint
⅛ teaspoon freshly ground pepper

1 In a heavy large saucepan or flameproof casserole, melt the butter over moderate heat. Add the onions and cook slowly, stirring, until softened but not browned, 8 to 10 minutes. Add the lettuce and turn it in the butter for a minute or two, just until wilted.

2 Add the peas, sugar, salt, chicken stock, and 3 cups water. Bring to a boil over high heat, reduce the heat to moderate, cover and simmer until the peas are very tender, 8 to 10 minutes for fresh peas, 3 to 5 minutes for thawed frozen peas.

3 Strain the soup. In a food processor, puree the solids with 1 cup of the cooking liquid. Pass this puree through a sieve into a large bowl. Gradually stir in the rest of the cooking liquid, mixing well.

4 Add the cream, mint, pepper, and additional salt to taste. Let cool to room temperature. Cover and refrigerate until well chilled, at least 6 hours, or overnight. Stir and adjust the seasoning, if necessary, before serving.

Fricassee of Mussels

Serve this richly sauced seafood with freshly cooked rice. If you want a vegetable in addition to those in the fricassee, buttered asparagus tips or tender young green beans would be ideal. For this or any recipe in which mussels are removed from the shell before serving, use small mussels. They are easier to eat and make a more elegant presentation.

SERVES 8 TO 10

8 pounds small mussels, scrubbed and debearded
6 tablespoons unsalted butter
1½ cups finely chopped onions
¼ cup finely chopped shallots
1 sprig fresh thyme or ¼ teaspoon crumbled dried thyme
4 sprigs fresh flat-leaf parsley
2½ cups dry white wine
2 medium leeks, white part only, cut into thin julienne strips
2 medium carrots, peeled and cut into thin julienne strips
2 medium stalks celery, cut into thin julienne strips
8 large egg yolks
1½ cups crème fraîche or heavy cream
⅛ teaspoon cayenne
⅛ teaspoon freshly grated nutmeg
Salt and freshly ground white pepper
4 tablespoons finely chopped flat-leaf parsley
6 cups Steamed Rice (page 39), for serving

1 Place the scrubbed mussels in a large bowl, cover with cold water, and stir in 2 or 3 large handfuls of flour. Refrigerate for at least 4 hours, or overnight. (While the mussels feast on the flour, becoming plumper and more succulent, they will also disgorge sand and excess salt.) After soaking, scoop the mussels up out of the dirty soaking water and rinse them thoroughly under cold running water.

2 In a large nonreactive flameproof casserole or stockpot, melt 4 tablespoons of the butter over moderately low heat. Stir in the onions and shallots, cover, and cook just until softened, about 5 minutes. Add the thyme and parsley sprigs, wine, ½ cup water, and mussels. Cover tightly and bring to a boil over high heat. Cook, shaking the pot vigorously once or twice, until all the mussels open, 5 to 7 minutes; discard any mussels that don't open.

3 Shell the mussels and place them in a bowl; set aside. Strain the mussel broth from the casserole through several thicknesses of dampened cheesecloth or a very fine mesh sieve. You should have 4 to 4½ cups; if necessary, pour the broth into a clean pot and reduce it to the correct amount. Set aside to cool.

4 Melt the remaining 2 tablespoons butter in a skillet. Add the julienned vegetables, cover, and sweat them over low heat until barely crisp-tender, 2 to 3 minutes. Remove from the skillet immediately and spread them out on a platter or tray to cool. *(The recipe can be prepared to this point up to 1 day ahead. The mussels, the broth, and the vegetables should be covered and refrigerated separately. Before proceeding, let the mussels and vegetables return to near room temperature and reheat the broth in a small saucepan.)*

5 About 30 minutes before serving, whisk the egg yolks and crème fraîche together in a large bowl. Gradually beat in the hot broth in a thin steady stream. Pour this hot sauce into a heavy large flameproof casserole. Cook over moderately low heat, stirring constantly, until the sauce has thickened to a smooth ivory cream, about 5 minutes. (Do not let the sauce come to a simmer or the egg yolks will scramble.) Add the cayenne and nutmeg and season with salt and pepper to taste.

6 Add the mussels and the vegetables and stir them in the sauce over low heat for a few minutes, just until piping hot. Stir in 3 tablespoons of the chopped parsley. Sprinkle with the remaining tablespoon parsley and serve at once with freshly cooked rice.

Italian Wild Cherries Jubilee

*E*verything old is *nuovo* again.

Though I feel most flambéed foods should be left to burn to the ground, I have always loved cherries jubilee. And when I discovered an Italian version in an English magazine not long ago, I couldn't wait to bring the hot news home. SERVES 8

2 cups Italian wild cherries in syrup (see Note)
1 teaspoon arrowroot
¼ cup kirsch
1 quart Vanilla Lovers' Vanilla Ice Cream (page 225), frozen hard

1 In a medium saucepan, heat the cherries in syrup over low heat until simmering. Mix the arrowroot with 2 tablespoons water, stirring to dissolve. Gradually stir the arrowroot mixture into the cherries. Simmer gently, stirring, until the sauce is clear and lightly thickened.

2 In a small saucepan, warm the kirsch over moderately low heat. Meanwhile, scoop the ice cream into individual dessert dishes. At the table, gently pour—without stirring—the well-warmed kirsch into the hot cherry sauce and ignite with a match. Spoon the flaming sauce over the ice cream and serve at once.

NOTE Italian wild cherries in syrup are available in jars in many specialty food stores.

DINNER AT TABLE MOUNTAIN

The Cape Malay Cooking of
South Africa

▲▲▲▲▲▲▲▲▲▲▲▲▲▲▲▲▲▲▲▲▲▲▲▲▲▲▲▲▲▲▲▲▲▲▲▲▲▲

Coconut and Carrot Sambal

Bobotie

Geel Rys

▲

Mixed Red Salad

▲

Double Espresso Ice Cream

▼

That the good things of the South African table should have
originated in Cape Town is certainly appropriate. Food was the
reason the Dutch decided to found a settlement at the foot of
majestic Table Mountain, which rises abruptly 3,500 feet above a
great sheltered bay near the Cape of Good Hope. . . . The first
settlers were sent to grow and provide food and water for the ships
sailing between Holland and the Dutch holdings in the East Indies.
It wasn't long before the Dutch began importing Malay slaves to
Cape Town. The spices and condiments these people brought with
them from the Indonesian archipelago soon overpowered the bland
dishes the Dutch hausfraus kept simmering at the back of the stove.
Today, Afrikaner cooking clearly shows the
Far Eastern influence. . . .

—HARVA HACHTEN,
Kitchen Safari

▲

Coconut and Carrot Sambal

*S*ambals, tangy relish-like salads of grated vegetables or fruits, are served as condiments at Malay feasts. Quince or apple sambals, for example, offset the richness of roast meats, while cucumber sambal is popular with everything spicy. Here I've combined shredded coconut and carrots in a sambal that goes especially well with lightly curried dishes like Bobotie.
SERVES 12

2 pounds crisp, bright orange carrots
1 teaspoon sugar, preferably superfine
¼ cup fresh lemon juice
1½ tablespoons peanut or safflower oil
¼ to ½ teaspoon cayenne, to taste
1 teaspoon coarse (kosher) salt
¾ cup unsweetened dessicated coconut shreds (see Note)

1 Peel the carrots, cut them into 2-inch lengths, and shred them in a food processor fitted with a medium shredding disc. *(This can be done up to 1 day in advance. Transfer the shredded carrots to an airtight container and refrigerate until about 90 minutes before serving. Transfer to a large serving bowl before proceeding.)*

2 In a small bowl, whisk together the sugar, lemon juice, oil, cayenne, and salt. Pour this dressing over the carrots and toss to moisten evenly. Cover tightly and refrigerate for 1 hour, stirring occasionally.

3 Add the coconut and toss to mix well. Cover again and return to the refrigerator for 30 minutes, stirring once or twice.

4 Adjust the seasoning with additional salt and/or lemon juice, if necessary, and toss once again before serving.

NOTE You can substitute an equal amount of grated fresh coconut if you like, but I prefer the concentrated flavor and pleasantly chewy texture of dessicated coconut in this sambal.

▼▼

Bobotie

▲▲

A LIGHTLY CURRIED CUSTARD OF LAMB, APPLES, APRICOTS, AND ALMONDS

*O*riginally created by the East Indian slave-cooks of the Dutch, this is one of those dishes that are, as South African writer Laurens van der Post says, ". . . so a part of the South African way of life that they have become almost sacramental substances." Though it goes by an Afrikäans name, bobotie can, I suspect, be traced back to the Indonesian *bebotok,* a dish of ground beef mixed with eggs and coconut milk, flavored with a spice mixture, and steamed. SERVES 12

¼ *cup whole blanched almonds*
2 *slices day-old homestyle white bread, crusts removed*
1 *cup milk*
4 *tablespoons unsalted butter*
2 *pounds lean ground lamb*
1½ *cups finely chopped onions*
½ *teaspoon minced garlic*
2 *tablespoons Madras curry powder*
1 *teaspoon powdered ginger*
¼ *cup diced dried apricots, preferably California apricots*
¼ *cup golden raisins*
1 *tablespoon sugar, preferably superfine*
1 *tablespoon fresh lemon juice*
1 *teaspoon freshly grated lemon zest*
1 *medium Granny Smith apple, peeled, cored, and diced*
3 *large eggs*
¼ *teaspoon freshly ground black pepper*
⅛ *teaspoon plus 1 large pinch cayenne*
Salt
¾ *cup heavy cream*
1 *large egg yolk*
⅛ *teaspoon freshly grated nutmeg*

1 Preheat the oven to 325 degrees. Spread the almonds out on a baking sheet and toast in the center of the oven, stirring once or twice, until light golden brown, about 10 minutes. Pour the nuts out onto a plate and let cool completely. Chop rather coarsely, then toss in a sieve to shake out any fine almond dust. *(This can be done up to a day in advance. Store the nuts in an airtight container until ready to proceed.)*

2 Tear the bread into large pieces. Put the pieces in a small bowl with the milk and let stand for 10 to 15 minutes. While the bread is soaking, melt 2 tablespoons of the butter in a heavy large skillet and cook the lamb over moderate heat, breaking up any lumps, just until no longer pink. With a slotted spoon, transfer the meat to a large bowl and set aside.

3 Add the remaining 2 tablespoons butter to the fat in the skillet, and melt over moderately low heat. Add the onions and cook, stirring, until soft and golden, 8 to 10 minutes. Add the garlic and cook for 1 minute. Sprinkle on the curry powder and ginger, and cook, stirring, for about 30 seconds longer. Stir in the apricots, raisins, sugar, lemon juice, and lemon zest and remove from the heat. Let cool for 2 to 3 minutes, then fold in the diced apple and chopped almonds. Scrape the contents of the skillet into the bowl of sautéed lamb and toss lightly to mix.

4 Squeeze the excess milk out of the soaked bread; reserve the milk and refrigerate in a covered container. Place the bread in a small bowl, add 1 egg, and whisk until light and fairly smooth. Blend the bread into the lamb and fruit mixture. Season with the black pepper, ⅛ teaspoon cayenne, and salt to taste. Mix well.

5 Spoon the mixture into a buttered baking dish about 9 x 12 x 2 inches; level and smooth the surface but do not pack down. Lay a protective sheet of plastic wrap over the surface and cover the pan tightly with aluminum foil. Refrigerate for 8 to 48 hours to let the flavors ripen and meld. Remove from the refrigerator 1 hour before baking.

6 Preheat the oven to 350 degrees. In a small bowl, combine the reserved milk (refrigerated in Step 4) with enough heavy cream to make 1½ cups of liquid. Add the remaining 2 eggs, the egg yolk, the pinch of cayenne, and the nutmeg; whisk until blended but not frothy. Ladle this custard mixture evenly over the meat. Place the bobotie in the middle of the preheated oven and bake for 30 to 40 minutes, or until the custard is set but still tender. Remove from the oven and let stand for 10 minutes before cutting and serving.

Geel Rys

▲▲

YELLOW RICE WITH CURRANTS

Geel rys is traditionally made with raisins, but currants are more interesting. SERVES 12

3 cups basmati rice
6 tablespoons unsalted butter
1½ cups finely chopped onions
2 cinnamon sticks, 3 inches each
1¼ teaspoons turmeric
¼ teaspoon saffron threads, crumbled and steeped in 3 tablespoons hot water
⅛ teaspoon cayenne
2 teaspoons coarse (kosher) salt, or to taste
1½ tablespoons sugar, preferably superfine
⅛ teaspoon ground allspice
½ cup dried currants

1 Pick over the rice to remove any foreign particles and wash it in several changes of cold water until the water no longer turns milky. Put the washed rice in a large bowl, cover with 6 cups fresh cold water, and soak for 30 minutes. Drain, reserving 3¾ cups of the soaking water.

2 In a heavy 4-quart saucepan or flameproof casserole, melt the butter over moderate heat. Add the onions and cook, stirring, until tender but not browned, about 5 minutes. Add the rice and stir for 1 or 2 minutes to coat with butter; do not let brown.

3 Add the reserved soaking water, the cinnamon sticks, the turmeric, saffron with the steeping water, cayenne, and salt. Bring to a boil. Give the bubbling mixture a good stir, then cover tightly and reduce the heat to its lowest level. Cook, without lifting the lid, for 20 minutes. Remove from the heat.

4 Uncover the pot (away from you) and let the steam escape for 1 or 2 minutes. With a large fork, fluff the rice quickly and lightly, taking care not to mash the grains. Combine the sugar and allspice, sprinkle mixture over rice, add the currants, and mix gently. Cover again and cook over lowest heat for 5 minutes longer. Remove the covered pot from the heat and let stand, undisturbed, for 10 minutes. Season with additional salt, if necessary, and fluff again before serving.

Mixed Red Salad

A slaai, or salad, is considered essential to a Cape Malay meal, and the Malays are particularly fond of beet slaais and onion slaais. Here I've included beets and red onions in a gorgeous red-lettuce salad that tastes as good as it looks. SERVES 12

6 small beets, 1 to 1½ inches in diameter
Orange juice (optional)
10 to 12 large handfuls loose red salad greens: red leaf lettuce, red oak-leaf lettuce,
   Lollo Roso, et cetera
1 large head radicchio, separated into leaves
1 teaspoon Dijon mustard
3 tablespoons red wine vinegar
½ teaspoon coarse (kosher) salt
Freshly ground black pepper
¾ cup extra-virgin olive oil
2 small red onions, thinly sliced and separated into rings

1 Preheat the oven to 350 degrees. Trim the beets, removing the leaves but leaving about 2 inches of the stems and 1 inch of the root tips attached. Scrub thoroughly but gently so as not to break the skins. (These precautions are designed to minimize bleeding and the loss of color and flavor, but some juice will always run out during cooking.) Place the beets in a shallow baking dish large enough to hold them without crowding and add water (or a mixture or orange juice and water) to a depth of ¼ inch. Cover tightly with aluminum foil and bake for about 45 minutes, or until tender. Test for tenderness by gently pressing the beets between your fingers and thumb; if the skins move slightly (indicating looseness), the beets are done. Uncover and let stand until cool enough to handle. Break off the stems and root tips; skins will slip right off. Strain the cooking juices through dampened cheesecloth into a clean bowl large enough to hold all the beets. Add the beets to the bowl and turn to moisten with the juices. Let cool completely, then cover, and refrigerate. *(The beets may be refrigerated for up to 4 days; do not freeze, as freezing alters the texture of beets.)*

2 Up to 24 hours before serving, cut the beets into uniformly thin slices. Cover and refrigerate the sliced beets in their cooking liquid until shortly before serving.

3 Wash the salad greens and radicchio thoroughly, drain well, and spin dry. Discard tough stems and tear large leaves into bite-size pieces. Layer the salad greens between paper towels or roll loosely in clean kitchen towels; refrigerate in plastic bags until serving time.

4 In a mixing bowl, combine the mustard, vinegar, salt, and pepper; whisk to blend. Whisking contantly, gradually add the oil, by droplets at first and then in a thin stream, to make an emulsified vinaigrette. Cover and set aside.

5 When ready to serve, place the chilled greens in a large salad bowl. Add about half the dressing and toss to mix. Drain and add the sliced beets; add the red onions to the bowl. Gradually pour on as much of the remaining dressing as is needed to coat everything lightly and evenly; toss the salad well. Season with additional salt and pepper, if necessary, and serve at once on chilled plates.

Double Espresso Ice Cream

This is an easy no-cook ice cream with a surprisingly sophisticated flavor and texture. Chocolate-covered espresso beans are widely available at candy and specialty shops, but if you can't find them, your ice cream will still be wonderful without them. Do not substitute coffee bean-shaped candies, coffee-flavored chocolates, or chocolate chips; they are much too sweet for a real espresso ice cream. MAKES ABOUT 1 QUART

½ cup (about 3 ounces) chocolate-covered espresso beans
1 can (14 ounces) condensed milk
2 cups heavy cream
½ cup very strong espresso, cooled
1 teaspoon vanilla extract

1 Coarsely crush the chocolate-covered espresso beans. (I like to seal them in a press-and-lock plastic bag and whack them with a rubber mallet.) Set aside.

2 In a large bowl, combine the condensed milk, cream, espresso, and vanilla. Stir well, cover, and refrigerate for 4 hours, or until very cold.

3 In an electric mixer on medium speed, beat the chilled espresso cream until thick and custard-like, 6 to 8 minutes.

4 Pour the mixture into an ice-cream maker and freeze according to the manufacturer's instructions until partially frozen. Stop the machine and quickly stir in the crushed chocolate-covered espresso beans. Continue churning until the ice cream is frozen.

PIGGING OUT IN THE DEEP SOUTH

▲▲▲▲▲▲▲▲▲▲▲▲▲▲▲▲▲▲▲▲▲▲▲▲▲▲▲▲▲▲▲▲▲▲

*Smothered Pork Chops from
Miss Ruby's Café*

Hoppin' John

*Whipped Sweet Potatoes with
Sweet Spices*

A Mess of Greens

Old-fashioned Corn Bread

▲

Lemon Buttermilk Ice

▼

As I told a friend at lunch the other day, I hardly ever eat red meat anymore.

"Me neither," she said. "Almost never."

"Excuse me, ladies," said the waiter, "but how do you want those cheeseburgers cooked?"

Rare. Blood-rare.

We both agreed that if it weren't for cheeseburgers, we could give up meat entirely.

Unless I ever get back to Paris, where I will stand in line in the pouring rain to get into one little restaurant that serves nothing but sliced steak with a secret sauce and crispy pommes frites. Hot french fries are also great with cold steak tartare, a combination I order anywhere I can get it, and with deviled beef bones, which are the only reason I roast beef anymore. I'm a pushover for potatoes. I like lots of them, nicely browned, in my corned beef hash. And the only reason I still eat pot roast is, what else are you going to eat with potato pancakes?

Lamb I could live without, except for ground lamb dishes like bobotie, kibbeh, or shepherd's pie, which I probably only love because it has mashed potatoes on top. And, of course, no couscous would be complete without skewers of lamb, especially delicious when grilled over an open fire. As is your basic bourgeois leg of lamb; butterflied and barbecued, it tastes like a whole other animal.

I'll even eat spareribs when they're cooked outdoors—especially when they're slow-cooked over hickory so they taste smoky as well as spicy. I eat bacon and ham, of course, but mostly just in sandwiches, and I order sausage and pepperoni pizza but, I mean, that's *pizza*. You know? Pizza doesn't count. It's like Chinese food; if you ask people who don't eat pork chops anymore how come they eat mu-shu pork, they always say, "That's different, it's Chinese food." I eat a lot of Chinese food. And, I'll confess, there's still one place in New Orleans and one place in New York where I can't resist the pork chops.

But basically, as you can see, I'm like everybody else these days. I hardly ever eat meat anymore.

▲

Smothered Pork Chops from Miss Ruby's Café

David Blackburn developed this dish at Miss Ruby's Café, where he is the . . . "Oh heavens, I don't know," says Miss Ruby (aka Ruth Bronz). "David works with me in the kitchen. I suppose if French food people saw how we do things here, they'd call him a sous-chef. Actually, if French food people saw how we do things here, they'd probably have a heart attack."

How they do things at 135 Eighth Avenue in New York City is, they cook wonderful American food, and periodically the whole menu changes and all the food is from a different part of America, but somehow it is always just what you feel like eating that day. If Mary Poppins were American and had a restaurant, it would be Miss Ruby's Café.

MAKES 6 HEARTY SERVINGS

6 large double loin pork chops
Flour for dredging
Salt and freshly ground black pepper
14 tablespoons butter
2 tablespoons peanut or safflower oil
6 medium-large onions, cut in half and sliced
¾ cup finely chopped celery heart
1 tablespoon chopped fresh thyme leaves
3 cups strong chicken stock

1 Dredge the chops in flour seasoned with salt and pepper to taste. In a heavy large skillet, melt 2 tablespoons butter with the oil. Add the chops and sauté just until golden brown on both sides; they will not be cooked through. Arrange them in a single layer in a baking pan. Set aside.

2 Preheat the oven to 350 degrees. Pour off any fat and scrape any burned bits out of the skillet. Add the remaining 12 tablespoons of butter to the skillet and melt over moderate heat. Add the onions and cook, stirring, until they are very dark brown—the secret of the dish lies in onions that are almost caramelized—about 30 minutes. Add the chopped celery heart and the thyme and stir together for a minute. Add the chicken stock and simmer gently for a minute or two, just to blend the flavors.

(Continued)

3 Pour this sauce evenly over the pork chops and seal the baking pan tightly with aluminum foil. Bake until the chops are falling-off-the-bone tender, about 1 hour. Miss Ruby suggests serving these gravy-smothered chops with mashed potatoes and Southern-style broad beans, but if someone were to give me Hoppin' John instead, I wouldn't push that off my plate either.

Hoppin' John

Recipes for Hoppin' John—even the old Southern "receipts"—are decent but often dull: cowpeas or black-eyed peas, a snippet of salt pork, water and maybe an onion cut up in it, maybe just a pinch of hot pepper. This blandness surprises, until one realizes that those who had the literacy and the leisure to write down "receipts" seldom ate rice and beans as a main course or actually cooked rice and beans themselves.

A Creole/Cajun approach makes this modern Hoppin' John honest and rich and colorful. SERVES 8 TO 10

1 pound dried black-eyed peas, rinsed and soaked overnight
8 cups Brown Pork Stock (pages 256–257) or water
6 ounces slab bacon, preferably double-smoked bacon, cut into ¼-inch cubes
1 tablespoon peanut or safflower oil
1 green bell pepper, seeded and finely chopped
1 red bell pepper, seeded and finely chopped (if unavailable, substitute another green pepper)
⅓ cup finely chopped celery
1 cup finely chopped onions
1 teaspoon finely chopped garlic
½ cup thinly sliced scallions, white and tender green
1 bay leaf
1 teaspoon chopped fresh thyme leaves or ⅓ teaspoon dried thyme
¼ to ½ teaspoon cayenne
¼ teaspoon freshly ground black pepper
Salt
2 tablespoons finely ground chopped flat-leaf parsley
Hot-pepper sauce
6 cups Steamed Rice (page 39), for serving

1 Drain the soaked black-eyed peas, rinse, and drain again. Put the peas in a heavy 4-quart flameproof casserole and add 6 cups of the Brown Pork Stock or water. Set over moderate heat and slowly bring to a simmer while you prepare the other ingredients, occasionally skimming the foam that rises to the top of the casserole.

2 In a heavy large skillet, slowly cook the bacon in the oil just until lightly crisped and golden; remove with a slotted spoon and set aside. To the hot bacon fat in the skillet add the chopped bell peppers, celery, onions, garlic, scallions, bay leaf, thyme, cayenne, and black pepper. Stirring constantly and vigorously, sauté over moderately high heat until the vegetables are softened and lightly browned. Scrape the pan, when necessary, to prevent sticking and burning, but do not lower the flame.

3 Transfer the contents of the skillet to the pea-cooking pot. Over moderate heat, deglaze the skillet with 1 cup of the remaining stock or water; pour the deglazing liquid into the pot. Stir in the bacon. Set the lid of the pot slightly askew and adjust the heat to maintain a slow steady simmer. Cook until the peas are very tender but not mushy, about 1 hour; stir frequently from the bottom of the pot to prevent sticking and scorching.

4 Remove ¾ cup of the cooked peas, not including any bacon, and puree in a food processor. Stir this puree back into the pot to thicken the rest of the peas. Season with salt to taste. (*The recipe can—and for maximum flavor should—be prepared ahead to this point. Let cool to room temperature, then cover and refrigerate for up to 2 days, or freeze for up to 2 months. Let return to room temperature and then reheat gently before proceeding.*)

5 The pea gravy should be rich but loosely flowing; thin it with a little more warm stock or water, if necessary, and then simmer for a few minutes to blend the flavors. Adjust the seasoning with more salt and pepper, if necessary. Add the parsley and stir in hot-pepper sauce to taste, mixing well. To serve, spoon some freshly cooked rice onto each plate and top with a ladleful of hot black-eyed peas.

Whipped Sweet Potatoes with Sweet Spices

Some sweet potatoes are thirstier than others. If yours are very fresh and moist, the amounts of cream and milk given here will probably be sufficient; drier potatoes may need a little more to drink before they loosen up. SERVES 8

½ teaspoon ground ginger
⅓ teaspoon freshly grated nutmeg
¼ teaspoon ground cinnamon
⅛ teaspoon ground cloves
3 pounds sweet potatoes
1 pound baking potatoes, preferably russets
1¼ cups heavy cream or crème fraîche
¼ cup milk
7 tablespoons unsalted butter, cut into 14 pieces
Salt and freshly ground white pepper

1 Preheat the oven to 400 degrees. In a small bowl, combine the ground ginger, nutmeg, cinnamon, and cloves; mix well, cover tightly, and set aside.

2 Bake the potatoes until tender throughout when pierced with a skewer or sharp knife, about 45 minutes for medium sweet potatoes and slightly longer for medium white potatoes. Or cook in a microwave oven, following the manufacturer's directions.

3 Cut the potatoes in half crosswise. Pass the sweet potato and white potato pulp through a ricer into a large bowl; stir to blend. Meanwhile, in a small saucepan, slowly heat the cream and milk until steaming hot; do not let boil.

4 Stir 8 pieces of the butter into the potatoes. As the butter melts, gradually add the hot cream and milk, whipping the puree with a large fork until smooth and creamy. Blend in the spice mixture, and season with salt and white pepper to taste. *(The recipe may be prepared ahead to this point. Let cool completely, then cover and refrigerate for up to 24 hours. Let return to room temperature before reheating in an uncovered serving dish in a microwave oven, stirring once or twice. Or reheat the potatoes in a covered casserole set in a pan of hot water in a moderate oven.)* With a fork, whip the remaining 6 pieces of butter into the hot puree. Season with additional salt and pepper, if necessary, and serve at once.

A Mess of Greens

5 pounds collard greens
2 smoked ham hocks
1 teaspoon hot-red-pepper flakes
½ teaspoon freshly ground black pepper
1 teaspoon coarse (kosher) salt
1½ teaspoons sugar
Hot-pepper sauce, for seasoning at table
Vinegar, for seasoning at table

1 Pick over the greens, discarding any leaves that are yellowing, insect-bitten, or very coarse and fibrous. Strip the stems up and off the leaves. Wash the leaves thoroughly in several changes of water, lifting them up out of the water each time to leave all grit and sand behind. Drain in a colander, shaking off excess water. Transfer to large plastic bags and seal airtight. Refrigerate until needed, as long as overnight.

2 At least 1 day in advance, put the ham hocks and 3 quarts water in a large nonreactive stockpot or casserole. Bring to a boil, then cover and reduce the heat to moderately low. Simmer until the hocks are tender, about 2 hours. Remove from the heat, uncover the pot, and let the hocks cool to room temperature in the water. When cool, cover and refrigerate overnight.

3 The next day, remove all the hardened fat from the surface of the liquid in the pot. Remove the ham hocks from the liquid. Shred or dice any lean meat and set aside, covered; discard the skin, fat, gristle, and bones. Over moderate heat, let the hock-cooking liquid slowly come to a boil. Meanwhile, tear the collard greens into large (but manageable) pieces.

4 Increase the heat under the pot to high until the liquid reaches a rolling boil. Add the collards, packing them down into the pot. Cover and cook for about 5 minutes, or until wilted and greatly shrunken in volume. Stir in the red-pepper flakes, black pepper, and salt. Reduce the heat to maintain a strong steady simmer and cook, covered, until almost tender, about 1 hour.

5 Add the reserved hock meat and stir in the sugar. Cover again and cook 30 to 60 minutes longer, until the greens are soft and juicy. *(The recipe can be made in advance. Let cool completely, then cover and refrigerate for up to 2 days. Or freeze the collards and the cooking liquid in separate containers for up to 1 month. Let come to room temperature, then reheat together until piping hot.)*

6 Drain very thoroughly, reserving the cooking liquid as "pot likker." Taste the greens, add more salt if necessary, and transfer to a warmed serving dish. Well-drained greens can go right on the dinner plate, but Southerners (and I) prefer theirs on the side, served in small bowls with a little of the pot likker for dunking corn bread. It is customary to have hot-pepper sauce and a cruet of vinegar on the table so guests can season their greens to taste.

Old-fashioned Corn Bread

*F*ollow the recipe for My Blue Heavenly Corn Bread (pages 184–185), using stone-ground white or yellow cornmeal. White is more authentically Southern than yellow, and makes a crunchier crust for dunking in pot likker and sopping up gravy. Yellow corn bread is "cornier," and its fuller flavor matches up well with the other big tastes on this menu. Either is good. And both—one pan of each—is even better.

Lemon Buttermilk Ice

*F*ive ingredients, no eggs, no cream, no whole milk, no cooking; easy, all-natural, low cost, intense flavor; keeps for days.

Don't say I never gave you anything. MAKES ABOUT 1½ QUARTS

2 cups sugar, preferably superfine
½ cup fresh lemon juice
1½ teaspoons freshly grated lemon zest
Pinch of salt
1 quart buttermilk

1 In a large bowl, combine the sugar, lemon juice, lemon zest, and salt; stir to blend.

2 Add the buttermilk and stir gently until the sugar dissolves. Cover and refrigerate for at least 4 hours, or overnight, if possible, to allow the flavor to develop fully.

3 Stir the chilled mixture well. Pour into an ice-cream maker and freeze according to the manufacturer's instructions.

INDIAN WITHOUT TEARS

▲▲▲▲▲▲▲▲▲▲▲▲▲▲▲▲▲▲▲▲▲▲▲▲▲▲▲▲▲▲▲▲▲▲▲

*Chick-pea and
Roasted Cashew Puree
with Toasted Indian Bread*

*Calcutta Popcorn with
Julie Sahni's Fresh Coriander
and Mint Chutney*

▲

Tandoori Shrimp

*Cucumber, Walnut, and
Dill Raita*

Buttered Basmati Rice

▲

Preserved Ginger Ice Cream

▼

Indian food? Ah." He smiled brightly, but I had already seen the flicker of fear in those blue Midwestern eyes.

"You don't like Indian food?"

He just didn't know much about it, he said diplomatically. But his new British bride was an expert. "Fiona loves that stuff."

She nodded happily. "I've a bunch of chums in London, we go out once a week and eat vindaloo till the tears are just streaming down our faces."

If only Tom would come too. All the other husbands came, she said, but not Tom.

"I went once," he said. "And I tasted everything they ordered—if you call it tasting when everything's so hot that after the first taste you can't actually taste anything at all. It's so hot that you break out in a sweat all over. Everybody sits there fanning themselves and gasping and crying—it's like a funeral in a steam bath. Eating Indian food is just . . . weird."

"It's not at all weird," said Fiona, "it's English. It's what we grow up with. We've a curry house on every corner, just as you have Chinese restaurants. My parents took me out for Indian. Why is that different from yours taking you for Chinese?"

"I never ate subgum chow mein till the tears ran down my face."

The bride sighed. "We argue about this a lot."

I didn't see them again until dinner was over and goodnights were being said. Tom pulled me aside. "I have to ask you something," he said quickly. "What we ate tonight, was that *real* Indian food?"

Absolutely. Tandoori shrimp, lightly spiced and seared in the shell. Buttered basmati rice. A cooling raita of cucumbers in yogurt—

"Tell me again," he said, "so I can order it while my wife orders vindaloo." He started to laugh. "My wife," he said happily. "She knows nothing about Indian food."

▲

Chick-pea and Roasted Cashew Puree

*I*rresistible with drinks, at a picnic, or on a festive Indian buffet table, this rich, discreetly healthy dip can be prepared almost entirely in advance. MAKES ABOUT 3 CUPS

3 cups home-cooked chick-peas or rinsed and drained canned chick-peas
¼ cup chick-pea cooking water or plain warm water
½ cup Fresh Roasted Cashew Butter (recipe follows)
¼ cup fresh lemon juice
2 large cloves garlic, cut in half, green shoots removed, peeled and
  crushed to a puree
1½ teaspoons ground roasted cumin (see Note)
1 teaspoon Garam Masala (recipe follows)
¼ teaspoon cayenne
½ teaspoon fresh ginger juice (see Note)
Salt and freshly ground black pepper
1 tablespoon peanut or safflower oil
Fresh coriander leaves, for garnish

1 In a food processor fitted with the steel blade, puree the chick-peas, gradually adding the chick-pea cooking water or plain water (not canned chick-pea liquid). Add the Fresh Roasted Cashew Butter, lemon juice, and garlic. Process until smooth and creamy.

2 Add the cumin, Garam Masala, cayenne, and ginger juice. Process on-and-off 4 or 5 times to blend. Transfer the puree to a colorful serving bowl and stir in salt and pepper to taste. (*The recipe can be made to this point up to 2 days ahead. Cover with plastic wrap and refrigerate. Let return to room temperature before proceeding.*)

3 Drizzle in the oil, whipping the puree vigorously with a large fork or whisk until light and smooth. Perk up the seasonings if refrigeration has dulled them and stir in a little more lemon juice if necessary. Garnish with fresh coriander leaves and serve with toasted pita bread.

(Continued)

NOTE Ground roasted cumin is an important seasoning for Indian, Middle Eastern, and Mexican dishes. To fully appreciate its heady aroma and intense "toasty" taste, make small amounts as needed.

In a heavy small skillet, heat 3 tablespoons cumin seeds over a moderate flame, shaking the pan constantly, until the seeds darken and become fragrant. This process takes only a few minutes and happens very suddenly, so be poised to pour the seeds onto a plate as soon as they are roasted. Let cool slightly. In a mortar with a pestle or in a spice mill or a coffee grinder reserved for spices, grind the seeds to a fine powder. Store in an airtight jar away from heat and sunlight.

NOTE To make fresh ginger juice, wrap minced ginger in cheesecloth and squeeze the cloth over a small bowl or jar. Covered and refrigerated, the juice will keep for up to 1 week. Stir well before using.

Fresh Roasted Cashew Butter

▲

The cashew butter sold in health food stores is costly and oily and often past its prime. Even the best doesn't compare with what you can make at home. Buy your cashews in Asian markets, where they're fresh and cheap. Some Indian shops price cashews according to size, and the small broken ones are a relative bargain. Store them—and all nuts—in your freezer to keep them fresher longer. MAKES ABOUT ½ CUP

1 cup raw cashew nuts
4 teaspoons peanut or safflower oil

1 Preheat oven to 325 degrees. Toss the cashews with a few drops of oil and roast on a baking sheet for 12 to 15 minutes, until they turn light golden brown. Remove from the oven immediately.

2 When the cashews have cooled slightly, place them in the bowl of a food processor fitted with the steel blade. Process for 60 seconds. Scrape down the sides of the bowl, re-cover, and run the motor for 30 seconds more. Stop, scrape down the sides again and add the remaining oil. Process for about 30 seconds longer to obtain a creamy cashew butter. (*Covered and refrigerated, this will keep its fresh-roasted taste for at least 2 weeks. Bring to room temperature and stir well before using.*)

Garam Masala

▲

Garam masala is a varied but always aromatic spice blend essential to Indian cooking. It can be bought ready-mixed at specialty stores and Indian markets but tastes much fresher when made at home. This is my own favorite blend. The recipe can be halved, if desired.

MAKES ABOUT ⅔ CUP

1 cinnamon stick, 2½ to 3 inches long
3 tablespoons cumin seeds
3 tablespoons coriander seeds
1 tablespoon whole black peppercorns
2 teaspoons cardamom seeds (removed from 1½ to 2 tablespoons
    green cardamom pods)
Scant 1 teaspoon (about 18) whole cloves
¼ teaspoon fragrant ground mace

1 Place the cinnamon stick between 2 sheets of wax paper; with a rubber mallet or rolling pin, break it into small pieces. In a heavy medium skillet, combine the cinnamon pieces, cumin seeds, coriander seeds, peppercorns, cardamom seeds, and cloves. Toast the spices over moderate heat, shaking the pan constantly, until they darken slightly and become fragrant, usually in 4 to 5 minutes. Immediately pour the spices out of the pan and let cool completely.

2 In a spice mill or a coffee grinder reserved for spices, grind the mixture to a fine powder. Transfer to a jar and stir in the ground mace, mixing well. Cover tightly and store away from heat and sunlight for up to 3 months.

Calcutta Popcorn

CRISP-FRIED INDIAN OKRA

*B*etcha can't eat just one.

Forget everything you (and I) ever heard about okra. Here it's fried crisp and crunchy and sprinkled with a heady mixture of spices. It's also simple and not at all greasy or messy if you make it right. I do all my deep-frying in a wok with a thermometer clamped to one side, so it's easy to keep the oil temperature constant. And I always use fresh oil; it's a little extravagance that makes a big difference. SERVES 8

1 teaspoon Garam Masala (page 97)
¾ teaspoon amchoor (optional, see Note)
¼ teaspoon ground cumin
¼ teaspoon cayenne
⅛ teaspoon freshly ground black pepper
⅛ teaspoon super fine sugar
2½ pounds firm fresh okra pods
Peanut or corn oil for deep-frying
Salt
Julie Sahni's Fresh Coriander and Mint Chutney (recipe follows),
*   as accompaniment*

1 In a small bowl, mix the Garam Masala, amchoor (if using), cumin, cayenne, black pepper, and sugar; set aside. Rinse the okra and dry very thoroughly. Remove the tops and tails and slice the pods ¼-inch thick.

2 In a wok or deep-fryer, heat the oil to a temperature of 350 degrees. Add as much okra as will fit without crowding. Raising and/or lowering the heat as necessary to maintain a fairly constant temperature of 350 degrees, cook until the pieces of okra are crisp and the cut ends lightly browned, about 4 minutes. (Do not let the okra darken further or it will become bitter.) With a mesh skimmer or a large slotted spoon, remove the okra from the oil and drain on paper towels. Keep warm in a low oven —I spread it out on pizza screens for extra crispness, but a baking sheet or heatproof platter will do—while you fry the rest in successive batches.

3 Toss the hot, crunchy okra with the spice mixture and season with salt to taste. If the spice mixture did not include amchoor, sprinkle the okra lightly with lemon juice just before serving.

NOTE Amchoor, a sundried mango powder used as a souring agent, is available at specialty stores and Indian markets.

▼▼

Julie Sahni's Fresh Coriander and Mint Chutney

▲▲

This quick, uncooked, vibrantly fresh chutney is the creation of Julie Sahni, author of *Classic Indian Cooking* and *Classic Indian Vegetarian and Grain Cooking*. When she served it with a first course, we all wanted to keep eating it straight through dinner; you might consider making a little extra in case your guests feel the same way. It also makes a great dipping sauce for non-Indian goodies like fried zucchini and fried onion rings and for just about any kind of vegetable fritter. MAKES ABOUT 1¾ CUPS

⅔ *cup distilled white vinegar*
¼ *cup sugar, preferably superfine*
2 jalapeño chilies, seeded and sliced
1 piece (1 inch) fresh ginger, peeled
1 teaspoon coarse (kosher) salt
1 cup, firmly packed, coarsely chopped fresh coriander with stems
1 cup, firmly packed, coarsely chopped fresh mint leaves with stems
1 small unripe mango, peeled, pitted, and chopped

1 In a blender, coarsely puree the vinegar, sugar, chilies, ginger, and salt. Add the coriander and mint a few tablespoons at a time, blending well after each addition.

2 Add the mango and blend to a puree. (*This chutney can be prepared up to 2 days ahead. Cover and refrigerate, but let come to room temperature before serving.*)

Tandoori Shrimp

Tandoori shrimp, swiftly seared in an Indian oven or on a backyard grill or even under a fiery broiler, are lightly charred but wonderfully juicy and richly flavored with ginger and fennel. SERVES 8 TO 10

3 pounds jumbo shrimp, in the shell
6 tablespoons fresh lime juice
2 teaspoons minced garlic
2 teaspoons minced fresh ginger
½ teaspoon fennel seeds, lightly crushed
⅓ cup plain yogurt
2 teaspoons ground cumin
2 teaspoons ground coriander
½ teaspoon paprika
½ teaspoon freshly ground black pepper
¼ to ½ teaspoon cayenne, to taste
¼ teaspoon coarse (kosher) salt
Peanut or safflower oil, for basting
Several sprigs fresh coriander, for garnish
Lime wedges, for garnish

1 Using kitchen shears, cut the legs off the shrimp. Slit each shell open down the back to the last segment and pull out the intestinal vein. Loosen the shells very slightly (so the marinade can get under them), but do not remove. Rinse the shrimp and pat dry.

2 In a large bowl, toss the shrimp with the lime juice, garlic, ginger, and fennel seeds. Marinate at room temperature for 30 minutes, stirring once or twice.

3 In a small bowl, combine the yogurt, cumin, coriander, paprika, black pepper, cayenne, and salt. Add the seasoned yogurt to the shrimp, stirring and turning them until evenly coated. Cover and refrigerate for 1½ hours, turning the shrimp in the marinade occasionally.

4 Drain the shrimp, reserving the marinade, and arrange them on skewers. *(The shrimp can be prepared to this point 1 hour in advance. Place the skewers on a large platter or tray, cover tightly with plastic wrap or aluminum foil, and refrigerate. Set the marinade aside at room temperature.)*

5 Light a charcoal grill or preheat the broiler; the fire must be quite hot so the skewered shrimp will cook quickly and stay moist. Brush the shrimp with oil. Grill or broil about 4 inches from the heat for 3 minutes. Turn the skewers over and brush the shrimp with oil again; grill until the shells are slightly charred and the meat inside is just opaque but still tender and juicy, 2 to 3 minutes.

6 Slide the hot shrimp off the skewers and onto a warmed serving platter. Pour the reserved marinade over the shrimp and toss. Garnish with sprigs of fresh coriander, and serve with lime wedges.

Cucumber, Walnut, and Dill Raita

*T*he use of walnuts and dill reflects the Persian influence on northern Indian cuisine and gives this refreshing yogurt salad a special texture and taste. SERVES 10

1 cup walnut halves
5 medium cucumbers, peeled, seeded, and cut into ¼-inch dice
4 cups plain yogurt
1 cup sour cream
¼ cup minced fresh dill
¼ teaspoon cayenne
½ teaspoon coarse (kosher) salt
¼ teaspoon freshly ground black pepper

1 Preheat the oven to 250 degrees. Scatter the walnuts on a baking sheet and toast in the oven for 15 minutes to crisp them and bring out their full flavor. Let the walnuts cool and then chop them into pieces about the same size as the cucumbers.

2 In a large bowl, combine the yogurt, sour cream, dill, cayenne, salt, and pepper. Fold in the diced cucumbers and mix well. *(The recipe can be prepared to this point several hours in advance. Set the walnuts aside at room temperature; cover the yogurt mixture and refrigerate.)*

3 Shortly before serving, stir the walnuts into the yogurt mixture and adjust the seasoning if necessary.

Buttered Basmati Rice

Basmati rice is an aromatic long-grain rice available in Indian and Pakistani markets, specialty food stores, and many supermarkets. The best, graded Number 1, is imported from India, has no broken grains, and has been aged for at least six months to decrease its moisture content and increase its delicate but extraordinary flavor and fragrance.

It is so good that sometimes all I want for supper is a cup of cool yogurt and a bowl of hot basmati rice. SERVES 8 TO 10

2 cups basmati rice
2 tablespoons unsalted butter
1 teaspoon coarse (kosher) salt

1 Pick over the rice to remove any foreign particles and wash it in several changes of cold water until the water no longer turns milky. Put the rice in a large bowl, cover with 4 cups fresh cold water, and soak for 30 minutes. Meanwhile, while the rice is soaking, bring 6 to 8 quarts of unsalted water to a boil in a deep pot.

2 Drain the soaked rice. Dribble it into the boiling water and stir briefly to keep it from sticking to the bottom of the pot as the water comes back to a rolling boil over high heat. Boil the rice rapidly, uncovered, for *exactly* 5 minutes. Meanwhile, when the rice has almost finished boiling, put the butter in a heavy 3- or 4-quart flameproof casserole and set over low heat to melt slowly.

3 Drain the boiled rice very thoroughly in a large sieve or colander, shaking off excess moisture. Immediately add the drained rice to the casserole and sprinkle with the salt. Over moderately low heat, gently turn and stir the rice until all the grains are separate, fluffy, and lightly buttered, usually in 2 to 3 minutes. Cover, turn the heat very low, and cook for a few minutes longer, just until steaming hot. If not to be served at once, the rice can be kept warm in a low oven for up to 15 minutes. *(The rice can be cooked up to 1 day in advance. Let cool completely, then transfer to a heatproof serving dish. Cover and set aside at room temperature for up to 2 hours, or refrigerate for longer keeping. Reheat in a microwave oven or large steamer.)* Season with additional salt, if necessary, and fluff the rice once more before serving.

Preserved Ginger Ice Cream

*E*xotic but easy to love, this ginger ice cream is surprisingly versatile. Serve it with fresh fruit salad after an Asian feast or perhaps with grilled peaches as a grand finale to any barbecue. MAKES ABOUT 1 QUART

2 cups heavy cream
1 cup milk
½ cup sugar
Pinch of salt
3 large egg yolks
2 teaspoons pure vanilla extract
⅓ cup finely chopped preserved stem ginger (see Note)
2 tablespoons syrup from the ginger jar

1 In a heavy medium saucepan, combine the cream, milk, sugar, and salt. Cook over moderate heat, stirring frequently, until the sugar dissolves and the mixture is hot, 6 to 8 minutes.

2 In a large bowl, beat the egg yolks lightly. Gradually whisk in the hot cream mixture in a very thin stream. Pour back into the saucepan and cook over moderately low heat, stirring constantly, until the custard thickens enough to lightly coat the back of a metal spoon, 5 to 7 minutes. (Do not let the temperature exceed 180 degrees.)

3 Pour the custard through a fine mesh strainer into a metal bowl. Set the bowl in a basin of ice and cold water and let stand, stirring occasionally, until the custard has cooled to room temperature. Add the vanilla extract. Stir in the chopped preserved ginger and syrup. Mix well, making sure the ginger doesn't clump together. Cover and refrigerate for at least 6 hours, or overnight, if possible, to allow the flavor to develop fully.

4 Stir the chilled mixture, pour into an ice-cream maker, and freeze according to the manufacturer's instructions. Let the ice cream soften slightly before serving.

NOTE Preserved stem ginger in syrup can be found in little green-glazed crocks in Chinese markets and in glass jars in specialty food shops and many supermarkets.

A SPLENDID TIME

▲▲▲▲▲▲▲▲▲▲▲▲▲▲▲▲▲▲▲▲▲▲▲▲▲▲▲▲▲▲

*Couscous and Roasted
Pepper Salad*

▲

A Grand Ragout of Vegetables

*Bert Greene's Long-baked
Tomatoes*

▲

Frozen Peanut Butter Pie

▼

A while ago this guy came to visit us from another commune. . . . We were talking about various things, about how our respective groups worked, shopping and cleaning up and so forth. We asked how his group did their cooking and he replied, rather nonchalantly, "Well, we used to just cook whenever somebody felt like it, but a few days ago somebody got uptight and decided we had to eat every day."

—CRESCENT DRAGONWAGON,
The Commune Cookbook

Ah, the sixties. Brown rice and Goldenberg's Peanut Chews. . . .

Chairman Mao said a revolution is not a dinner party, but you could have fooled us. We had food and music wherever we went. The greening of America was a picnic on the grass of city parks and country communes, a banquet on blankets that stretched from the Sheep Meadow through Yasgur's Farm all the way to the Haight-Ashbury. We were going to feed the world just by passing stuff from blanket to blanket.

And why not? Anything was possible when mushrooms were magic, bananas were electric, Lucy was in the sky with diamonds, and rocking horse people ate marshmallow pies.

"Grandma, what were 'the munchies?'" they'll ask me, when I'm sixty-four.

I never ate an actual marshmallow pie, nor did anyone ever give me an honest-to-God Alice B. Toklas brownie. I had a nuclear family and they didn't want bread that was made out of zucchini. I couldn't stand brown rice and I couldn't think of anything that Boone's Farm Apple Wine went *with*.

But I loved the sixties. Twenty-five years ago we rushed home with the new Beatles album and put a big pot of something on the stove and called up everyone we knew and told them to hurry over. No one listened to a Walkman when Sgt. Pepper taught the band to play. No one ate Soup For One. *A splendid time is guaranteed for all*, the Beatles sang.

And for a little while, they were right.

▲

Couscous and Roasted Pepper Salad

Most Moroccan cooks disdain quick-cooking couscous and no Moroccan cook would serve cold couscous. But two American wrongs make a right here: this salad is easy enough to enjoy often, light enough to be a first course or side dish, and flavorful enough to become, with the addition of a little leftover cooked lamb or chicken, a simple but satisfying supper. And it is the only couscous salad I've ever tasted that tates like a real couscous. SERVES 8 AS A FIRST COURSE

½ *teaspoon ground cumin*
½ *teaspoon ground ginger*
¼ *teaspoon cinnamon*
¼ *teaspoon freshly ground black pepper*
Large pinch powdered saffron
Large pinch cayenne
¾ *cup warm water*
2 cups chicken stock
2 tablespoons unsalted butter
1 teaspoon coarse (kosher) salt
2 cups quick-cooking couscous
1 red bell pepper
1 green bell pepper
6 tablespoons mild olive oil
⅔ *cup slivered blanched almonds*
1½ *teaspoons sambal oelek (see Note)*
1¼ *teaspoons ground roasted cumin (page 96)*
2 tablespoons fresh lemon juice
⅓ *cup finely chopped red onion*
2 tablespoons chopped fresh coriander
Salt and freshly ground black pepper
Sprigs of fresh coriander, for garnish
Romaine lettuce, for serving

(Continued)

1 In a heavy flameproof 3-quart casserole, combine the cumin, ginger, cinnamon, pepper, saffron, and cayenne. Gradually whisk in the warm water, dissolving the spices. Add the stock, butter, and salt, and bring to a boil over moderate heat. Add the couscous in a steady stream and stir for a few seconds, until it begins to bubble gently. Cover the pot tightly and remove from the heat at once. Let stand for 10 minutes.

2 Uncover the pot and use a large fork to loosen and fluff the steamy couscous grains without mashing them. Transfer the couscous to a large shallow pan and spread it out evenly; then stir it up and smooth it out again once or twice. As soon as it is cool enough to handle, after about 10 or 15 minutes, rake the couscous with your fingers, aerating and separating the grains and gently breaking up any lumps. Set aside uncovered if it still seems damp, or cover with a clean cloth if it feels fluffy and dry.

3 Roast the peppers under a broiler or over the flame of a gas stove or, best of all, on an open grill, turning until charred and blistered on all sides. Place them in a paper bag and close tightly. Set aside for 15 to 20 minutes; the steam that forms in the bag will loosen the charred skin of the peppers and make them easy to peel.

4 Meanwhile, heat 1 tablespoon of the olive oil in a heavy skillet. Add the almonds and stir over moderate heat until lightly golden. Remove the nuts from the pan immediately and set aside to cool.

5 Peel the peppers, slit them open, and discard seeds, ribs, and stems. Cut the flesh lengthwise into ¼-inch strips and then crosswise into ¼-inch dice. Lay the diced peppers on paper towels to drain off excess moisture.

6 In a small bowl, combine the sambal oelek, ground roasted cumin, and lemon juice. Whisk in the remaining 5 tablespoons of olive oil to make a dressing for the salad.

7 In a serving bowl large enough to hold all the ingredients, toss the couscous with the roasted peppers, almonds, onions, and chopped coriander. Season with salt and pepper to taste. Mix the dressing again and stir it into the salad, moistening the couscous lightly and evenly. Cover and set aside in a cool place for 2 to 4 hours to allow the dressing to be absorbed and the flavors to blend and "ripen"; do not refrigerate. Just before serving, adjust the seasonings, toss once more, and garnish with a few sprigs of fresh coriander. Serve with tender leaves of romaine lettuce.

NOTE Sambal oelek is an Indonesian paste of hot red chilies. Because it contains no seasonings except salt, it can be used in many Asian cuisines and in Middle Eastern and North African dishes. Sambal oelek is widely available at specialty food stores and Oriental markets and can be mail-ordered from Maison Glass, 111 East 58th Street, New York, NY 10012. Store in the refrigerator after opening.

A Grand Ragout of Vegetables

We did not, of course, measure in the sixties—not time, not the length of our hair, and certainly not food. The recipe then might have read: *Fill an infinitely expandable pot with all the freshest vegetables you can find or grow. Season them richly and cook just until they are done and taste wonderful. Serves however many you are.*

What made my ragout better than others that followed that same free-form formula was what I did *not* put in it: tamari, sesame oil, kelp, sunflower seeds, wheat germ, nuts, soy grits, and/or sprouts of any kind. What I did put in my vegetables was good olive oil and Mediterranean herbs because real people have been doing that for centuries, and that's my definition of natural.

This gorgeous garden-in-a-pot can be made with more of this and less of that, depending on taste and availability. You can use frozen baby peas but everything else should be absolutely fresh. Cut sliced vegetables into approximately ¼-inch slices; cut diced vegetables into approximately ½-inch dice.

This was my father-in-law's favorite dish (and he was no hippie, believe me). Every time I make it now, I smile because I remember his delight whenever I made it for him then. We get by with a little help from our families, too. SERVES 8 TO 10

1 bunch broccoli, about 1½ to 2 pounds
6 cups sliced onions
4 tablespoons mild olive oil
2 teaspoons chopped garlic
8 cups sliced cabbage
3 cups peeled and diced all-purpose potatoes
2 cups peeled and diced carrots
½ to ¾ cup sliced celery
2 cups peeled and diced turnips
1 cup peeled and diced parsnips
1 cup sliced fennel
3 cups diced zucchini and/or yellow squash
1½ teaspoons Mediterranean Herbs (recipe follows)
Salt and freshly ground black pepper
3 tablespoons fruity green extra-virgin olive oil

1½ cups cooked chick-peas
½ pound slender young green beans, trimmed and cut into 2-inch lengths
1½ cups tiny tender peas, thawed if frozen

1 Prepare the broccoli. Cut the top of the broccoli into florets and set aside. Cut off and discard the tough ½- to 1-inch base at the end of each broccoli stalk. Peel the stalks to expose the tender flesh. Halve or quarter them lengthwise and then cut them into pieces about 1 to 1½ inches long; set aside, separate from the florets.

2 In a heavy large casserole, cook the onions in the mild olive oil over low heat until softened, 5 to 8 minutes. Add the garlic and cook for a minute longer, stirring. Add the cabbage, potatoes, carrots, celery, turnips, parsnips, fennel, zucchini and/or yellow squash, and the broccoli stalks. Rub the Mediterranean Herbs between your palms for a few seconds to release the full fragrance and flavor, then sprinkle it over the vegetables. Season with salt and pepper to taste. Drizzle 2 tablespoons of the extra-virgin olive oil over all. Stir and toss to mix thoroughly. Cover, and cook very slowly for about 30 minutes, stirring occasionally. Add the chick-peas and cook for 5 to 10 minutes longer, just until all the vegetables are tender. Remove from the heat, uncover, and set aside.

3 Meanwhile, bring a large pot of lightly salted water to a boil. Add the broccoli florets and boil, uncovered, until barely crisp-tender. Remove the florets immediately and plunge them into cold water to stop the cooking; drain and pat dry. Blanch and cool the green beans in the same manner, allowing 2 to 3 minutes boiling time for tiny haricots verts and a few minutes longer for larger beans. Set the blanched vegetables aside in a bowl with the peas. (*The recipe can be prepared to this point up to 1 hour ahead. Cover the bowl of cool blanched vegetables with plastic wrap. Leave the casserole uncovered. Do not refrigerate anything.*)

4 Shortly before serving, cover the casserole and reheat over moderate heat, stirring frequently, until heated through. Gently fold in the peas, broccoli florets, and green beans. Blend in the remaining tablespoon of extra-virgin olive oil. Cover and simmer a few minutes longer, just until the ragout is hot and juicy throughout. Adjust the seasonings with more salt and pepper if necessary, and serve at once.

Mediterranean Herbs

▲

This well-balanced blend of herbs takes no time at all to make and tastes much fresher than the herbes de Provence that's sold in those pricey clay pots. MAKES ABOUT 3½ TABLESPOONS

2 tablespoons dried thyme
2 teaspoons dried oregano
1½ teaspoons dried savory
1¼ teaspoons fennel seeds
½ teaspoon dried rosemary
¼ teaspoon dried marjoram

1 Crumble the herbs and mix well. Cover tightly and store in a cool, dry place.

2 Just before using, rub the required amount between your palms for a few seconds to release the full fragrance and flavor of the mixture.

Bert Greene's Long-baked Tomatoes

Bert Greene was as warm and wise and witty as the cookbooks he wrote. I never met anyone who didn't love Bert and I don't know anyone who doesn't miss him. SERVES 8

8 tablespoons extra-virgin olive oil
8 ripe red tomatoes
Coarse (kosher) salt and freshly ground black pepper
½ cup fresh basil leaves
½ cup fresh flat-leaf parsley leaves
3 large cloves garlic

1 Preheat the oven to 450 degrees. Pour 2 tablespoons of the olive oil into a large shallow baking pan (use 2 smaller pans if necessary) and swirl to coat the bottom of the pan lightly. Cut the tomatoes in half crosswise and gently squeeze out the seeds. Arrange the tomatoes, cut side up, in the baking pan.

2 With a knife or in a food processor, finely chop the basil, parsley, and garlic together. (If using a processor, add 1 tablespoon of the remaining olive oil to the herbs in the processor bowl to facilitate chopping.) Season the tomatoes lightly with coarse salt and freshly ground pepper and spread an equal portion of the herb-garlic mixture over each. Drizzle on the remaining olive oil and place the pan in the middle of the preheated oven.

3 When the oil in the pan begins to sizzle—after about 10 minutes— reduce the heat to 350 degrees and continue to bake for about 90 minutes. Every 30 minutes, baste the tomatoes with the richly flavored oil in the bottom of the pan. When the tomatoes are done, they will have shriveled considerably and turned black on the bottom and their flavor will be wonderfully concentrated and intense. Arrange the tomatoes on a large platter and serve hot, warm, or at room temperature; do not refrigerate and/or reheat.

Frozen Peanut Butter Pie

Groovier than marshmallow.... SERVES 8 TO 12

*7 to 8 ounces packaged chocolate wafers, processed and finely crushed
  to yield 1½ cups crumbs*
2 tablespoons superfine sugar
Pinch of coarse (kosher) salt
6 tablespoons unsalted butter, melted
½ cup plus 2½ tablespoons creamy peanut butter
*8 ounces cream cheese, preferably preservative-free bulk cream cheese,
  at room temperature*
¾ cup milk, at room temperature
1 cup confectioners' sugar, sifted
1 cup cold heavy cream

1 In a medium bowl, toss the crumbs, sugar, and salt together. Add the melted butter and mix thoroughly. Pat the mixture evenly onto the bottom and sides of a well-buttered 9-inch pie pan. Refrigerate for at least 1 hour, or until firm, before filling.

2 Meanwhile, prepare the filling. In the large bowl of an electric mixer, cream the peanut butter and cream cheese together until soft and smooth. Gradually beat in the milk. Add the sugar a little at a time, beating until smooth. In another bowl, whip the ceam until it holds a soft shape. Gently but thoroughly fold the whipped cream into the peanut butter mixture.

3 Pour about two-thirds of the filling into the chilled pie crust and level the surface with a rubber spatula. Carefully spoon or pour on the remaining filling and lightly smooth the surface again. Freeze, uncovered, until firm, then seal airtight in plastic wrap and return to the freezer. *(The pie may be made ahead and if very well wrapped, will keep perfectly in the freezer for up to 2 weeks.)* Unwrap and let stand at room temperature for about 30 minutes, or until easy to cut but not really soft, before serving.

FROM RUSSIA WITH LOVE

▲▲▲▲▲▲▲▲▲▲▲▲▲▲▲▲▲▲▲▲▲▲▲▲▲▲▲▲▲▲▲▲▲

Oysters and Caviar

▲

Pelmeni with Mustard and
Sour Cream Sauce

Kasha with Wild Mushrooms
and Toasted Walnuts

Endive and Beet Salad

▲

The New Year's Eve
Fruit Compote

▼

It is said that whole villages in Siberia still turn out one afternoon before the onset of winter to make a vast batch of *pel'meni*. The women make the dough and chop the meat, the men do the folding. For their exacting work the latter enjoy a glass of vodka every hundredth pel'men'. . . . The villagers have an immediate feast after their work, with which ice-cold vodka is obligatory. The rest of the *pel'meni* are deep frozen in goatskin bags in the snow. *Pel'meni*-eating contests take place periodically.

—LESLEY CHAMBERLAIN,
The Food and Cooking of Russia

Leslie Newman had just hit her 1,340th pelmeni. From there, she segued into fruit compote, the final touch on her 10th New Year's Eve party where she feeds about 200 of her friends promptly at 12:01 A.M. She cooks everything herself—from scratch. "It was going to be 1,600 pelmeni, but you reach a point," Mrs. Newman said. "Let 'em eat kasha."

—*The New York Times*, January 1, 1985

▲

Oysters and Caviar

FOR EACH GUEST

2 or more oysters on the half shell, freshly opened
Beluga caviar
1 lemon wedge, wrapped in cheesecloth

ON THE TABLE

Small peppermills, filled with black peppercorns
Thinly sliced French bread and/or crustless white-bread toast
Unsalted butter

TO DRINK

Brut champagne

1 Prepare the oysters and caviar just before serving. With a nonmetallic utensil (i.e., a porcelain, horn, or bone spoon or even a doctor's wooden tongue depressor), carefully spoon some caviar around the rim of each oyster shell; gently nudge and plump the oyster to make it appear nestled in the caviar. Cover loosely with plastic wrap and refrigerate while you prepare the remaining oysters and caviar. Serve at once with a well-chilled brut champagne worthy of the caviar.

2 To eat, grind a few grains of pepper over the oyster *only* and squeeze a few drops of lemon juice over the caviar *only*. Lift the shell to your lips and tip the oyster and caviar together into your mouth. The taste is astonishing, so exquisite and intense that you'll want a bit of bread and butter between oysters.

Pelmeni

▲▲▲

SIBERIAN BOILED BEEF DUMPLINGS

MAKES APPROXIMATELY 10 DOZEN DUMPLINGS

One: The Outsides

2 1-pound packages wonton wrappers of medium thickness (see Note)

1 On your work surface, set up a little assembly line. To the left, the wonton wrappers loosely stacked in a plastic bag large enough to reach into easily. In front of you, a cutting board and a sharp, plain-edged, 2½-inch round cookie cutter. To the right, a flat platter or tray covered with a clean dry towel. Now, working from left to right:

▲ Remove a few wonton wrappers at a time from the bag. Stack on cutting board.

▲ Center cookie cutter on top and press down to cut out circles.

▲ Transfer circles to tray and cover with towel to keep from drying out. Repeat, stacking circles on tray, until all have been cut.

▲ Wrap stacks of circles in plastic wrap and seal in airtight plastic bags. *(Refrigerate for up to 4 days, or freeze for up to 1 month. Frozen wrappers should be completely defrosted in their airtight wrappings, preferably in the refrigerator, before using.)*

2 This takes less time to do than write about.

Two: The Insides

4 to 5 pounds lean, meaty first-cut flanken
12 cups Brown Beef Stock (pages 122–123)
3 tablespoons unsalted butter
2 cups finely chopped onions
1½ teaspoons very finely chopped garlic
1½ tablespoons very finely chopped flat-leaf parsley
3 tablespoons minced fresh dill

1 teaspoon freshly ground black pepper
1½ teaspoons coarse (kosher) salt, or to taste
1 large egg white, lightly beaten

3 In a large stockpot, bring 6 to 8 quarts of water to a vigorous boil over high heat. Add the flanken. As soon as the water returns to a boil, lower the heat and simmer for 2 minutes. Drain. Run the flanken under cold water to rinse off any scum and drain again. Wash and dry the stockpot.

4 Return the flanken to the pot. Add the Brown Beef Stock and 4 cups water and bring to a boil. Lower the heat and cook, partially covered, until the meat is meltingly tender, about 2 hours. The cooking liquid should barely simmer and never boil, and any scum or foam that forms should be carefully skimmed from the surface.

5 Remove the flanken and discard all bones, gristle, and obvious fat; put the meat in a bowl with 1 or 2 ladlefuls of the cooking broth to keep it moist. Strain the remaining broth through several thicknesses of dampened cheesecloth and let cool completely. Cover and refrigerate overnight, then remove the congealed fat from the surface.

6 The trimmed flanken can be chopped immediately after cooking or it can be refrigerated overnight and gently reheated in a little stock before chopping; what is essential is that it be chopped while just slightly warm, not when very hot or cold. With a knife, chop the meat fairly fine but not to a paste; the filling must have texture. Scoop the chopped meat into a large mixing bowl, cover with plastic wrap, and set aside while you prepare the remaining ingredients.

7 In a heavy medium skillet, melt the butter. Add the onions and cook, stirring, over moderately low heat until soft and golden, 8 to 10 minutes. Add the garlic and cook for about 2 minutes longer.

8 Scrape the onions and garlic into the bowl of chopped beef. Stir in 2 tablespoons of cooking broth. Add the parsley, dill, pepper, and salt; mix lightly but thoroughly. Add the egg white and stir to blend. If necessary, add another tablespoon of broth to bind the filling, but take care that it does not become pasty or wet. Cover and refrigerate for at least 4 hours; the filling will be easier to work with when cool.

(Continued)

Outsides (wrappers)
Insides (filling)
Cooking broth

9 Another assembly line. Gather together and arrange the following, from left to right. First, the wrapper circles (completely defrosted, if they were frozen). Next, the prepared filling, which should be cool. Then, a small bowl of water and a clean brush. An ordinary salad fork or dinner fork. Finally, 1 or 2 large baking sheets or metal trays (if you have 2, you can fill the second while the first is in the freezer), each covered with a clean kitchen towel.

10 Before you begin, find or clear a flat space in your freezer large enough to accommodate the baking sheet.

11 Place 1 teaspoon of filling just below the center of each wrapper. Lightly moisten your brush and run it around the edges of the wrapper. Fold the upper half over the lower half and pinch the edges together, enclosing the filling in a half-moon shaped dumpling. Seal by pressing the edges firmly with the tines of a fork; this ensures that the pelmeni won't come open when cooked, and it also gives them a nice homemade look. Place the finished pelmeni on the baking sheet or tray; leave a little space between them and keep them covered with the towel.

12 Once the tray is filled, place it in the freezer, uncovered. When the pelmeni are frozen firm, divide them into conveniently sized batches and store in airtight plastic freezer bags. Repeat with the remaining filling and wrappers. The pelmeni are ready to be cooked as soon as they are frozen, or they can be kept in the freezer for up to 1 month; do not defrost before cooking.

13 The strained and degreased cooking broth will be used to cook the pelmeni. If the pelmeni will not be cooked within 3 days, the broth should be frozen at the same time as but separate from the pelmeni. Let the broth come to room temperature before proceeding.

Flanken-cooking broth, at room temperature
Frozen pelmeni
6 to 8 tablespoons unsalted butter, melted
Freshly ground black pepper
Coarse (kosher) salt
Mustard and Sour Cream Sauce (page 123), as accompaniment
Cider vinegar for seasoning at table

14 Generously butter a large baking dish or shallow bowl to hold the cooked pelmeni; cover loosely with aluminum foil and set aside. Preheat the oven to 150 degrees to keep the pelmeni warm.

15 Pour the stock and 8 cups water into a wide shallow pan (you can use more or less water, as necessary for cooking) and bring to a vigorous boil. Add as many frozen pelmeni as will fit in one layer without crowding. As soon as the broth comes back to a boil, reduce the heat to keep the dumplings from breaking apart. Cook, uncovered, at a steady even simmer for 10 minutes. With a slotted spoon, remove the cooked pelmeni to the baking dish and sprinkle with melted butter to keep them from sticking together. Sprinkle generously with black pepper and very lightly with salt. Cover loosely and keep warm in the preheated oven while you cook the remaining pelmeni. When all have been cooked, serve at once with a bowl of Mustard and Sour Cream Sauce and/or a cruet of cider vinegar.

Leftovers (as rare and precious as Fabergé eggs) can be gently reheated with, and eaten in, a bowlful of the broth, or they can be panfried until lightly crisp and golden, and eaten with a sprinkling of vinegar.

NOTE I prefer thin ($\frac{1}{32}$-inch) wonton wrappers for wontons but find them too fragile for pelmeni. Wonton wrappers of medium ($\frac{1}{16}$-inch) thickness, usually sold in 1-pound packages of 80, hold up better here, and their "toothsomeness" is more compatible with the hearty pelmeni filling. I have also had good results with the $\frac{1}{16}$-inch rounds marketed as "pot-sticker skins" by the Chinese and "gyoza skins" by the Japanese. The bad news is that all of the above are 3½-inch wrappers and must be cut into 2½-inch rounds for pelmeni. The good news is that 1) this job can be delegated to the noncooks around us and 2) the wrapper scraps, when deep-fried, make an irresistible snack.

Brown Beef Stock

▲

To keep stock from becoming cloudy, skim scrupulously and do not stir at any time during cooking or straining. MAKES ABOUT 3 QUARTS

3 pounds shin or shank of beef, in thick crosscut sections
3 pound meaty beef bones, cut into 3- to 4-inch pieces
¾ pound yellow onions, peeled and quartered
½ pound carrots, washed and cut into chunks
2 large cloves garlic, unpeeled

BOUQUET GARNI

4 sprigs parsley
1 sprig thyme
1 bay leaf

1 large ripe tomato or 2 canned Italian plum tomatoes, chopped and drained
¼ teaspoon coarse (kosher) salt

1 Preheat the oven to 425 degrees. Lightly oil a roasting pan (or 2 pans) large enough to hold all the ingredients. Add the shin and beef bones and roast them, turning once, for 20 minutes. Scatter the onions and carrots in the pan and roast for 20 minutes longer, stirring once or twice.

2 With a slotted spoon, transfer the browned meat, bones, and vegetables to a large stockpot. Pour off and discard the fat from the roasting pan. Add 2 cups water to the pan and deglaze over moderate heat, scraping up any browned particles and caramelized pan deposits that cling to the bottom. Pour this deglazing liquid into the stockpot and add 5 quarts water. Bring to a boil over moderate heat, skimming to remove any scum or foam on the surface. Add the garlic, bouquet garni, tomato, and salt. Adjust the heat to maintain a slow steady simmer and cook, partially covered, for 4 hours. Occasionally skim any fat off the surface.

3 Line a sieve with several thicknesses of dampened cheesecloth and strain the stock without pressing down on the solids or stirring the liquid. Discard the solids. Let the stock cool completely, then cover and refrigerate. When the stock has set to a jelly, remove the congealed fat from the surface.

4 Transfer the degreased stock to a clean stockpot or large saucepan. Set the pan half off the heat. Bring to a strong simmer and cook, uncovered, skimming the impurities that rise on the cooler side of the pan, until the stock is reduced to about 3 quarts. Strain and let cool completely. Transfer to covered containers and refrigerate *(The stock may be refrigerated for up to 5 days, or frozen for several months.)*

Mustard and Sour Cream Sauce

MAKES ABOUT 2 CUPS

2 cups sour cream
2 tablespoons prepared hot English mustard
2 tablespoons finely chopped fresh dill
Salt and freshly ground black pepper

1. In a small bowl, combine the sour cream, mustard, dill, and sugar. Season with salt and pepper to taste, and stir to blend. Set aside for 30 to 60 minutes to let the flavors meld. *(The sauce can be covered and refrigerated for up to 24 hours, but should be cool rather than cold when served.)*

2 Stir again before serving.

Kasha with Wild Mushrooms and Toasted Walnuts

This dish combines three of the most characteristic ingredients of Russian cookery. A last-minute enrichment of walnut oil brings out all the glorious nutty flavor of the kasha grain and the subtle smokiness of the wild mushrooms. SERVES 12

1 ounce dried cèpe or porcini mushrooms
4 to 5 cups hot chicken stock
4 tablespoons unsalted butter
1½ cups chopped onions
½ pound fresh shiitake mushrooms or cultivated mushrooms, trimmed and sliced
2 large eggs, lightly beaten
2 cups medium kasha
Salt
1 cup coarsely chopped or broken walnuts, about 4 ounces
¼ teaspoon plus 2 tablespoons walnut oil
3 tablespoons finely chopped flat-leaf parsley

1 Soak the dried cèpes in 2 cups of the hot chicken stock until soft, about 30 minutes. Remove the cèpes and gently squeeze dry over the bowl of soaking liquid. Rinse the cèpes quickly under cool running water and pat dry. Coarsely chop the cèpes and set aside. Strain the soaking liquid through a strainer lined with a damp paper towel. Add enough chicken stock to make a total of 4 cups liquid; set aside in a medium saucepan.

2 In a heavy large skillet, melt 2 tablespoons of the butter. Add the onions and cook over moderately low heat, stirring occasionally, until soft but not brown, about 10 minutes. Push the onions to one side, off heat. Add the remaining 2 tablespoons butter to the skillet and sauté the fresh mushrooms over moderate heat until tender, about 5 minutes. Add the reserved chopped cèpes and cook with the onions and fresh mushrooms, stirring, for 2 minutes. Transfer to a bowl and set the skillet aside, unwashed, for cooking the kasha.

3 Bring the reserved cèpe-soaking liquid to a boil over moderate heat; set aside over low heat. In a large bowl, mix the eggs into the kasha until the grains are thoroughly moistened and all the egg has been absorbed. Place the egg-coated kasha in the skillet and cook over moderately high heat, stirring constantly to break up any lumps, until the grains are hot, dry, and mostly separate, about 4 minutes.

4 Add the hot cèpe-soaking liquid to the kasha. Stir to moisten thoroughly, then cover tightly and steam over low heat for 10 minutes. Stir in the mushroom mixture and season with salt to taste. Cover and cook until all the liquid is absorbed and the grains are fluffy and separate, about 10 minutes. Remove from the heat and let stand, uncovered, stirring occasionally with a large fork, until the kasha has cooled to room temperature. *(The recipe can be prepared ahead to this point. Transfer the kasha to a covered container and refrigerate for up to 3 days, or freeze for up to 1 month. Let return to room temperature before proceeding.)*

5 A few hours before serving, preheat the oven to 300 degrees. Toss the walnuts with ¼ teaspoon of the walnut oil. Place on a baking sheet and roast for 10 minutes to crisp them and bring out their full flavor.

6 About 30 minutes before serving, preheat the oven to 350 degrees. Mix the toasted walnuts into the kasha and transfer to an attractive shallow baking dish. Cover tightly and bake, stirring 2 or 3 times, for 20 minutes or until heated through. Stir in the remaining 2 tablespoons of walnut oil and the parsley. Season with salt to taste. Fluff the kasha with a large fork and serve while still hot.

Endive and Beet Salad

SERVES 10 TO 12

10 to 12 medium beets, 1½ to 2 inches in diameter
10 to 12 medium Belgian endives
1½ teaspoons Dijon mustard
3 tablespoons red wine vinegar
¾ teaspoon coarse (kosher) salt
Freshly ground black pepper
¾ cup olive oil
¾ fresh orange juice

1 Preheat the oven to 350 degrees. Trim the beets, leaving about 2 inches of stem and 1 inch of root attached. Scrub thoroughly but gently, being careful not to break the skins. Place the beets in a shallow baking dish large enough to hold them without crowding and add water (or a mixture of orange juice and water) to a depth of ¼ inch. Cover tightly with aluminum foil and bake for about 1 hour, or until tender. Test for tenderness by gently pressing the beets; if the skins move slightly, the beets are done. Uncover and let stand until cool enough to handle. Break off the stems and root tips, then rub the beets lightly; the skin will slip right off. Strain the cooking juices through dampened cheesecloth into a clean bowl large enough to hold all the beets. Add the beets to the bowl and turn to moisten with the juices. Let cool completely, then cover and refrigerate for up to 4 days; do not freeze, as freezing alters the texture of the beets.

2 Up to 24 hours before serving, cut up the beets for the salad. Cut each beet into ¼-inch slices, cut the slices into ¼-inch strips, and cut the strips crosswise into ¼-inch dice. Cover and refrigerate the diced beets in their cooking liquid until 1 hour before serving.

3 Slice off the tough bottom ends and separate the leaves. Wash the endives but do not soak (soaking makes them bitter); dry well. Seal in plastic bags and refrigerate until ready to serve.

4 In a small bowl, combine the mustard, vinegar, salt, and pepper; whisk to blend. Whisking constantly, gradually add the oil, by droplets at first and then in a thin stream, to make an emulsified vinaigrette. Set aside until ready to serve.

5 One hour before serving, remove the diced beets from their cooking liquid; drain well and place in a clean bowl. Pour the orange juice over the beets and toss lightly. Cover and refrigerate, stirring once or twice, until ready to serve.

6 To serve, fan out the endive leaves on chilled salad plates. Mix the vinaigrette again and drizzle a generous tablespoon evenly over each portion of endive. Drain the diced beets and toss with ⅛ teaspoon salt. Lay a scarlet band of beets across each fan of leaves and serve at once.

▼▼▼

The New Year's Eve Fruit Compote

▲▲▲

This is The Dessert That Spans the Years. By which I mean not only that we make it every New Year's Eve, but that when I find some at the back of the fridge in the middle of February, it's at least as good as it was on December thirty-first (which is more than you can say for most things at the back of the fridge). It keeps particularly well if the fresh fruits are not added until just before serving. But I don't suggest making even the cooked compote base weeks in advance; it occupies too much refrigerator space, which is at a premium during the holiday season. Instead, take advantage of the compote's longevity for weeks *after* the party by preparing it as follows.

Even if you're entertaining no more than twelve, a day or two before your party make a full recipe of the compote through Step 2. At this point, remove half of the compote base to a covered container and reserve in the refrigerator. To the other half of the compote base, which is to be served immediately, add only one-half the specified amounts of bananas, cherries, and berries, and follow the recipe through to the end. Serve as directed.

(Continued)

After the ball is over, the remaining half of the compote base (the half you squirreled away in the refrigerator) can be enjoyed for another month. Gently warmed, it is delicious with cinnamon-scented whipped cream or Thick Yogurt Cream (page 142) and becomes a whole new festive dessert when topped with homemade ice cream. It also makes a lovely filling for a lattice-crusted pie. And eaten simply as is, cold and unadorned, it's just right after a steaming bowl of soup.

MAKES 25 TO 30 SERVINGS

1 pound pitted sweet prunes
¾ pound dried apricots, preferably California apricots
¾ pound dried apples
¾ pound dried peaches
¾ pound dried pears
Super fine sugar
1 to 2 cups Armagnac
3 ripe medium bananas
1 pound fresh or thawed frozen dark sweet pitted cherries
3 cups fresh blueberries, strawberries, and/or raspberries

1 Using kitchen shears, cut the prunes, apricots, and apples in half and cut the peaches and pears in thirds or quarters; dip the blades of the shears in hot water frequently to prevent sticking. In a heavy large non-reactive pot, combine the dried fruit with water to cover by 3 to 4 inches (usually about 4 quarts). Bring to a boil. Reduce the heat to moderate and simmer, uncovered, until the fruit is soft and very tender, about 20 minutes. Remove from the heat and let cool, stirring occasionally, for 30 minutes.

2 Transfer the stewed fruit and its cooking liquid to a serving bowl large enough to accommodate all the remaining ingredients as well. Stir in sugar to taste; this dessert should not be overly sweet. Add 1 cup of the Armagnac; its strong alcoholic flavor will mellow as the compote base ripens. Mix well. Cover and refrigerate for 1 to 3 days.

3 No more than 2 hours before serving, peel and slice the bananas and add them to the compote base. Add the cherries. Taste the compote and add more sugar and/or Armagnac if necessary; a little more Armagnac is almost always necessary. Stir well. Finally, fold the berries into the compote very gently so as not to crush them. Set aside in a cool place but do not refrigerate again before serving; this compote is most enjoyable when only lightly chilled.

AN ARABIAN NIGHT

▲▲▲▲▲▲▲▲▲▲▲▲▲▲▲▲▲▲▲▲▲▲▲▲▲▲▲▲▲▲▲▲▲▲▲▲

Bidon Lebna

▲

Kibbeh-Bil-Sanieh

Batinjan-Bil-Laban

Carrot and Orange Salad

▲

*Compote of Apricots with
Toasted Almonds
and Thick Yogurt Cream*

▼

Greet guests at the door, saying *"Ahlan wa sahlan!,"* which is usually translated as "Welcome." The actual translation is "kinfolk and level ground," meaning that the guests will be welcome and safe (like members of the same tribe) and comfortable (flat ground makes an easier campsite).

—ANNE MARIE WEISS-ARMUSH,
Arabian Cuisine

▲

Bidon Lebna

THYME-SCENTED GOAT CREAM CHEESE
WITH OLIVE OIL

I made this for the first time in the South of France in a house called Cassiopeia in a summer when it never rained once. My friend Rassam had come for the weekend and he felt like cooking, so we called ten, twelve, twenty friends and invited them to feast with us on Sunday. Saturday morning we nibbled our way through the open market and carried the best of everything back to our kitchen. Then we decided what to do with it.

And for the rest of the day and half of the night, we cooked and tasted and argued and laughed until there were so many dishes of food everywhere that we had to eat our supper sitting on the kitchen floor. We ate bread and fat black olives and a loose, creamy, thyme-scented cheese beaten with olive oil—"bidon lebna" he called it, fake lebna, because we had made it with French goat cheese instead of the rich Lebanese goat yogurt his mother used to drain to make the real lebna of his childhood. That memory was suddenly very vivid to him. He smiled as he rubbed his bread around the bottom of the dish to get the last smear of cheese, the last slick of pungent oil.

In New York City, twenty years later, goat yogurt is easy to find. I could make the real lebna. But I don't. I still make the "bidon lebna" I made with Rassam. It is for me now what it was for him then—a taste of long ago and far away. MAKES ABOUT 2 CUPS

12 ounces (weighed without rind, if any) full-flavored goat cheese,
    at room temperature
6 ounces cream cheese, preferably preservative-free bulk cream cheese,
    at room temperature
3 tablespoons fruity green extra-virgin olive oil
1½ teaspoons finely chopped fresh thyme leaves
Pinch of cayenne
Toasted pita bread, for serving
Black olives, for serving

(Continued)

1 In a shallow bowl, mash the cheeses with a fork until soft and well blended. Gradually add 2½ tablespoons of the olive oil, whipping the cheese mixture with your fork until the oil is fully incorporated and the cheese is loose and creamy. Fold in the thyme and cayenne; there is often enough salt in the goat cheese to make additional salt unnecessary. Mix well and transfer to an attractive serving dish no more than 2 inches deep. *(The recipe can be made to this point up to 24 hours in advance. Cover with plastic wrap and refrigerate. Let return to room temperature and whip lightly once again before proceeding.)*

2 Drizzle the remaining ½ tablespoon of olive oil over the top of the lebna. Serve with triangles of toasted pita bread and olives.

LESLIE
NEWMAN

Kibbeh-Bil-Sanieh

BAKED MEAT AND WHEAT WITH PINE NUTS AND CURRANTS

*T*echnically, this is a meat loaf. But it's a meat loaf like foie gras is liver and caviar is fish eggs.

One of the gastronomic glories of the Arab world, kibbeh is a spiced mixture of lean meat, fine bulgur, and grated onion enjoyed in countless variations. Pounded (or processed) to a paste, kibbeh is shaped into balls, patties, or little torpedos; stuffed with any of a dozen fillings or not stuffed at all; fried, grilled, simmered, or baked; served hot or warm or cool with yogurt or tahini or lemon juice and olive oil or, or, or. . . . Or not cooked at all: kibbeh naye is like steak tartare but better.

I like Kibbeh-Bil-Sanieh best of all. The easiest of the stuffed kibbehs, the one you are most likely to see at a dinner party in Syria or Lebanon, "kibbeh-in-a-tray" is two crisp layers of meat-and-wheat filled with a juicy layer of sautéed meat, onions, pine nuts, and currants. Made up to a month in advance and frozen in its baking pan (freezing actually improves its texture!), it need only be basted with spiced butter and briefly baked before serving. A garnish of fresh pomegranate seeds is dazzling and delicious, but optional.

This recipe requires a total of 3 pounds mixed lamb and beef. If possible, have the butcher grind the lamb and beef together. If not, combine the two ground meats now and mix thoroughly before proceeding.

SERVES 12 AS A MAIN COURSE

One: The Shell Mixture

2 cups fine bulgur
Coarse (kosher) salt
1 tablespoon unsalted butter
1¼ teaspoons ground allspice
⅛ teaspoon mace
⅛ teaspoon cayenne
¾ teaspoon freshly ground black pepper
1 onion, about 8 ounces, cut into chunks
¾ pound ground leg of lamb
¾ pound ground beef round
3 ice cubes

(Continued)

1 In a sieve, rinse the bulgur under cool running water. Transfer to a bowl and add fresh water to cover by at least 1 inch. Set aside to soak for 10 minutes. Drain in a large sieve (or in 2 sieves) lined with a double thickness of cheesecloth. Wrap the bulgur in the cheesecloth and squeeze it dry. Spread the bulgur out in a tray and rake it with your fingers to break up any lumps. To keep the grain from becoming mushy, sprinkle it with ¾ teaspoon salt and place the tray in the refrigerator, uncovered, while you prepare the remaining ingredients.

2 In a microwave oven or over low heat, melt the butter; remove from the heat and let cool to room temperature. In a small bowl, combine the allspice, mace, cayenne, black pepper, and 1 teaspoon salt; mix the seasonings well.

3 In a food processor fitted with the steel blade, process the onion to a puree. Remove half the puree and set aside. To the puree in the processor, add half the meat (both lamb and beef), half the seasoning mixture, and ½ tablespoon of the cooled melted butter. Process to a paste by letting the motor run nonstop for 15 seconds. Scrape into a large bowl. Repeat with the remaining pureed onion, meat, seasonings, and butter. Combine the 2 batches, cover airtight with plastic wrap, and refrigerate for 30 minutes.

4 Divide both the meat mixture and the bulgur into thirds. Put one third of the meat in the food processor. Sprinkle one third of the bulgur over the meat and add 1 ice cube. Process nonstop for 20 seconds, until the meat and wheat blend into a dough-like ball riding on the processor blade. Uncover the processor, discard any ice chips, and scrape the blended meat and bulgur—the kibbeh—into a large metal bowl. Repeat with the remaining 2 batches of meat and bulgur and 2 ice cubes. Combine the 3 processed batches.

5 Dip your hands in a bowl of ice water, shake off the excess, and knead the kibbeh to a smooth, soft, and no-more-than-slightly sticky paste; when necessary, lightly dampen your palms and fingers with ice water again to keep them and the kibbeh cool. Cover airtight with plastic wrap and refrigerate until cold.

Two: The Filling

SPICED STOCK

½ cup lamb or beef stock (not canned broth) or water
⅛ teaspoon ground cinnamon
⅛ teaspoon ground allspice
⅛ teaspoon sugar

½ cup dried currants
4 tablespoons unsalted butter
2 cups chopped onions
½ cup pine nuts
¾ pound ground leg of lamb
¾ pound ground beef round
¾ teaspoon ground allspice
½ teaspoon ground cinnamon
⅛ teaspoon freshly grated nutmeg
Generous pinch of cayenne
½ teaspoon freshly ground black pepper
Coarse (kosher) salt

6 In a small saucepan, combine the stock, cinnamon, allspice, and sugar for the spiced stock and set over low heat until barely bubbling. Remove from the heat. Add the currants and set aside to steep.

7 In a heavy large skillet, melt 3 tablespoons of the butter over moderate heat and sauté the onions until soft and lightly golden, 8 to 10 minutes; push to one side, off heat. Add the pine nuts to the skillet and cook, stirring, until lightly toasted; push aside with the onions. Melt the remaining tablespoon butter and add the meat. Cook, breaking up the meat with a metal spatula, just until no longer pink. Add the allspice, cinnamon, nutmeg, cayenne, black pepper, and salt to taste; stir to blend with the meat and onions. Add the currants and spiced stock, mix well, and remove from the heat. Let stand until cool but no longer; if you are not ready to assemble the Kibbeh-Bil-Sanieh, cover and refrigerate the filling to keep it from drying out.

(Continued)

Shell mixture
Filling
4 tablespoons unsalted butter
3 tablespoons safflower or peanut oil
⅛ teaspoon allspice
⅛ teaspoon cinnamon
Pinch of cayenne
⅛ teaspoon coarse (kosher) salt
Pomegranate seeds, for garnish (optional)

8 Butter 2 8-inch-square baking pans. Divide the shell mixture into 4 *unequal* portions: 2 scant quarters and 2 generous quarters. Spread 1 scant quarter over the bottom of the first pan, smoothing it with cool, damp hands. Cover evenly with half the filling. Top with 1 generous quarter of the shell mixture, dampen your hands again, and smooth and level this layer, covering the filling completely. Following the same procedure, layer the remaining shell mixture and the remaining filling in the second baking pan.

9 In a small saucepan, melt 2 tablespoons of the butter over low heat or in a microwave oven. Brush a little over each kibbeh, just a thin glaze to seal the surface and keep it from drying out; discard any unused butter in the pan. Cover the 2 pans tightly with plastic wrap and refrigerate for 8 to 24 hours before baking and serving. *(Or freeze, unbaked, for up to 1 month. To freeze, gently press a sheet of plastic wrap directly on the surface of each kibbeh, covering it completely. Wrap each pan airtight in a double thickness of heavy aluminum foil and place in the coldest part of the freezer until firmly frozen. Then, 24 to 48 hours before serving, remove the layers of heavy foil and transfer the kibbeh to the refrigerator to thaw completely.)*

10 With a sharp knife, score the kibbeh (thawed if frozen) to a depth of about ¼ inch, cutting an attractive geometric design—diamonds are traditional—to mark and decorate the portions. Wipe the knife blade and run it around the sides of the pan. Cover the pans with plastic wrap and return to the refrigerator.

11 One hour before serving, remove the kibbeh from the refrigerator. Preheat the oven to 350 degrees. In a small saucepan, melt the remaining 2 tablespoons butter with the oil. Add the allspice, cinnamon, cayenne, and salt and stir to blend. Spoon 2 tablespoons of the mixture evenly over the top of each kibbeh, letting a little run down between the kibbeh and the sides of the pan. Place the pans on the lower shelf of the preheated oven, leaving several inches of space between them. Bake for 25 minutes. Increase the heat to 400 degrees and move the kibbeh to the upper shelf of the oven. Sprinkle with the remaining spiced butter-oil mixture and bake for about 10 minutes longer, until the tops are lightly crisped but not hard; because the kibbeh can overcook very quickly, it should be checked frequently towards the end of this period. Remove from the oven and let stand for 3 to 4 minutes before serving.

12 To serve, cut down through the scored lines that divide each kibbeh into portions. Moisten with buttery pan juices and scatter pomegranate seeds, if desired, over each serving.

Batinjan-Bil-Laban

EGGPLANT AND MINTED YOGURT SALAD

The ancient Hebrews scattered mint leaves on the floor so that each footstep would produce a fragrant aroma. . . .

*T*raditionalists would fry the eggplant, but baking is quicker, easier, and lighter. Prepared twenty-four hours in advance, this richly spiced salad for all seasons is irresistible with—or without—lamb, beef, or chicken. I have never had any leftovers. SERVES 12 TO 15

3 large eggplants, peeled, cut in half lengthwise, and sliced ¼-inch thick
2 teaspoons coarse (kosher) salt
6 cups plain yogurt, preferably whole-milk yogurt
2 teaspoons minced garlic
¾ teaspoon ground roasted cumin (page 96)
1 tablespoon crushed dried mint leaves (see Note)
⅛ teaspoon cayenne
Freshly ground black pepper
⅔ cup mild olive oil
Small fresh mint leaves, for garnish

1 Sprinkle the eggplant slices with the salt and let drain in a colander for at least 30 minutes. (This draws off excess and sometimes bitter juices and also reduces the amount of oil the eggplant will absorb when cooked.)

2 Preheat the oven to 450 degrees. Meanwhile, in a large serving bowl, mix the yogurt, garlic, cumin, dried mint, cayenne, and salt and pepper to taste.

3 Rinse the eggplant slices and pat dry. Brush with the olive oil and place on nonstick or lightly oiled baking sheets. Set the sheets in the oven and bake, turning once, until the eggplant slices are tender and lightly browned, 15 to 20 minutes.

4 Drain the eggplant briefly on paper towels. While still slightly warm, fold the slices into the yogurt mixture, immersing them completely (don't mind if the eggplant gets mashed a bit). Cover and refrigerate for 24 hours, turning 3 or 4 times.

5 Remove from the refrigerator 1 to 2 hours before serving so that the salad will be cool, not cold. Stir well and garnish with small fresh mint leaves.

NOTE In Mediterranean and Middle Eastern countries dried mint is preferred for its intense flavor in certain salads and stews. In this country, I've found the best dried mint in spice shops and Middle Eastern markets; to clean, crush, and release its full fragrance, rub through a sieve just before measuring and using.

▼▼

Carrot and Orange Salad

▲▲

SERVES 12 TO 15

3 medium navel oranges
3 to 3½ pounds crisp young carrots
1 teaspoon sugar, preferably superfine
4½ tablespoons fresh lemon juice
¾ cup safflower or peanut oil
¾ teaspoon coarse (kosher) salt

1 Using a zester, remove the zest of the oranges in long thin shreds. Chop the shreds into pieces ¼ to ½ inch long; cover and set aside. Squeeze half of 1 zested orange and reserve 1½ tablespoons of the juice. Place the remaining zested oranges in a plastic bag (to keep them from drying out) and refrigerate for some other purpose.

2 Peel the carrots, cut into 3-inch lengths, and shred in a food processor fitted with a medium shredding disk; there should be 12 to 14 cups of shredded carrots. Transfer to a large serving bowl. Add 3 tablespoons of the chopped orange zest and toss to mix.

3 In a small bowl, stir the sugar, lemon juice, and reserved orange juice until the sugar dissolves. Whisk in the oil and season with the salt. Pour this dressing over the carrots and mix well. Cover tightly and refrigerate for at least 4 hours, stirring occasionally. *(The recipe can be prepared to this point up to 1 day ahead.)* Just before serving, adjust the seasoning with additional salt and/or lemon juice, if necessary, and toss once again.

Compote of Apricots with Toasted Almonds

"The word apricot has had a life-history as pleasant as it is interesting. From the Latin for early-ripening, *praecoquus* (from which is also derived the word precocious), it passed through Byzantine Greek into Arabic as *al-barquq*. From the Arabic-speaking world it passed on to Portugal and Spain as *albaricoque*, thence to France, and finally assumed its English form by false analogy with the unconnected Latin word *apricus*, meaning sunny."

—SIR HARRY LUKE,
The Tenth Muse

SERVES 12

1 cup whole blanched almonds
1½ pounds dried California apricots
1½ cups sugar
4 whole green cardamom pods
Zest of 2 small lemons, removed in narrow julienne strips and chopped
    into ¼- to ½-inch pieces
1½ teaspoons fresh lemon juice
¾ cup Muscat de Beaumes-de-Venise
3 tablespoons fresh orange juice
2 cups Thick Yogurt Cream (recipe follows), for serving

1 Up to 2 weeks before serving, toast the almonds. Preheat the oven to 325 degrees. Spread the almonds out on a rimmed baking sheet and toast in the center of the oven, stirring 2 or 3 times, until light golden brown, about 10 minutes. Pour the nuts onto a plate and let cool completely. Pack in a tightly covered jar and store in a cool dry place. On the day of serving, chop the nuts rather coarsely; place them in a sieve and shake out any fine almond dust.

2 Two to 3 days before serving, rinse the apricots well and place in a large bowl. Add tap water to cover by about 1 inch and set aside to soak overnight.

3 Drain the apricots, reserving the soaking liquid. In a heavy nonreactive 4- to 6-quart pot, combine 3½ cups of the soaking liquid with the sugar, cardamom pods, lemon zest, lemon juice, and ½ cup of the Muscat de Beaumes-de-Venise. Bring to a simmer, stirring until the sugar dissolves, and cook gently for about 3 minutes to bring out the flavor of the ingredients. Add the apricots and bring to a simmer again. Then lower the heat to just below a simmer, the liquid quivering but not quite bubbling, and cook until the apricots are tender but still hold their shape, about 10 minutes.

4 With a slotted spoon, remove the apricots to a serving bowl. Over moderate heat, stirring frequently, reduce the apricot-cooking liquid to a thick syrup. Remove from the heat. Stir in the orange juice and the remaining ¼ cup Muscat de Beaumes-de-Venise, blending well. Let stand for 5 minutes. Pour the syrup evenly over the apricots. Let cool to room temperature, then cover and refrigerate for at least 8 hours or up to 1 week. Remove from the refrigerator 30 to 60 minutes before serving, so the compote's flavors and fragrances will not be muted by extreme cold.

5 To serve, top each small portion of rich, sweet apricots in syrup with a dollop of Thick Yogurt Cream and a generous scattering of toasted almonds.

Thick Yogurt Cream

*E*asier than whipped cream, cheaper than crème fraîche, lighter than sour cream, more festive than straight yogurt, this is a delicious dessert-time alternative to all of the above. MAKES ABOUT 2 CUPS

3 cups plain low-fat yogurt
1½ cups sour cream
Generous pinch of coarse (kosher) salt

1 In a large bowl, combine the yogurt, sour cream, and salt; stir until well blended. Line a colander or large sieve with several thicknesses of dampened cheesecloth. Set the colander over a bowl and slowly pour in the yogurt–sour cream mixture. Let drain for 30 minutes. With a rubber spatula, gently turn and stir the mixture up from the bottom. Continue to drain, stirring occasionally, for about 4 hours longer, or until the yogurt mixture has reduced to about 2 cups and resembles rich clotted cream—thicker than crème fraîche but not as thick as cream cheese.

2 Discard the liquid in the bowl. Transfer the thickened yogurt to a covered container and chill for at least 6 hours before using. The yogurt cream will keep in the refrigerator for at least 1 week.

FED UP

▲▲▲▲▲▲▲▲▲▲▲▲▲▲▲▲▲▲▲▲▲▲▲▲▲▲▲▲▲▲▲▲▲

*Poached Chicken with
Mediterranean Tuna
Mayonnaise*

▲

*Escarole Soup with Eggs
and Cheese*

Crusty Bread

▲

Applesauce for Grown-ups

Grandma's Butter Cookies

▼

All cooks have something they like to cook when they're tired of cooking, something they fix for themselves when they're fed up with food. Real chefs don't eat beurre blanc, not on their day off anyway.

The word *restaurant,* from the Latin *restaurare,* is literally a place that "restores or refreshes" so it is ironic that restaurateurs restore themselves with home-style cooking. Before preparing three-star dinners at Les Frères Troisgros, the late Jean Troisgros would often take his own supper at a rundown country café where the grandmotherly *patronne* offered no menu but simply set before him a roast chicken with fried potatoes and a glass of beer. He ate with great gusto.

For those who toil in fantasy fields—those who make food or music or touchdowns or love for a living—the hardest job is just keeping your passion alive. If pleasure is your business, what do you do when you're overworked? What do you eat when you're fed up?

A food-writer friend asked me to come over one afternoon and taste four new dishes. She'd open a bottle of wine, we'd have lunch. She needed an opinion, she said. She'd been working for days on this assignment about foie gras.

Foie gras? Like French, like goose livers, like *foie gras?*

Oh yes, she'd make a gorgeous terrine of foie gras and a lovely sauté of fresh foie gras with apples and then a whole foie gras with——

"I'll be right over," I said.

"What are you cooking now?"

"Me?" I said. "Nothing, some dumplings."

"Bring them," she said. "I'd love dumplings for lunch. I'm so sick of this damned foie gras."

▲

Poached Chicken

This is the Chinese way to poach chicken and, as far as I'm concerned, it's the only way. The hot bird (or any part thereof) goes straight from the poaching pot into an icy bath that chills the flesh instantly, sealing in all the juices that are lost during the usual slow-cooling process. With no guesswork about timing, the simple technique called "white-cooking" gives you white meat that is moist, tender, and perfectly cooked every time.

As a bonus, the cooking liquid can be reduced and used in making the soup that is served next on this menu. SERVES 8

4 whole chicken breasts, not skinned or boned, split into 8 halves
2 cups Mediterranean Tuna Mayonnaise (recipe follows)
Capers, for garnish
Ripe red tomatoes, sliced, for garnish
Niçoise olives, for garnish

1 In a large pot with a tight-fitting lid, bring about 4 quarts of water to a vigorous boil over high heat. Add 4 of the chicken breast halves. As soon as the water returns to a boil, cover the pot tightly, reduce the heat to moderately low, and simmer strongly for exactly 6 minutes. Turn off the heat and let the chicken steep, covered and undisturbed, for 16 minutes. Do not lift the lid at any time during the cooking and steeping process.

2 Toward the end of that process, fill a large metal bowl with very cold water and scatter in about 2 dozen ice cubes. Remove the cooked chicken pieces from the pot and immediately plunge them into the ice water. Let stand for 16 minutes. Remove the chicken pieces and pat dry. Cover and refrigerate while you prepare the rest of the chicken.

3 Skim the water in which the chicken was poached and then bring it to a boil again. Cook and steep the remaining 4 pieces of chicken; chill in a fresh ice-water bath and pat dry. *(The recipe can be prepared to this point up to 1 day ahead. Wrap the chicken tightly and refrigerate. Strain and degrease the chicken-poaching liquid, then reduce by about two-thirds or until you have a lightly flavorful stock to use in soups or sauces; let the stock cool completely, cover, and refrigerate for up to 4 days, or freeze for up to 2 months.)*

(Continued)

4 Remove and discard the skin and bones of the chicken breasts. Cut away any clinging cartilage and trim ragged edges so that all 8 pieces are neatly shaped. Nap each piece evenly with 2 to 3 tablespoons of Mediterranean Tuna Mayonnaise, dot with capers, and serve with sliced tomatoes and niçoise olives. Pass the remaining sauce separately.

Mediterranean Tuna Mayonnaise

*T*his luxurious and earthy sauce is prepared in minutes and keeps for days. It's one of the few things I make just to have around, to serve with raw vegetables or over poached chicken or just to dip a breadstick into while I'm cooking. MAKES ABOUT 2 CUPS

2 large cloves garlic
4 anchovy fillets
1 can (6 to 7 ounces) Italian tuna in olive oil, drained and broken up with a fork
1½ tablespoons fresh lemon juice
Pinch of cayenne
1½ cups mayonnaise, preferably homemade
3 tablespoons fruity green extra-virgin oilve oil
Salt and freshly ground white pepper

1 Cut each garlic clove in half lengthwise and remove the green sprout, if there is one; cut each half-clove into 2 or 3 pieces. Rinse the anchovy fillets in cool water and pat dry; cut each into 2 or 3 pieces. Combine the garlic and anchovies in a food processor and mince finely. Add the tuna, lemon juice, cayenne, and 1 cup of the mayonnaise. Process until well blended, 15 to 20 seconds. Scrape down the sides of the processor bowl, add the remaining ½ cup of mayonnaise, and process until smooth and creamy.

2 With the motor running, add the olive oil in a thin steady stream; continue processing for 5 seconds after all the oil has been incorporated. Transfer the sauce to a bowl and season with salt and freshly ground white pepper to taste. Cover and refrigerate overnight. *(This sauce can be made ahead and will keep in the refrigerator for up to 3 days.)* If using as a dip, remove from the refrigerator about 30 minutes before serving.

Escarole Soup with Eggs and Cheese

*T*his is my "raggedy soup," a soup of green and golden "rags" that restores me when I'm feeling raggedy myself. Serve with country bread, thickly sliced, and country wine, freely poured.

SERVES 8 GENEROUSLY AS A MAIN COURSE

1½ pounds escarole
4 tablespoons unsalted butter
1 cup chopped onions
12 cups chicken stock
3 large eggs
⅓ cup freshly grated imported parmesan cheese, preferably Parmigiano-Reggiano
Pinch of freshly grated nutmeg
Pinch of cayenne
Salt and freshly ground black pepper

1 Take apart the heads of escarole, discarding the tough cores and any bruised or wilted leaves. Wash the rest of the leaves very thoroughly in several changes of cool water; pat dry. Chop or tear coarsely.

2 In a heavy large flameproof casserole, melt the butter over moderately low heat. Add the onions and cook, stirring occasionally, just until tender but not browned, 5 to 8 minutes. Raise the heat to moderate, add the escarole, and turn it in the butter until wilted, 3 to 4 minutes. Stir in 4 cups of chicken stock and bring to a boil. Cover, reduce the heat to moderately low, and simmer gently until the escarole is tender, usually 30 to 40 minutes.

(Continued)

3 Add the remaining 8 cups of stock and simmer for about 5 minutes to blend the flavors. *(The recipe can be prepared to this point up to 1 day ahead. Let cool, cover, and refrigerate.)*

4 Shortly before serving, beat the eggs lightly in a mixing bowl. Stir in the grated cheese, nutmeg, and cayenne; set aside. Bring the soup to a boil over high heat, then reduce the heat to moderate and simmer strongly for a few minutes, until very hot. Lower the heat even further, until the soup is barely simmering. Gradually swirl in the egg mixture in a steady stream while stirring the soup with a fork in a large figure eight; the mixture will form shreds and flakes (like those in egg-drop soup but more solid because of the cheese). Remove from the heat. Season with salt and pepper to taste and serve at once in large soup bowls.

LESLIE
NEWMAN

Applesauce for Grown-ups

This is the most apple-y applesauce in the whole world and when it's cooking, your house smells like the nicest house in the whole world.
MAKES ABOUT 2 QUARTS

6 pounds apples, McIntosh, Macoun, Ida Red, Northern Spy, alone or in
    combination
2 tablespoons fresh lemon juice
Pinch of coarse (kosher) salt
¼ cup apple cider
1 cup sugar, preferably superfine
¼ cup Calvados or applejack
⅓ teaspoon cinnamon
2 tablespoons cold unsalted butter, cut into 8 pieces

1 Peel and core the apples. Chop coarsely and place in a heavy large nonreactive pot (I use an 8-quart enameled cast-iron casserole). When about half the apples have been prepared, toss them with 1 tablespoon of the lemon juice. Chop and add the remaining apples. Add the remaining tablespoon of lemon juice and the pinch of salt, and toss again. Pour the cider over the apples and cover the pot tightly.

2 Cook over moderately low heat, stirring frequently, until the apples are tender and have formed a sort of lumpy puree, about 30 minutes. Stir in the sugar and the Calvados and cook for a few minutes until the sugar dissolves. Uncover and simmer, stirring vigorously and mashing any large lumps, for about 5 minutes longer, or just until the applesauce is soft and thick enough to mound in a spoon. Remove from the heat.

3 Stir in the cinnamon and beat in the butter, 3 or 4 pieces at a time. (*The applesauce can be made in advance. Let cool completely, cover, and refrigerate for up to 1 week, or freeze for up to 2 months. Let come to room temperature before reheating in a microwave oven or a 300-degree conventional oven.*) Serve warm, plain or topped with Vanilla Lovers' Vanilla Ice Cream (page 225) or cinnamon-scented whipped cream.

Grandma's Butter Cookies

No, Virginia, there is no Betty Crocker. And I have my doubts about Aunt Jemima. But these are a real Grandma's butter cookies. You can tell by the fork marks—anybody who's ever been offered one of these cookies gets all misty-eyed and says, "Oh, that's just what my Grandma did, she pressed them down with a fork this way and then that way." And while they're telling you, they eat about twelve of them.

The Grandma in question is my children's Grandma (my husband's mother). When I questioned her foolishly and endlessly about the recipe —What size egg yolks? How hot is not too hot? Why had she used salted butter?—she just smiled and said, "Nobody told me what to do, so this was what I did."

And this is what I do to restore my sometimes overprocessed mixmastered microwaved battery-dead plastic and rubber soul. Making cookies with just a bowl and a wooden spoon and an old fork makes cooking seem like magic again. MAKES ABOUT 3 DOZEN

8 tablespoons (1 stick) lightly salted *butter, at room temperature*
7 tablespoons (½ cup minus 1 tablespoon) sugar
½ teaspoon pure vanilla extract
2 large egg yolks, at room temperature
1¼ cups sifted all-purpose flour

1 Using a wooden spoon, blend the softened butter and the sugar together in a mixing bowl until creamy. Add the vanilla extract and the egg yolks and mix well. Finally, add the flour and mix just until all the ingredients are thoroughly and smoothly blended; do not work the dough any more than is necessary or the cookies will be tough. Cover the bowl tightly and refrigerate for 1 or 2 hours, just until the dough is firm enough to handle easily.

2 When ready to bake, preheat the oven to 375 degrees. Break off pieces of dough and roll them lightly between your palms to form balls about 1 inch in diameter; again, do not overhandle. Place the balls about 2 inches apart on an ungreased cookie sheet (or 2 sheets, if necessary). Flatten with the tines of a fork, pressing first this way and then that way *(Grandma's directions, verbatim)* to make a grid or ticktacktoe mark; the flattened cookies should be about ¼ inch thick. Dip the fork in warm (not hot) water occasionally to keep it from sticking to the dough.

3 Bake in the preheated oven until the edges of the cookies are golden, about 8 to 10 minutes. Rotate the cookie sheet once to ensure even baking and watch the cookies carefully after they've cooked for about 6 minutes so they don't get too brown. With a metal spatula, transfer the cookies from the baking sheet to a rack and let cool completely; they will be chewy while warm but will become buttery-crisp when cool. Store in a cookie tin. Grandma says they also freeze very nicely, but I've never had any left to freeze.

LIGHT IN AUGUST

▲▲▲▲▲▲▲▲▲▲▲▲▲▲▲▲▲▲▲▲▲▲▲▲▲▲▲▲▲▲▲

Mojitos

▲

Fresh Herb and
Cheese Custards

▲

Mussels in Sorrel Sauce
Crusty Bread

▲

Red Fruits in Vanilla Cream

▼

August is a good time to go exploring in the herb garden, to go beyond rosemary and thyme and tarragon and get into chervil and mint and savory, among others. Remember that the tomato vine does not actually entwine with the basil bush and the mozzarella tree, and that tomatoes taste deliciously different with dill and feta or with chervil and chopped chives and Roquefort crumbled in a little cream. Let lovely lemony sorrel turn plain old moules marinière into a feast of Mussels in Sorrel Sauce.

If you want to enjoy August to the fullest, learn how it's done in countries that have August weather as much as four months a year. Try Indian ways with coriander and Thai ways with mint and purple basil; slice a hot grilled steak into a salad tossed with crisp rice noodles and Oriental herbs. Tempt guests with intriguing spices like fennel seed and ground roasted cumin and with vibrant seasonings like ginger and tamarind and with the amazing variety of chilies used to fire up appetites in torrid zones. When you can't stand the heat, cook more in your imagination and less in your kitchen.

▲

Mojitos

CUBAN RUM AND MINT COCKTAILS

Maricel Presilla, a terrific Cuban cook and food historian, took me to Victor's Cafe 52 in New York and said they made this famous Cuban drink there called a mojito and I had to have one. So I had one. And then I had another one.

Now I will always have to have them.

This is all Maricel's fault, but I forgive her because she gave me the recipe. MAKES 1 DRINK

4 to 5 small fresh mint leaves
½ tablespoon sugar or 1 tablespoon if you are Cuban
2 tablespoons fresh lime juice
2 ounces white rum
Club soda, chilled
Dash of sweet vermouth (optional)
Small sprig of mint, for garnish

1 Place the mint leaves and the sugar in a wine glass. Crush lightly with the back of a spoon so that the mint releases its flavorful oils. Smear the rim of the glass with the mint leaves.

2 Add 3 ice cubes, or more if you don't want to get thoroughly drunk.

3 Pour the lime juice and rum into a cocktail shaker, and shake well. Then pour this into the glass with the ice and the mint and stir everything together. Fill up the glass with ice-cold club soda. You can stir in a dash of sweet vermouth, if you like (I don't). Serve garnished with a sprig of fresh mint.

Fresh Herb and Cheese Custards

A flan for all seasonings. After trying feta and dill, consider combining chèvre and basil. Or English Cheddar and, instead of an herb, a dash of sharp English dry mustard. Or Monterey Jack and, instead of an herb, finely chopped jalapeño peppers—in which case, grated dry Monterey Jack cheese might replace the parmesan to make a completely California custard. SERVES 8

4 large eggs
1½ cups heavy cream
⅛ teaspoon freshly grated nutmeg
⅛ teaspoon cayenne
¼ teaspoon freshly ground white pepper
2 teaspoons minced flat-leaf parsley
1 tablespoon minced fresh dill
1 tablespoon snipped fresh chives
1½ cups finely crumbled Greek or Bulgarian feta cheese, about 8 ounces
1 cup freshly grated imported parmesan cheese, preferably Parmigiano-Reggiano

1 Preheat the oven to 400 degrees. In a medium bowl, whisk together the eggs, cream, nutmeg, cayenne, and white pepper. Add the parsley, dill, and chives. Stir in the feta and parmesan cheese and blend well. Because the cheeses are salty, you probably won't need to add salt.

2 Using a small ladle to stir and scoop from the bottom of the bowl, divide the mixture evenly among 8 individual soufflé molds or custard cups (about 8 ounces each). Place them several inches apart on a large baking sheet.

3 Bake on the middle shelf of the oven for about 20 minutes, until the custards are puffed and golden. Serve at once.

Mussels in Sorrel Sauce

I love mussels in the summer, especially at the shore, where I can find shiny black beauties not much bigger than my thumbnail. They are so tasty and tender—and cheap—that I could eat them every night, simply steamed in wine. Unfortunately, by August I feel as if I *have* eaten them every night. This is when I dress up my mussels a little. Robed in a light ivory sauce with ribbons of tart green sorrel, they are suddenly irresistible again. SERVES 8 TO 10

8 pounds mussels, scrubbed and debearded
Flour
4 large egg yolks
1⅓ cups crème fraîche or heavy cream
2 cups dry white wine
6 tablespoons unsalted butter
2 cups finely chopped onions
2 teaspoons finely chopped garlic
¼ cup finely chopped flat-leaf parsley
¾ cup Sorrel Semi-puree (recipe follows)
Dash of cayenne
Dash of freshly grated nutmeg
2 teaspoons fresh lemon juice
Salt and freshly ground black pepper
Crusty bread, for serving

1 After scrubbing and debearding the mussels, put them in a large bowl, cover with cold water, and stir in 2 or 3 large handfuls of flour. Refrigerate for at least 4 hours, or overnight; the mussels will become plump and succulent, while also disgorging sand and salt. After soaking, scoop the mussels out of the dirty soaking water and rinse them under cold running water.

2 Set a large heatproof bowl to warm in a low (about 150 degrees) oven. In another large bowl, whisk together the egg yolks and crème fraîche until blended; set aside at room temperature.

(Continued)

3 Put the mussels in a large nonreactive flameproof casserole or stockpot. Add the wine, butter, onions, garlic, and parsley; stir to mix well. Cover tightly and bring to a boil over high heat. Cook, shaking the pot vigorously once or twice, until all the mussels open, usually about 5 to 7 minutes. Discard any that do not open.

4 Using a slotted spoon, transfer the mussels as rapidly as possible to the bowl in the oven. Cover loosely, using aluminum foil if necessary, and keep warm in the oven.

5 Strain the mussel broth from the casserole through several thicknesses of dampened cheesecloth or a very fine mesh sieve. Gradually beat this hot strained broth in a thin stream into the egg-yolk/cream mixture. Rinse and dry the casserole, then pour the sauce back into it.

LESLIE
NEWMAN

6 Set the casserole over low heat and whisk the Sorrel Semi-puree into the sauce. Add the cayenne, nutmeg, and lemon juice. Season with salt and black pepper to taste. Strain in any juices that have accumulated in the bowl of mussels. Cook, stirring, for 2 to 3 minutes, until the sauce is hot and slightly thickened; do not let it come to a simmer or it will curdle.

7 Pour the sauce over the mussels and then tip the contents of the bowl back into the pot. Serve immediately, ladling the mussels and their sauce into heated soup plates and passing a big basket of crusty bread.

Sorrel Semi-puree

▲

MAKES ABOUT ¾ CUP

1 pound fresh young sorrel
2 tablespoons unsalted butter
Generous pinch of coarse (kosher) salt

1 Pick over the sorrel, stripping off the stems and discarding any yellowing leaves. Wash the tender leaves thoroughly in several changes of water, lifting them out of the water each time to leave grit and sand behind. Dry in a salad spinner, or shake off excess water and drain on paper towels. Coarsely tear or chop the leaves.

2 In a large nonreactive skillet, melt the butter over moderate heat. Add the sorrel and cook, stirring, until wilted, about 1 minute. Continue to cook, turning the sorrel in the butter and pressing and mashing the leaves with a heavy spoon, until they have melted into a loose but tender puree, 5 to 10 minutes. Stir in the salt. Remove from the heat and let cool to room temperature. *(If not used immediately, the pureed sorrel can be transferred to a covered container and refrigerated for up to 3 days, or frozen for up to 2 months.)*

Red Fruits in Vanilla Cream

Dorine Gillet was, everyone agreed, the best cook in the tiny French Riviera town where I lived many summers ago. Her airy soufflés aux fruits de mer tasted richly of the sea, and the pizzas she rolled out on her kitchen table and baked in a thermostat-less oven could put chefs to shame then and now. This dessert, incredibly rich and good, was one of her simplest dishes, a recipe with no fixed amounts or proportions and only one absolute rule: The fruit must be at its finest.

Strawberries
Raspberries
Fresh lemon juice
Ripe peaches
Crème fraîche (not heavy cream, which is not thick enough for this dessert)
Vanilla sugar (see Note)

1 Wash and hull the strawberries; cut the big ones in half and leave the smaller ones whole. Gently wash—never under running water—the raspberries. Put all the berries in a big bowl and squeeze a few drops of lemon juice over them. (Dorine says a little, just a little, lemon juice always brings out the flavor of red fruits.) Peel, stone, and slice some ripe peaches over the bowl, so the juices drip in, and mix them with the berries.

2 Pour a generous amount of crème fraîche over all; this is as much a cream as a fruit dessert. With a rubber spatula, fold the thick cream and the fruit together (over and under, as if folding egg whites into a soufflé), just until mixed. Sprinkle with vanilla sugar to taste and gently mix again; it's all right if the fruit gets crushed a little, but not too much. Cover and refrigerate for at least 1 hour, and stir again just before serving. You can make this several hours ahead, but not the night before.

NOTE To make vanilla sugar, simply hold a vanilla bean over a bowl of sugar, slit it lengthwise, and then bury it in the sugar. Keep the bowl tightly covered. Replenish the sugar from time to time, as you use it, and replace the vanilla bean when its fragrance fades.

THE LAST CRAB OF SUMMER

▲▲▲▲▲▲▲▲▲▲▲▲▲▲▲▲▲▲▲▲▲▲▲▲▲▲▲▲▲▲

Buster Crabs Béarnaise

▲

Andouille and Oyster Gumbo
Steamed Rice

▲

Fresh Lime Ice Cream

▼

The hell with rosebuds. Gather ye soft-shell crabs—and corn and tomatoes and peaches—while ye may.

There's a lot of confusion about soft-shell crabs, even among people who eat a lot of soft-shell crabs. One such person told me he went around for years thinking they were soft-*shoe* crabs. And there are college graduates who believe soft-shells are a special species of crab and that they are eaten alive.

Wrong. Unlike oysters and clams, which often *are* eaten alive, soft-shell crabs are always DOA on your plate. For that matter, they're not even alive when cooked, as lobsters and hard-shell crabs often are.

Hard-shells and soft-shells are actually the same critter, an Atlantic blue crab that molts its hard shell every spring and doesn't grow a new hard shell until the autumn. They're a lot like you and me—as soon as the weather's warm, they want to get out of the house, but when the beaches turn cold again, it's "Gimme Shell-ter."

▲

Buster Crabs Béarnaise

No relation to the movie star, the buster crabs of New Orleans are very small soft-shell crabs that have just molted (or "busted") out of their hard shells. Lest the little darlings feel naked, the good folk of that city quickly take them home and throw a big blanket of béarnaise over them. Me, I always lay a little lump crabmeat on them as well; I'm an old softie when it comes to soft-shells.

Get out your best china and invite your best friends. This is a spectacularly good dish. SERVES 8 AS A FIRST COURSE

8 small soft-shell crabs, cleaned
Milk
1 cup Creole Béarnaise Sauce (recipe follows)
¾ cup all-purpose flour, approximately
½ teaspoon coarse (kosher) salt
¼ teaspoon freshly ground black pepper
⅛ teaspoon cayenne
3 tablespoons safflower or corn oil
4 tablespoons unsalted butter
¾ cup lump crabmeat, picked over to remove any cartilage
½ teaspoon fresh lemon juice

1 Place the crabs in a shallow dish or pan just large enough to hold them in a single layer. Add cold milk to barely cover, pouring it gently down the side of the dish so as not to bruise the fragile crabs. Cover and refrigerate for 30 to 60 minutes.

2 Shortly before cooking the crabs, prepare the Creole Béarnaise Sauce and keep warm as directed in the recipe. Preheat the oven to 200 degrees and place a large heatproof platter in it, ready to receive the crabs.

3 In a large shallow dish, blend the flour, salt, pepper, and cayenne. Carefully remove one crab at a time from the milk and hold it up to drain for a few seconds. Dredge lightly in the seasoned flour. Lay the floured crabs, not touching, on a baking sheet or tray.

(Continued)

4 In a heavy large skillet, heat the oil with 2½ tablespoons of the butter. Add the crabs, shell side down, and cook over moderate heat until golden brown, about 2 minutes. Turn and cook 2 to 3 minutes longer, until crisp and golden on the other side. Transfer the crabs to the platter in the oven to keep them hot; do not cover or crowd them.

5 In a heavy small skillet or sauté pan, melt the remaining 1½ tablespoons butter over low heat. Add the lump crabmeat, cover, and let it steam in the butter, stirring once or twice, just until heated through, 2 to 3 minutes. Stir in the lemon juice and remove from the heat.

6 Stir to remix the béarnaise sauce. Crown each crisp crab with a few lumps of warm crabmeat, top with about 2 tablespoons of sauce, and serve at once.

Creole Béarnaise Sauce

▲

MAKES ABOUT 1 CUP

1 tablespoon minced fresh tarragon or 1 teaspoon crumbled dried tarragon
1 tablespoon minced scallions, tender green only
¼ cup dry white wine
3 tablespoons white wine vinegar
3 large egg yolks
⅛ to ¼ teaspoon cayenne
12 tablespoons (1½ sticks) unsalted butter, melted
Salt and freshly ground white pepper

1 If you are using dried tarragon, rub the leaves between your palms to release their full flavor. In a heavy small nonreactive saucepan, combine the tarragon, scallions, wine, and vinegar. Boil slowly until the liquid is reduced to a glaze of about 1 tablespoon; set aside to cool slightly. (*This can be done up to 1 hour in advance.*)

2 Combine the egg yolks and cayenne in the bowl of a food processor. Process on-and-off to break the yolks. Stir 1 teaspoon warm water into the tarragon glaze to loosen it, then scrape the glaze into the processor bowl.

3 Heat the melted butter until bubbling hot. With the processor motor running, gradually pour the hot butter down the food chute in a thin steady stream. Continue to process for about 10 seconds after all the butter has been added. Season with salt and pepper to taste and process for 5 seconds longer.

4 To keep warm, transfer to a heatproof bowl, lay plastic wrap directly on the surface of the sauce, and place the bowl in a pan of very warm but not hot water. Or keep it warm in a wide-mouthed thermos jar. If the sauce thickens while standing, lighten it by whisking in a little warm water and a few drops of lemon juice just before serving.

▼▼▼

Andouille and Oyster Gumbo

▲▲▲

Gombo a la Creole, Louisiana gumbo, is perhaps the state's single most famous dish. . . . Like the people of South Louisiana, this native dish is a happy blending of just about everything. In fact, in the patois of the area, gumbo means "all together" or "all at once" as in the expression gumbo ya-ya, which means everyone talking at once.

—*Pirate's Pantry, Treasured Recipes of Southwest Louisiana*

▲

Gumbo's a taste, a feeling, a party.

—PAUL PRUDHOMME,
The Prudhomme Family Cookbook

Yes, indeed. And this is my favorite gumbo—a rich, roux-dark, soup-stew packed with plump oysters and spicy smoked sausage and smoothly thickened with gumbo filé, the earthy herb powder discovered by the Choctaw Indians. Filé is available in specialty stores across America and in every corner grocery store in New Orleans, but apparently there are still some folks who want to make their own. On December 1, 1988, *The*

(Continued)

New Orleans Times-Picayune printed a recipe that begins, "Gather sassafras leaves in the month of August, preferably during a full-moon period. . . ." SERVES 10

1 cup peanut or corn oil
1 cup all-purpose flour
2 cups finely chopped onions
1½ cups finely chopped green bell peppers
¾ cup finely chopped celery
¼ cup thinly sliced scallions, white part only
1 tablespoon very finely chopped garlic
¾ pound andouille sausage or other good-quality smoked sausage, such as kielbasa, cut into ¼-inch dice (see Note)
2 small bay leaves
1½ teaspoons finely chopped fresh thyme leaves or ½ teaspoon dried thyme
½ to ¾ teaspoon cayenne
¾ teaspoon freshly ground black pepper
10 cups hot chicken stock
1 teaspoon Worcestershire sauce
Salt
4 dozen freshly shucked oysters, liquor reserved
½ cup thinly sliced scallions, tender green only
3 tablespoons finely chopped flat-leaf parsley
1 tablespoon filé powder
6 cups Steamed Rice (page 39), for serving
Hot-pepper sauce, for seasoning at table

1 First make your roux. In a heavy large skillet (preferably cast iron), heat the oil over moderate heat until very hot but not smoking. Gradually add the flour, about ⅓ cup at a time, whisking rapidly to blend. Cook, stirring constantly with a long-handled spoon, until golden. Reduce the heat to moderately low. Continue stirring the roux, lowering the heat even further as it darkens, until it gives off a nut-like fragrance and turns a rich medium brown—a few shades darker than peanut butter.

2 Immediately (but carefully—spattering roux is also known as "Cajun napalm"!) add the chopped onions, peppers, celery, white of scallions, and garlic. Stir over moderate heat for 5 minutes. Add the diced andouille and cook for 5 minutes. Add the bay leaves, thyme, cayenne, and pepper and cook, stirring constantly, for 5 minutes longer. Gradually add 6 cups of the hot chicken stock, stirring rapidly to blend. Transfer the mixture to a heavy large flameproof casserole. Rinse the skillet with the remaining 4 cups of stock and pour this enriched liquid into the casserole. Stir in the Worcestershire sauce and add just a little salt, underseasoning now to allow for the saltiness of the oysters and oyster liquor that will be added later.

3 Partially cover the casserole and simmer over moderately low heat for 1 hour, stirring occasionally. *(The recipe can be prepared ahead to this point. Let cool completely, cover, and refrigerate for up to 2 days, or freeze for up to 1 month. Let return to room temperature and then reheat to a simmer before proceeding.)*

4 Over moderate heat, simmer the gumbo, uncovered, for about 5 minutes. Pass the oyster liquor through a fine sieve and into the pot. If the gumbo is very thick, add a little hot chicken stock or water. Increase the heat to moderately high and cook, stirring, until the soup comes to a boil. Add the oysters. Reduce the heat to moderate and simmer just until their edges curl, 2 to 3 minutes. Remove from the heat, and stir in the scallion greens and parsley. Gradually add the filé powder, blending it smoothly into the gumbo. Taste, and add more salt and more cayenne, if necessary.

5 Serve at once, mounding about ½ cup of rice in the center of each soup bowl and ladling the gumbo around it. Have a bottle of hot-pepper sauce on the table for those who like theirs extra spicy.

NOTE Andouille (pronounced ahn-*doo*-ee) is a flavorful Cajun smoked pork sausage used in bean dishes, rice dishes, and hearty soups; it is also delicious grilled. Andouille can be ordered from K-Paul's Louisiana Mail Order, 501 Elysian Fields, PO Box 770034, New Orleans, LA 70177-0034; telephone: 1-800-654-6017. Both regular and hot andouille are available, but these are Cajun definitions; most cooks will find regular andouille quite hot enough. Andouille can also be ordered from Aidells Sausage Company, 1575 Minnesota Street, San Francisco, CA 94107; telephone: 1-415-285-6660.

Fresh Lime Ice Cream

This ice cream is so light but so intense and so refreshing even after a rich repast that everyone who tastes it wants to make it. And it's so easy to make. MAKES ABOUT 1½ QUARTS

½ cup plus 1 tablespoon fresh lime juice
1 tablespoon plus 1 teaspoon grated lime zest
2 cups sugar, preferably superfine
Pinch of salt
2 cups heavy cream
2 cups milk

1 In a large bowl, combine the lime juice, lime zest, sugar, and salt; stir to mix well.

2 Gradually add the cream and then the milk; stir gently until the sugar dissolves. Cover and refrigerate for at least 4 hours or overnight, if possible, to allow the flavor to develop fully.

3 Stir the mixture, pour it into an ice-cream maker, and freeze according to the manufacturer's instructions.

AND THE DAYS GROW SHORT

▲▲▲▲▲▲▲▲▲▲▲▲▲▲▲▲▲▲▲▲▲▲▲▲▲▲▲▲▲

Smoked Chicken, Celery Root,
and Tongue
in Horseradish Rémoulade

▲

Alsatian Lentil Soup

▲

Mixed Leaf Salad

▲

Warm Compote of
Autumn Fruits
with Armagnac Ice Cream

▼

As the days grow short, some faces grow long. But not mine.

Every autumn, when the wind turns cold and darkness comes early, I am suddenly happy. It's time to start making soup again.

▲

Smoked Chicken, Celery Root, and Tongue Salad

SERVES 10 TO 12

1 pound skinless and boneless smoked chicken breast, sliced
¾ pound cooked lean beef tongue, sliced
1½ to 2 pounds small to medium celery roots
½ teaspoon coarse (kosher) salt
1 tablespoon fresh lemon juice
Horseradish Rémoulade (recipe follows)
Freshly ground white pepper
2 tablespoons finely chopped parsley
Crusty bread, for serving

1 Cut the smoked chicken and the tongue into narrow strips. Cover with plastic wrap and set aside.

2 Scrub the celery roots well. With a very sharp knife, slice off the tops and bottoms, and remove the skin. Cut the roots into halves or quarters and cut out any spongy cores. Immerse the trimmed roots in a bowl of acidulated water to prevent darkening. Remove one piece at a time and cut into matchstick strips in a food processor fitted with a 3-millimeter julienne disk. (Or use a knife to cut the roots into ⅛-inch slices and then into ⅛-inch strips.) Toss with coarse salt and lemon juice.

3 In a large serving bowl, combine the julienned celery root with the strips of chicken and tongue; toss lightly to mix. Add the Horseradish Rémoulade and mix very thoroughly. Season with white pepper and additional salt to taste. Stir in the chopped parsley. *(The salad can be prepared up to 1 day ahead. Cover tightly and refrigerate until 1 hour before serving.)* Serve cool, not cold, with crusty bread.

Horseradish Rémoulade

MAKES ABOUT 1¼ CUPS

1 cup mayonnaise, preferably homemade
2 tablespoons crème fraîche or heavy cream
2 tablespoons Dijon mustard
⅛ teaspoon cayenne
½ tablespoon fresh lemon juice
2 teaspoons prepared horseradish (bottled horseradish in vinegar)

1 In a small bowl, whisk together the mayonnaise, crème fraîche, mustard, cayenne, and lemon juice.

2 Place the prepared horseradish in a small strainer and press the vinegar out of it with the back of a spoon. Whisk the drained horseradish into the dressing, blending well. Cover and set aside.

Alsatian Lentil Soup

MAKES 10 TO 12 HEARTY MAIN COURSE SERVINGS

6 tablespoons unsalted butter
2 cups chopped onions
1½ cups diced carrots
¾ cup sliced leeks, white part only
6 tablespoons all-purpose flour
12 cups hot Brown Beef Stock (pages 122–123)
1½ pounds lentils, rinsed and picked over to remove any grit
¼ pound lean slab bacon, preferably double-smoked
1 large bay leaf
1 teaspoon chopped fresh thyme leaves or ¼ teaspoon crumbled dried thyme
⅓ teaspoon Quatre-Épices (page 68)

⅓ teaspoon sugar
5 fresh bratwurst, about 1 pound
Salt and freshly ground black pepper
3 tablespoons finely chopped flat-leaf parsley

1 In a heavy large saucepan or flameproof casserole, melt the butter over moderately low heat. Add the onions, carrots, and leeks. Cover and cook slowly, stirring once or twice, until the vegetables are tender but not brown, 5 to 8 minutes. Blend in the flour and cook, stirring, for about 2 minutes. Remove from the heat.

2 Gradually add 3 cups of the hot Brown Beef Stock, stirring until smooth. Add the remaining stock and 6 cups water. Stir in the lentils, bacon, bay leaf, thyme, Quatre-Épices, and sugar. Bring to a boil over moderate heat. Reduce the heat to moderately low, cover, and simmer slowly, stirring occasionally, for 45 minutes.

3 With a sharp fork or skewer, prick each bratwurst in 2 or 3 places; add to the soup. Simmer, covered, for about 30 minutes, until the lentils are very tender. Remove the bacon and bratwurst to a cutting board; cover loosely and set aside.

4 Remove the pot from the heat. Ladle 4 cups of the soup into a food processor and puree until fairly smooth. Stir this puree back into the pot to thicken the soup. Over moderately low heat, let the soup come to a simmer again.

5 Meanwhile, trim the bacon of visible fat; dice the lean meat and return it to the soup. Slice the bratwurst and add it to the soup. Season with salt and pepper to taste. Cover and simmer for about 5 minutes to heat the meats through and let the flavors blend. (*The soup can be served immediately but is even better when reheated. Let cool to room temperature, cover, and refrigerate for up to 2 days, or freeze for up to 2 months. Let return to room temperature, then reheat gently until steaming.*)

6 If the soup is too thick, thin with a little warm water. Adjust the seasonings, if necessary, and stir in the parsley. To serve, put a ladle in the pot and put the pot on the table. Hot homemade soup should look like hot homemade soup.

Mixed Leaf Salad

SERVES 12

About 1½ pounds loose salad greens: green and red leaf lettuce, oak-leaf lettuce,
  Bibb lettuce, Boston lettuce, et cetera
¾ teaspoon Dijon mustard
3 tablespoons lemon juice
½ teaspoon coarse (kosher) salt
Freshly ground black pepper
¾ cup extra-virgin olive oil

1 Wash the salad greens thoroughly, lifting them out of the water each time to leave any sand or grit behind. Drain well and spin dry. Discard all tough stems and tear large leaves into bite-size pieces. Layer the salad greens between paper towels or roll loosely in clean kitchen towels; refrigerate in plastic bags until serving time.

2 In a mixing bowl, combine the mustard, lemon juice, salt, and pepper; whisk to blend. Whisking constantly, gradually add the oil, by droplets at first and then in a thin stream, to make an emulsified vinaigrette. Cover and set aside.

3 When ready to serve, place the chilled greens in a large salad bowl. Add about half the dressing and toss to mix. Gradually add as much of the remaining dressing as is needed to coat the leaves lightly and evenly; toss the salad well. Season with additional salt and pepper, if necessary, and serve at once.

Warm Compote of Autumn Fruits

SERVES 10 TO 12

8 ounces pitted sweet prunes
6 ounces dried apricots, preferably California apricots
6 ounces dried apples
6 ounces dried peaches
6 ounces dried pears
Super fine sugar
½ to ¾ cup Armagnac
Armagnac Ice Cream (recipe follows), for serving

1 Using kitchen shears, cut the prunes, apricots, and apples in half and cut the peaches and pears in thirds or quarters; dip the blades of the shears in hot water frequently to prevent sticking. In a large heavy non-reactive pot, combine the dried fruit with water to cover by about 3 inches. Bring to a boil. Reduce the heat to moderate and simmer, uncovered, until the fruit is soft and very tender, about 20 minutes. Remove from the heat and let cool, stirring occasionally, for 30 minutes.

2 Transfer the stewed fruit and cooking liquid to a large serving bowl and stir in sugar to taste; this dessert should not be overly sweet. Add ½ cup of the Armagnac; its strong alcoholic flavor will mellow as the compote base ripens. Mix well. Cover and refrigerate for 1 to 3 days. Let come to room temperature before proceeding.

3 Shortly before serving, reheat the compote in a microwave oven or a slow conventional oven. Add a little more sugar and/or Armagnac, if necessary, and stir gently but well. Serve warm, not hot, topping each portion with a scoop of Armagnac Ice Cream.

Armagnac Ice Cream

People who say they can't stand boozy ice cream won't be able to resist this subtle variation on vanilla. They'll put away two bowls full while they're wondering what it is. MAKES ABOUT 1 QUART

2 cups heavy cream
1 cup milk
½ cup sugar
Pinch of coarse (kosher) salt
3 large egg yolks
1 teaspoon vanilla extract
3 tablespoons Armagnac

1 In a heavy medium saucepan, combine the cream, milk, sugar, and salt. Cook over moderate heat, stirring frequently, until the sugar dissolves and the mixture is hot, 6 to 8 minutes.

2 In a large bowl, beat the egg yolks lightly. Gradually whisk in the hot cream mixture in a thin stream. Return the mixture to the saucepan and cook over moderately low heat, stirring constantly, until the custard thickens enough to lightly coat the back of a metal spoon, 5 to 7 minutes. (Do not let the temperature exceed 180 degrees or you will have scrambled eggs instead of custard.)

3 Strain the custard into a metal bowl. Set the bowl in a basin of cold water and ice and let stand, stirring occasionally, until the custard has cooled to room temperature. Stir in the vanilla extract and the Armagnac. Cover and refrigerate for at least 4 hours, or until very cold.

4 Pour the chilled custard into an ice-cream maker and freeze according to the manufacturer's instructions. Let the ice cream soften slightly before serving.

BARBECUE IN A BLIZZARD

▲▲▲▲▲▲▲▲▲▲▲▲▲▲▲▲▲▲▲▲▲▲▲▲▲▲▲▲▲▲▲▲

North Carolina Chopped Barbecue
Sassy Slaw
Smallville Potato Salad
My Blue Heavenly Corn Bread
▲
Frozen Fruit Salad

▼

Wanting the best of everything, I wait till everything is at its best. I don't buy corn on the cob when I have to put on a coat to go get it. And I won't eat tomatoes until they're good enough to make a whole meal of. So I know what Alice Waters means when she writes in her *Chez Panisse Cookbook,* "My definition of freshness is that the perfect little lettuces are hand-picked from the hillside garden and served within a few hours."

But, hey, just because it's a snowy February night in Manhattan is no reason not to have a barbecue.

I'm not talking ribs with onion loaf or a chicken you pour sauce over and stick in the microwave; I'm talking *barbecue.* North Carolina chopped barbecue. Have some while you're waiting for those little lettuces to grow.

▲

North Carolina Chopped Barbecue

Nothing could be finer. And it can be made a month in advance. And it's actually very simple to make: Let it simmer for two and one-half hours, then let it roast for two hours, then (when it's falling apart anyway) chop it up and mix it with sauce. Just allow enough time to simmer, roast, chop, and sauce in one continuous process. If you let the meat get cold or dry out between steps, it will not absorb the sauces properly or have the texture of authentic Tarheel barbecue. SERVES 12 TO 15

2 pork picnic shoulder roasts, 6 pounds each, bone in, rind removed
12 cloves garlic, peeled
3 cups cider vinegar

MOPPING SAUCE

The 12 garlic cloves that cooked with the pork
1 teaspoon coarse (kosher) salt
¼ cup reserved pork-simmering liquid
¾ teaspoon sugar
1 tablespoon cayenne
¼ teaspoon freshly ground black pepper
3½ cups cider vinegar

MIXING SAUCE

1½ cups reserved Mopping Sauce
¼ cup reserved pork-simmering liquid
⅓ cup smoky-flavored barbecue sauce (see Note)
Salt
Hot-pepper sauce, for seasoning at table

1 Place the roasts, the garlic, and the 3 cups of vinegar in a very large deep stockpot or flameproof casserole. (If necessary, divide the roasts, garlic, and vinegar evenly between 2 smaller pots.) Add water to cover by at least 2 inches and bring to a boil over high heat. Reduce the heat, partially cover, and simmer for 2½ hours, adding boiling water as needed to keep the meat covered.

(Continued)

2 Remove the roasts from the pot, reserving the cooked garlic cloves and ½ cup of the pork-simmering liquid. Place the roasts on a rack in a large roasting pan. Preheat the oven to 350 degrees.

3 Meanwhile, prepare the Mopping Sauce. In a large bowl, mash the cooked garlic to a paste with the salt. Add ¼ cup of the reserved pork-simmering liquid, the sugar, cayenne, pepper, and 3½ cups of vinegar and mix well. Remove 1½ cups of the Mopping Sauce and set it aside to be used later in the Mixing Sauce.

4 Use the remaining Mopping Sauce to baste the pork as it roasts. With a clean new dishmop or paintbrush, baste the roasts with Mopping Sauce and place them in the 350-degree oven. Immediately reduce the heat to 300 degrees. Cook for 2 hours, basting every 15 minutes and turning once or twice. Use all of the Mopping Sauce (but none of the reserved Mopping Sauce).

5 Remove the pork from the oven and transfer to a large chopping board. Spoon or pour all fat out of the roasting pan and set the pan aside. Do not wash it. The pork roasts should be a little crusty on the outside and very tender and moist inside. Discard the bones and remove any fat. With a heavy large knife, chop/shred the lean pork fairly fine. Transfer to a large bowl and cover loosely to keep warm and moist.

6 Proceed immediately to make the Mixing Sauce. Place the empty, unwashed roasting pan over very low heat and add ½ cup of the reserved Mopping Sauce. Scrape the pan to loosen caramelized juices and browned bits, stirring quickly and constantly so none of the flavorful liquid evaporates. Pour every last drop of this "essence of barbecue" back into the remaining reserved Mopping Sauce. Add the ¼ cup of reserved pork-simmering liquid. Stir in the smoky-flavored barbecue sauce and season with salt to taste. This Mixing Sauce will mellow considerably as the barbecue "ripens."

7 Add half the Mixing Sauce to the chopped pork and mix well. Gradually blend in the remaining Mixing Sauce. Let cool, cover tightly, and refrigerate for at least 12 hours to let the flavor develop. *(Chopped barbecue can be prepared in advance and refrigerated for up to 2 days, or frozen for up to 2 months.)* Let return to room temperature before reheating, covered, in a microwave oven or a 300-degree conventional oven. Adjust the seasonings as necessary and serve hot. Cole slaw—or my version of it, Sassy Slaw—is traditional with chopped barbecue, and hot-pepper sauce is a must.

NOTE Real barbecue is, of course, cooked over an open pit of hickory coals, but this is difficult to manage in my living room. A good-quality bottled smoky-flavored barbecue sauce, used sparingly and only as a seasoning, gives the Mixing Sauce an authentic Tarheel tang. Look for one that's got a good balance of heat and smoke and isn't too sweet.

Sassy Slaw

Get this pretty, peppery salad ready twenty-four to forty-eight hours in advance. It's so good that I once made it for two hundred people—and so easy that I *still* love to make it. SERVES 10 TO 12

2 pounds green cabbage, cored and shredded
1 small turnip, peeled and shredded
2 carrots, peeled and shredded
4 red radishes, chopped
⅔ cup finely chopped red onions
¼ cup very finely chopped flat-leaf parsley
3 tablespoons minced fresh dill
1 cup mayonnaise
½ cup cider vinegar
1 teaspoon sugar, preferably superfine
¼ teaspoon freshly ground black pepper
⅛ teaspoon freshly ground white pepper
¼ to ½ teaspoon hot-red-pepper flakes
½ teaspoon coarse (kosher) salt

1 In a large salad bowl, toss together the cabbage, turnip, carrots, radishes, red onions, parsley, and dill.

2 In a small bowl, whisk together the mayonnaise, vinegar, sugar, black pepper, white pepper, hot red pepper, and salt. Add this dressing to the slaw and toss, mixing very thoroughly. Add additional salt to taste and toss again. Cover and refrigerate, stirring occasionally, for 24 to 48 hours. (The longer it stands, the creamier and more peppery the slaw becomes.) Just before serving, adjust the seasonings if necessary and stir again.

Smallville Potato Salad

By the time my husband and I got around to writing our third Superman movie, Clark Kent was going home for his class reunion. One of the dishes on the menu at that Smallville High dinner dance was an old-fashioned all-American potato salad just like this. SERVES 12

4½ pounds red or white new potatoes
2 teaspoons coarse (kosher) salt
1½ cups mayonnaise
1½ tablespoons Dijon mustard
6 tablespoons pickle juice from a jar of bread-and-butter pickles
¾ teaspoon dry mustard
¼ teaspoon cayenne
¾ cup chopped red and/or green bell peppers
¾ cup chopped celery
⅓ cup finely chopped red onions
Freshly ground black pepper
4 hard-boiled large eggs, roughly chopped
3 tablespoons finely chopped flat-leaf parsley, for garnish

1 Scrub but do not peel the potatoes and steam or boil just until tender when pierced with a skewer or small sharp knife. Drain well.

2 While they are still hot, peel the potatoes and cut them into approximately ¾-inch cubes. In a serving bowl large enough to hold all the ingredients, toss the warm potatoes with 1½ teaspoons salt; set aside to cool. (If necessary, divide the potatoes and other ingredients between 2 smaller bowls.)

3 In a small mixing bowl, whisk the mayonnaise, Dijon mustard, pickle juice, dry mustard, and cayenne together to make a dressing.

4 Add the chopped peppers, celery, and onions to the bowl of potatoes and toss together. Stir in the dressing, mix well, and season with salt and pepper to taste. Gently fold in the chopped eggs. (*The salad can be prepared up to 1 day ahead. Cover and refrigerate, but remove from the refrigerator 1 to 2 hours before serving; like most potato salads, this is better slightly cool than very cold.*) Adjust the seasoning if necessary and sprinkle with chopped parsley before serving.

My Blue Heavenly Corn Bread

*U*nlike orange beets, golden raspberries, and green bagels, blue cornmeal is not a novelty. Native Americans have been growing, drying, and grinding blue corn in the Southwest for centuries. It makes pricey packaged corn chips, but in home-baked bread it comes into its own—rich and moist with a tender crumb and a deep earthy flavor. It keeps well too, and can be baked, cut, and buttered in advance and then quickly reheated as explained in the recipe.

This corn bread is also delicious when made with white or yellow cornmeal, especially with white water-ground cornmeal.

MAKES 2 EIGHT-INCH PANS (18 PIECES)

2 cups flour
2 cups blue cornmeal (see Note)
2 tablespoons plus 2 teaspoons baking powder
¼ cup sugar
2 teaspoons coarse (kosher) salt
3 cups milk
4 large eggs, lightly beaten
8 tablespoons (1 stick) unsalted butter, melted
Butter, at room temperature, to butter the corn bread after baking

1 Preheat the oven to 425 degrees. Sift the flour, cornmeal, baking powder, sugar, and salt into a large mixing bowl. Add the milk and eggs and stir just until blended; do not overmix. Stir in the melted butter.

2 Pour the batter into 2 well-buttered 8-inch square cake pans. Bake for about 25 minutes or until a tester comes out clean and the surface of the corn bread shows irregular patches of golden brown. Cool the pans on a rack for 5 minutes. Serve immediately. *(At this point, the corn bread can be prepared for serving later: Run a knife around the sides of the first pan and invert the corn bread onto a large flat plate. With a bread knife, cut the bread in half horizontally; carefully lift off the top layer and set aside. Spread the bottom layer with softened butter. Carefully put the layers together again and cut the corn bread into 9 squares. Place the baking pan upside down over the plate, covering the squares, and invert to return the corn bread to the pan. Repeat this process with the second pan. Let both pans cool to room temperature, then cover snugly with aluminum foil. Set aside in a cool place for up to 6 hours, or refrigerate for up to 24 hours and then bring back to room temperature. About 30 minutes before serving, preheat the oven to 325 degrees. Place the foil-covered pans of corn bread in the oven for about 10 minutes, or until heated through.)*

NOTE Blue cornmeal is available in specialty food stores and can also be mail-ordered from Blue Corn Connection, 8812 Fourth Street, NW, Albuquerque, NM.

Frozen Fruit Salad

We called it frozen fruit salad, but my favorite teenage dessert (circa 1955) was actually semi-frozen. This was my mother's inspired improvement on the more common "Five-Cup Salad," which was made with (ugh) canned mandarin oranges instead of peaches and which was merely cold rather than elegantly icy.

You will not believe how good this is. I mean, you could serve this to people from France. Just put out the garbage before they come so they don't see the cans. MAKES ABOUT 12 SERVINGS

3 cans (8 ounces each) sliced elberta peaches, drained
3 cans (8 ounces each) crushed pineapple, drained
3 cups shredded sweetened coconut
3 cups miniature white marshmallows
3 cups sour cream

1 Cut the peaches into pieces a little smaller than the marshmallows. In a large freezer-proof serving bowl, combine the peaches, pineapple, coconut, and marshmallows. Add the sour cream and mix well. Cover and refrigerate for at least 6 hours or overnight, allowing the flavors to blend and the marshmallows to soften.

2 At this point, you have two choices. You can place the bowl in the freezer, stirring occasionally, until the fruit salad is semi-frozen—not hard but frosty and a little crunchy-chewy (especially the coconut shreds) —and then serve it right away. Or you can leave the fruit salad in the freezer to freeze solid and then let it thaw to a semi-frozen state before serving. I prefer the first method but sometimes find it more convenient to follow the second. Either way, you'll have to figure out the exact timing for yourself because it depends on what kind of bowl you're using and how cold your particular refrigerator and your particular freezer are; make it once and you'll know.

GRECIAN HARMONIES

▲▲▲▲▲▲▲▲▲▲▲▲▲▲▲▲▲▲▲▲▲▲▲▲▲▲▲▲▲▲▲▲▲▲▲▲▲

*Taramasalata with Fennel and
Cucumbers*

Lemon Veal Meatballs

▲

Pastitsio

Mixed Green Salad

*Carrot, Orange, and
Pomegranate Salad*

▲

Paula's Black Grape Ice

▼

In every Greek home and in good Greek restaurants, it is a pleasure to see the cook eagerly watching over his pots and kettles.
Such a sight recalls Athenaeus' description of an ancient cook
teaching his apprentices (all cooks should read Athenaeus for real
inspiration):

> I sit nearby and . . . explain principles and result . . .
> "Play fortissimo with the fire. Make the tempo even. The
> first dish is not simmering in tune with the others next
> it" . . . You see, I serve no course without study, I min-
> gle all in a harmonious scale . . . Some things are related
> to each other by fourths, by fifths, or by octaves. These
> I join by their own proper intervals and weave them in
> a series of appropriate courses . . . "What are you join-
> ing that to?" "What are you going to mix with that?"
> "Look out, you are pulling a discordant string."
>
> —VILMA LIACOURAS CHANTILES,
> *The Food of Greece*

The harmonies of home cooking are less grand and less studied than
those of haute cuisine but no less satisfying. Here, everything—the colors
on the plate, the vibrant tastes, the varied textures—everything is *anala-*
gos, in proportion and beautifully balanced.

▲

Taramasalata

This pale pink carp roe dip is rich but light, whetting the appetite for what's to come. MAKES ABOUT 3½ CUPS

8 slices day-old homestyle white bread, crusts removed
½ small yellow onion, peeled and cut into chunks
6 ounces tarama (see Note)
1 cup mild olive oil
6 tablespoons fresh lemon juice
3 tablespoons heavy cream
2 tablespoons finely chopped red onion
Greek olives, for garnish
Cucumber slices, for dunking
Fennel, cut into small squares, for dunking

1 Tear each slice of bread into 2 or 3 pieces. Put the bread in a small bowl, sprinkle with water, and let soak until soft and moist. Squeeze out excess water.

2 In a food processor fitted with the steel blade, process the yellow onion until finely chopped. Add the bread and the tarama and process to a smooth paste. With the motor running, slowly add ⅔ cup of the olive oil in a thin steady stream. Continue processing while slowly drizzling the lemon juice and then the remaining olive oil through the feed tube; the taramasalata will develop the consistency of a thick mayonnaise.

3 Transfer to a large bowl. Whisk in the cream, 1 tablespoon at a time, to lighten the taramasalata. Fold in the chopped red onion. Cover tightly and refrigerate for at least 4 hours, or overnight if possible. *(The recipe can be prepared up to 2 days in advance.)* Garnish with Greek olives and serve with cucumber slices and small squares of fennel for dunking. Or, for a large gathering, use a pastry bag to pipe the taramasalata onto pieces of cucumber and fennel. Leftover taramasalata will keep in the refrigerator for up to a week (try a big dollop in a freshly baked potato for lunch.)

(Continued)

NOTE Tarama is salted carp roe, an inexpensive "caviar" of tiny orange eggs that is sold in jars in specialty food stores and Middle Eastern markets and scooped from wooden tubs in old-fashioned Greek groceries. Because tarama is highly salted, it will keep for at least a month in a tightly covered and refrigerated container.

LESLIE
NEWMAN

Lemon Veal Meatballs

MAKES 50 TO 60 ONE-INCH MEATBALLS

2 pounds ground veal
1/2 cup finely chopped onions
1/2 cup fresh breadcrumbs
2 tablespoons finely chopped flat-leaf parsley
2 tablespoons finely chopped fresh dill
1/2 teaspoon freshly grated lemon zest
1/2 teaspoon ground coriander
1 teaspoon coarse (kosher) salt, or to taste
1/4 teaspoon freshly ground black pepper
2 large eggs, lightly beaten
4 tablespoons mild olive oil
1/2 lemon

1 In a large bowl, break up the meat, loosening it with your fingers. Scatter the onions, breadcrumbs, parsley, dill, and lemon zest over the meat; toss lightly, just to distribute the ingredients evenly. Sprinkle with the ground coriander, salt, and pepper. Add the beaten eggs. Using your hands, mix gently but well. Cover and refrigerate for 24 hours.

2 Shape into 1-inch balls that are light but compact (loosely formed meatballs will fall apart when sautéed) and arrange them in a single layer on a baking sheet or large tray. Cover the tray with aluminum foil and refrigerate for at least 4 hours before cooking. (*The meatballs can be prepared ahead to this point and refrigerated for up to 1 day, or frozen for up to 1 month. Freeze the meatballs on the tray until firm, then transfer to a tightly covered container; thaw in the refrigerator before proceeding. Thawed meatballs should be kept cold; just before sautéing, lay the meatballs on paper towels to blot up excess dampness.*)

3 Divide the olive oil evenly between 2 heavy large skillets (preferably nonstick). Heat the oil and add the cold meatballs, leaving a little space between them so they will cook evenly. Sauté over moderate heat; shake the pans often to roll the meatballs around until lightly browned on all sides but still slightly pink inside, about 5 to 6 minutes. Turn off the heat. Quickly squeeze a little lemon juice into each skillet and stir. Using a slotted spoon, transfer the meatballs to warmed serving trays or to a chafing dish. Serve at once.

Pastitsio

ZITI WITH GREEK MEAT SAUCE, RICH CUSTARD SAUCE, AND THREE CHEESES

*P*astitsio is the world's richest macaroni and cheese, and this is arguably the world's richest pastitsio. Made in advance for maximum flavor, it is refrigerated for a day or two or frozen for up to a month and then effortlessly reheated shortly before serving. Note that Step One (the preparation of the meat sauce) can and should be done twenty-four to forty-eight hours before Steps Two, Three, and Four, which should be completed in an uninterrupted sequence. SERVES 20

One: The Greek Meat Sauce

4 tablespoons unsalted butter
2 cups finely chopped onions
1¼ teaspoons finely chopped garlic
2½ pounds ground beef round
½ teaspoon crumbled dried oregano
⅛ teaspoon crumbled dried thyme
1½ teaspoons ground cinnamon
¾ teaspoon ground allspice
¼ teaspoon freshly grated nutmeg
½ teaspoon hot-red-pepper flakes
½ teaspoon freshly ground black pepper
2¾ cups chopped canned Italian tomatoes, with any juices exuded during chopping
3 tablespoons tomato paste
¾ cup dry red wine
1½ teaspoons freshly grated orange zest
1 teaspoon sugar
1 teaspoon coarse (kosher) salt
3 tablespoons finely chopped flat-leaf parsley

1 In a heavy large skillet, melt the butter over moderately low heat. Add the onions and cook until softened but not browned, about 6 minutes. Add the garlic and cook, stirring, for 2 minutes longer.

2 Remove the onions and garlic and set aside. Add the beef to the skillet. Increase the heat to moderate and cook, constantly stirring and breaking up the meat, just until no longer pink; do not let it brown. Return the onions and garlic to the skillet. Add the oregano, thyme, cinnamon, allspice, nutmeg, red-pepper flakes, and black pepper; stir to blend with the meat and onions.

3 Add the tomatoes and any juice that has accumulated. Stir in the tomato paste, wine, orange zest, sugar, and salt. Bring to a boil, then immediately reduce the heat to low. Cover and simmer gently for 25 minutes. Uncover and continue simmering, stirring frequently, until most of the liquid in the pan has evaporated and the sauce is thick, usually about 3 minutes. Stir in the parsley and additional salt to taste. Remove from the heat.

4 Let the sauce cool completely, then transfer to a covered container and refrigerate for 24 to 48 hours to let the flavors meld. Remove any fat from the surface of the chilled sauce. Reheat gently just until warm, not hot, before assembling the pastitsio.

Two: The Ziti

1 tablespoon peanut or corn oil
1 pound ziti
2 tablespoons unsalted butter, melted

5 In a deep pot, bring a large quantity of salted water to a rolling boil over high heat. Add oil to keep the water from foaming over. Gradually add the ziti, about ¼ pound at a time. Boil, stirring occasionally to prevent clumping, until tender but still firm.

6 Drain well in a colander, shaking off excess moisture. Transfer to a large bowl and toss with the butter until evenly coated to prevent sticking. Cover and set aside while you prepare the Rich Custard Sauce.

(Continued)

12 tablespoons (1½ sticks) unsalted butter
1 cup flour
4 cups cold milk
3 cups heavy cream
6 large egg yolks, at room temperature
1½ cups ricotta cheese, at room temperature
1 tablespoon freshly grated lemon zest
½ teaspoon freshly grated nutmeg
⅛ teaspoon cayenne
Salt and freshly ground white pepper

7 First make a roux. In an enameled cast-iron 6-quart casserole, melt the butter over moderately low heat. Gradually blend in the flour and cook, stirring, for 2 minutes. Remove from the heat. Set aside until the roux has stopped bubbling and cooled slightly, 2 to 3 minutes.

8 Slowly add the cold milk, whisking vigorously to prevent lumping. Whisk in 2 cups of the cream. Set over moderate heat and stir constantly, scraping the bottom and sides of the pot, until the sauce is steaming but not bubbling hot. Lower the heat and cook just below a simmer, stirring, until the sauce is thickened and smooth, usually 5 to 8 minutes. Remove from the heat. (If lumps form when you make a cream sauce, simply whirl the sauce in a food processor for 10 to 15 seconds and it will smooth out miraculously. Strain through a fine-mesh sieve and reheat, if necessary, before proceeding.)

9 In a large mixing bowl, beat the egg yolks lightly with the remaining cup of cream. Slowly dribble in 2 cups of the hot sauce, beating vigorously. Now reverse the process, whisking the egg-yolk mixture back into the remaining hot sauce in the casserole. Add the ricotta cheese, ½ cup at a time, whisking until smooth after each addition. Stir in the lemon zest, nutmeg, cayenne, salt, and pepper. Scrape the sides of the pot clean with a rubber spatula.

Greek Meat Sauce
Ziti
Rich Custard Sauce
Coarse (kosher) salt
1 cup finely crumbled Greek feta cheese
1 cup freshly grated imported parmesan cheese, preferably Parmigiano-Reggiano

10 Reheat the Greek Meat Sauce just until warm, not hot. Taste, and adjust the seasonings if necessary.

11 Preheat the oven to 350 degrees. Generously butter the bottom, corners, and sides of a sturdy roasting pan or baking dish about 16 x 11 x 3 inches.

12 Spread half the ziti over the bottom of the pan. Sprinkle with a generous pinch of coarse salt. Ladle 3 cups of the Rich Custard Sauce evenly over the ziti. Sprinkle ½ cup of the feta cheese and ½ cup of the parmesan cheese over the custard sauce. Cover with the meat sauce.

13 Spread the rest of the ziti over the meat sauce. Sprinkle the ziti with the remaining ½ cup feta cheese. Cover as evenly as possible with the remaining custard sauce, spreading it into the corners with a rubber spatula. Use the spatula to level and smooth the surface of the pastitsio.

14 Bake in the middle of the preheated oven for 25 minutes. Sprinkle the surface with the remaining ½ cup of parmesan cheese. Bake 20 to 25 minutes longer, until bubbling hot, golden-crusted, and set throughout. (Do not overcook; remember that the pastitsio will cook further when reheated.) Remove from the oven and let cool completely, preferably on a rack so that air can circulate freely around the pan.

Five: Freezing, Reheating, and Serving

15 To freeze the cooled pastitsio for up to 1 month, lay a protective sheet of plastic wrap directly on the surface and then cover the pan airtight with a double thickness of heavy aluminum foil. Place in the coldest part of the freezer (and don't stack anything on top of it) until firmly frozen.

16 Two to 3 days before serving, transfer the pastitsio to the refrigerator to thaw. About 4 hours before serving, remove the pastitsio from the refrigerator, strip off the foil and plastic coverings, and let stand at room temperature.

(Continued)

17 About 2 hours before serving, preheat the oven to 350 degrees. Bake the pastitsio for about 1 hour, or until hot throughout. (Test by inserting a skewer deep into the center; if the skewer comes out hot, the pastitsio is hot.) Remove from the oven and let stand for at least 15 minutes before cutting into squares and serving. Pastitsio is traditionally served warm rather than piping hot, because it is more flavorful when warm.

Mixed Green Salad

SERVES 20

20 large handfuls mixed greens: Boston lettuce, red leaf lettuce, Bibb lettuce,
  watercress, radicchio, arugula, et cetera
1½ teaspoons Dijon mustard
⅓ cup red wine vinegar
1 teaspoon coarse (kosher) salt
Freshly ground black pepper
1¼ cups extra-virgin olive oil

1 Wash the salad greens thoroughly, lifting them out of the water each time to leave any sand or grit behind. Drain well and spin dry. Discard all tough stems and tear large leaves into bite-size pieces. Layer the greens between paper towels or roll loosely in clean kitchen towels; refrigerate in plastic bags until serving time.

2 In a mixing bowl, combine the mustard, vinegar, salt, and pepper; whisk to blend. Whisking constantly, gradually add the oil, by droplets at first and then in a thin stream, to make an emulsified vinaigrette. Cover and set aside.

3 When ready to serve, place the chilled greens in a very large salad bowl. Add about half the dressing and toss to mix. Gradually add as much of the remaining dressing as is needed to coat the leaves lightly and evenly; toss the salad well. Season with additional salt and pepper, if necessary, and serve at once.

Carrot, Orange, and Pomegranate Salad

It's difficult to give precise measurements for this ravishing and refreshing salad. Some carrots are sweeter than others and some lemons are tarter than others, so sometimes you might need a little more or a little less sugar, in which case you then might like a little more or a little less salt. Whatever. As long as all those flavors are balanced. And vibrant.

SERVES 18 TO 20

4 medium navel oranges
5 pounds crisp bright-orange carrots
1½ teaspoons sugar, preferably superfine
6 tablespoons fresh lemon juice
1 cup safflower or peanut oil
1 teaspoon coarse (kosher) salt
2 large pomegranates, seeded (about 2 cups seeds)

1 Using a zester, remove the zest of the oranges in long thin shreds. Chop the shreds into ¼- to ½-inch pieces; cover and set aside. Squeeze half of 1 zested orange and reserve 2 tablespoons of the juice. Place the remaining zested oranges in plastic bags (to keep them from drying out) and refrigerate for some other purpose.

2 Peel the carrots, cut into 3-inch lengths, and shred in a food processor fitted with the medium shredding disk; there should be 16 to 18 cups of shredded carrots. Transfer the carrots to a large serving bowl. Add 4 tablespoons of the chopped orange zest and toss to mix.

3 In a small bowl, stir the sugar, lemon juice, and reserved orange juice until the sugar dissolves. Whisk in the oil and season with salt. Pour this dressing over the carrots and mix well. Cover tightly and refrigerate for at least 4 hours, stirring occasionally. (*The recipe can be prepared to this point up to 1 day ahead.*)

4 Shortly before serving, adjust the seasoning with a little additional salt and/or lemon juice if necessary. Add about 1½ cups of the pomegranate seeds and toss to distribute them evenly. Sprinkle the remaining pomegranate seeds over the surface of the salad.

Paula's Black Grape Ice

My friend Paula Wolfert attributes this simple but intensely flavorful (and beautifully colored) dessert to *her* friend Simonetta Ponzone, who "worked out the addition of the ruby port wine by sniffing every bottle in her immense cabinet of liqueurs after tasting a black grape puree and deciding it needed 'a little something.' " (This taste-and-sniff technique, incidentally, is the best way I know of determining whether a potential ingredient will work in a given dish.) SERVES 18 TO 20

3 pounds black grapes, stems removed
3 cups sugar
1 cup plus 2 tablespoons fresh lemon juice
9 tablespoons ruby port wine
Heavy cream, whipped (optional)

1 The day before you plan to serve, puree the grapes in a blender or food processor and push the pulp through a sieve to remove skins and seeds.

2 Combine the sugar and 1½ cups water in a saucepan and cook, stirring over medium heat, until the sugar is dissolved. Boil the syrup for 5 minutes. Pour the syrup into a mixing bowl and allow it to cool; then stir in the grape puree and all the lemon juice. Whisk until well blended. Pour into two 8-cup molds or metal pans and freeze until mushy in the center but set around the rim. Using an electric beater, beat the ice until smooth. Return to the freezer and freeze overnight.

3 Several hours before serving, remove from the freezer and beat once more. Add the port wine and mix well. Refreeze the ice until firm. Serve in small portions, with a dollop of softly whipped cream, if desired.

COOK'S NIGHT OUT

▲▲▲▲▲▲▲▲▲▲▲▲▲▲▲▲▲▲▲▲▲▲▲▲▲▲▲▲▲▲▲▲▲▲▲

*Hearts of Romaine
with Buttermilk Bacon
Blue-Cheese Dressing*

▲

Steak by David

Roasted Potato Wedges

▲

*Peaches with the Last of
the Wine*

▼

Not only are cookbooks for men inherently sexist (because there are no cookbooks for women), they are also written for the wrong men. The Bachelor/Playboy/Lonely Guy doesn't need all those gastronomic survival guides addressed to him; for better or for worse, he's already learned how to make supper, because he *has* to.

The man who needs help is the man who's happily married to a woman who loves to cook. Suddenly, after twenty years, she has to go out of town for a week, enrolls in grad school, takes a night job. Left alone in front of a full refrigerator, this man could starve to death. Everything is raw, he cries, the shrimp are in shells, I don't know what these leaves are, there is nothing to eat.

Here is something wonderful to eat, a feast noncooks can cook for themselves and those they love.

▲

Hearts of Romaine
with Buttermilk Bacon
Blue-Cheese Dressing

There is absolutely nothing wrong with blue-cheese dressing except that it usually comes out of a bottle, either in places where the waitress says, "Frenchrussianorbluecheese?" or, occasionally, in otherwise tasteful homes where it's hidden at the back of the fridge behind all the Perrier. Sure, what comes out of that bottle is mediocre at best, but that's because what went into it was mediocre at best. When it's made from real ingredients by a real cook in a real kitchen, blue-cheese dressing is every bit as honorable as a walnut oil and balsamic vinaigrette. SERVES 8

⅔ cup mayonnaise, preferably homemade
1⅓ cups buttermilk
3 scant tablespoons plus 2 teaspoons rendered bacon fat, at room temperature
   or slightly warmer
1 tablespoon red wine vinegar
1 teaspoon very fine chopped garlic
¼ cup finely crumbled blue-veined cheese (see Note)
⅛ teaspoon cayenne
Salt and freshly ground white pepper
2 large heads of romaine lettuce (1¼ to 1½ pounds each)

1 In a medium bowl, whisk the mayonnaise and the buttermilk together until smooth. Stir in all the bacon fat, vinegar, garlic, blue cheese, cayenne, salt and pepper. Mix well. You should have about 2¼ cups of dressing. Cover and refrigerate for at least 4 hours to let the flavors meld. (The dressing can be made up to 1 week ahead.)

2 Remove from the refrigerator about 30 minutes before serving; the dressing should be cool but not ice-cold when added to a salad. If it has thickened, thin it with a little more buttermilk. Adjust the seasonings, if necessary, and stir well before using.

(Continued)

3 Discard the tough outer leaves and trim off the bottom of the romaine. Slice lengthwise through the hearts, cutting each head into quarters. Divide among 8 salad plates. Spoon 3 to 4 tablespoons of the dressing over each quarter.

NOTE Do not use a soft or creamy blue cheese. Roquefort is fine, of course, but Danish blue cheese will do, and a good American cheese like Maytag blue is ideal in this very American salad dressing. All these cheeses are most easily crumbled when very cold.

▼▼

Steak by David

▲▲▲

Nobody does steak better than my husband, David. Here, in his own words, is how.

People who don't know me very well think that because I'm married to this great cook I must spend a lot of time "helping out" in the kitchen and doing supportive stuff with salad dressings. People who *do* know me know that all I ever do in the kitchen is say, "Smells good, hon." The only two things I do that relate to the preparation of sustenance are: (1) mix a great martini and (2) broil a great steak. Since my wife neither drinks the former nor eats the latter, I do this mainly for myself and selected friends, all of whom have said, "Hey, man, you make the best martini and/or steak."

Since this is a cookbook, I'll just sip the martini while I tell you how to do the steak. The main thing is, everything everybody says you're not supposed to do is what I do, and I'm right and they're wrong. Like, experts say, "Never salt the meat because that dries it out under the flame." To that I say, "Bushwah." You never ate juicier beef than this. Here's the ingredients:

1 sirloin steak, 1½ to 2 inches thick
1 salt shaker
1 pepper mill

1 First turn up the broiler as high as you can. While it's heating up, making the kitchen smell like something is already cooking even though there's nothing on yet, take your steak out. It should be 1½ to 2 inches thick and it should be a sirloin. Sure it costs. But how often do you have steak? And what's the point of buying a lousy tough cut of meat that costs too much anyway when you can spend a little more and take care of your cholesterol count for the whole month. Right? Right.

2 Salt the steak on one side, liberally. I mean, really salt the sucker. Then grind pepper all over it. Then stick it under the broiler and let it go about 8 minutes. Pull it out. Don't burn yourself. Turn it over and do the same routine on the flip side. The salt. The pepper. Shove it under the flame again. About 8 minutes later, check it. Here's how I check it—I cut into it a little. *Everybody* says you can't do that or all the juices will run out. Everybody is wrong. It's so hot and seared that it cauterizes itself the second you put it back under the fire. I like it medium rare. If you like it well done, there's no point to even bothering to make this great recipe because you could just as well put your shoe in the microwave for all you care about taste.

That's it.

Roasted Potato Wedges

SERVES 8

1 large garlic clove
3 tablespoons extra-virgin olive oil
6 large baking potatoes, preferably russets, scrubbed and dried but not peeled
1½ teaspoons Mediterranean Herbs (page 112)
½ teaspoon coarse (kosher) salt

1 Eight to 12 hours before serving, prepare the garlic oil. Place the garlic clove on a cutting board. Lay the blade of a large heavy knife flat on the clove. Bring your fist down hard on the blade, splitting the clove and loosening the peel; lift off the peel. Hit the blade a second time to smash the garlic into pieces and release its essential oils. Scrape the crushed pulp into a small bowl, add the olive oil, and stir. Cover tightly and set aside in a cool place.

2 About 45 minutes before serving, preheat the oven to 450 degrees. Cut the potatoes in half lengthwise, then cut each half into 3 or 4 long wedges. Place all the wedges in a large mixing bowl and strain the garlic oil over them. Toss to coat evenly. Rub the herbs between your palms for a few seconds to release their full fragrance and flavor, then sprinkle them over the potatoes. Add the salt and toss well.

3 On a large baking sheet, arrange the wedges in rows, laying them flat on a cut side so they are all facing in the same direction. Roast for 15 minutes. Using tongs, quickly flip each wedge over onto the other cut side. Roast for 10 to 15 minutes longer, until all the potato wedges are golden brown and crisp on the outside and very tender inside. Transfer to a warmed platter, sprinkle with additional coarse salt to taste, and serve at once.

Peaches with the Last of the Wine

Give everyone a last glass of the red wine you've been drinking and a dripping-ripe peach to slice into it. Pass the sugar bowl and the spoons.

SUNDAY DUNCH

▲▲▲▲▲▲▲▲▲▲▲▲▲▲▲▲▲▲▲▲▲▲▲▲▲▲▲▲▲▲▲▲▲▲▲

Rillettes of Smoked Trout

*Creamed Herring with Oranges
and Lemons*

Smoked Fish

Hungarian Cucumber Salad

Three Onion Flan

▲

My Mother's Banana Bread

▼

Brunch got its name because it's served between breakfast and lunch and it's served instead of breakfast and lunch.

I serve dunch.

I can't imagine eating anything people eat at brunch until at least an hour after my normal lunchtime. I don't want to wake up and smell the hollandaise.

Hollandaise sauce is what covers the Eggs Benedict restaurants serve on Sunday at "champagne brunches"—as if what sparkles in the glass is always Dom Perignon and as if what happened Saturday night is always worth celebrating on Sunday.

Brunch must have been James Bond's favorite meal.

Like I said, I serve dunch. Dunch is between lunch and dinner, closer to lunch but not so close that you will also have to make a serious dinner later. Dunch is around two, two-thirty. Dunch is when—after you wake up Sunday morning with nothing in particular to celebrate except that the entire paper got delivered and that nobody bothered you while you read it—dunch is what you put down the paper for and make. It is *never* Eggs Benedict.

▲

Rillettes of Smoked Trout

MAKES ABOUT 2 CUPS

2 smoked trout, each about 8 ounces, skinned, boned and filleted
1½ tablespoons fresh lemon juice
Pinch of cayenne
⅓ to ½ cup crème fraîche or heavy cream
⅓ to ½ cup fruity green extra-virgin olive oil
Salt and freshly ground black pepper
Thin toast or crisp crackers, for serving

1 Break each trout fillet into 3 or 4 pieces; place all the pieces in the bowl of a food processor fitted with the steel blade. Process on-and-off 3 or 4 times, just until very coarsely chopped.

2 Add the lemon juice, cayenne, crème fraîche, and olive oil; use the smaller amount of cream and of oil if the trout is moist and the larger amount if it's dry, but in either case use *equal* amounts of cream and oil. (The strong taste of the olive oil will mellow considerably as the rillettes ripen.)

3 Process on-and-off 3 or 4 times, scraping down the sides of the bowl each time. The mixture should not be like mousse but should have a definite rillette-like texture with shreds of trout bound together in a flavorful paste. Season to taste with salt and pepper. Taste and add more lemon juice, if necessary.

4 Spoon, do not pack, the rillettes into an attractive terrine or small serving bowl. Smooth the surface lightly without pressing it down. Cover tightly and refrigerate for at least 12 hours. *(The rillettes can be made up to 2 days ahead.)*

5 Serve cool, not cold, with thin toast or crisp crackers. Radishes, sliced paper-thin, taste wonderful with this terrine.

NOTE Do not try to double this recipe or your overloaded food processor will puree half the trout and leave the rest in chunks. If you are having a large gathering and wish to prepare 4 cups of rillettes, just make the recipe twice. It's very quickly done.

Creamed Herring with Oranges and Lemons

This is the kind of recipe that you look at and you think, this is either *very* good or *very* bad.

Trust me. SERVES 8 AS A FIRST COURSE OR AS PART OF A BUFFET

2 pounds herring "tidbits" in wine sauce (see Note)
1 large navel orange
1 large lemon
4 whole coriander seeds
1 red onion, 8 to 10 ounces
1½ cups sour cream
4 teaspoons red wine vinegar
Salt and freshly ground white pepper

1 Drain the herring and discard the onion slices accompanying it. Put the herring pieces in a large serving bowl.

2 Trim off the ends of the orange and the lemon, and cut each in half. Using either the 2-millimeter slicing disk of a food processor or a very sharp knife, slice one half of the orange and one half of the lemon very, very thin; add the slices to the herring. Squeeze the remaining orange and lemon halves and add their juices. Add the coriander seeds.

3 Using either the 2-millimeter slicing disk of a food processor or a knife, slice the onion very, very thin. Add to the herring and toss lightly to mix.

4 Stir the sour cream and vinegar together, and add to the herring. With a rubber spatula, gently turn and fold until all the ingredients are well blended. Season to taste with salt and white pepper. Cover and refrigerate for at least 4 hours to let the flavors blend. (*The recipe can be prepared up to 12 hours ahead.*) Adjust the seasonings, if necessary, and stir well before serving.

NOTE Jars of imported and domestic brands of herring in wine sauce are available in fine food stores and many supermarkets.

Inspired by a recipe from Craig Claiborne.

Smoked Fish

Since my Nova-and-lox childhood, a remarkable—and ever-increasing —variety of smoked fish has become available in specialty food stores across America. At New York's Zabar's, for instance, the current catch includes:

Smoked salmon (Nova Scotia, Irish, or Scottish)
Lox (popularly grouped with smoked fish, but actually brine-cured)
Smoked whitefish (either pieces cut from large fish or the whole
    smaller fish known as chubs)
Smoked sturgeon
Sable (smoked cod, sometimes called poor man's sturgeon, that
    many—myself included—like better than sturgeon)
Smoked trout
Smoked eel (wonderful, but don't bring it to the table whole or
    normally sensible people will start acting like idiots)
Kippered herring (great with eggs)
Smoked mackerel
Smoked tuna
Nantucket smoked bluefish (moist and flavorful, a Newman family
    favorite)
Smoked mussels and smoked scallops (which I personally don't
    care for)
Black pepper-crusted versions of the smoked salmon, mackerel, and
    bluefish (in all of which I find the pepper gimmicky and
    overpowering)

Smoked Fish isn't just fish, of course, it's all the stuff that goes with it, like:

Platters of sliced ripe tomatoes (no basil, please) and sliced red onions
Little dishes filled with Greek black olives, capers, and lemon wedges
Butter and cream cheese and/or scallion cream cheese and/or
    vegetable cream cheese, as preferred
Baskets of bagels, bialys, onion rolls, and assorted light and/or
    dark breads, as preferred.

In some families, it is also customary to put out a tray of mild cheese, such as Muenster, Swiss, and Havarti.

Hungarian Cucumber Salad

When serving this salad with fish, I sometimes add a tablespoon or two of chopped fresh dill. SERVES 10 TO 12

2½ to 3 pounds long European-style cucumbers, peeled
1½ teaspoons coarse (kosher) salt
½ cup distilled white vinegar
⅔ cup very cold water
1 tablespoon sugar, preferably superfine
Freshly ground white pepper

1 Slice the cucumbers very thin, using the 2-millimeter slicing disk of a food processor or a mandoline. Transfer the cucumber slices to a large bowl, sprinkle with the salt, and toss lightly to mix. Cover with plastic wrap and refrigerate for 1 hour.

2 Pour off the liquid that has accumulated in the bowl and squeeze the juice out of the cucumbers.

3 In a small bowl, whisk the vinegar, water, sugar, and pepper until the sugar dissolves. Pour this dressing over the cucumbers and turn the slices to coat them evenly. Cover and refrigerate, stirring occasionally, for 4 to 12 hours. Taste, and adjust the seasoning with a little more salt, if necessary. Use a slotted spoon to serve the salad in small individual bowls.

Three Onion Flan

*T*wo things are essential to the success of this lovely dish. First, the leeks must be very well washed to rid them of every last grain of grit or sand. Slit and rinse before chopping and then rinse again (and perhaps again) after chopping; pat dry. Second, the flan must be baked until the top is not golden but browned—not as dark as mahogany and certainly not burned, but a fairly even light- to medium-brown; if the top is too pale, the flan will taste bland and insipid rather than rich and sweet.

SERVES 8 AS A FIRST COURSE OR SIDE DISH OR AS PART OF A
BUFFET; SERVES 4 AS A LIGHT MAIN COURSE WITH A SALAD

5 tablespoons unsalted butter
2 cups chopped leeks, white part only
1 tablespoon peanut or safflower oil
6 cups chopped onions
¼ teaspoon sugar
1½ tablespoons all-purpose flour
3 large eggs
1½ cups heavy cream
Pinch of cayenne
Pinch of freshly grated nutmeg
¼ cup freshly grated Emmenthaler cheese
Salt and freshly ground white pepper
1 tablespoon snipped fresh chives

1 In a heavy large skillet, melt 2 tablespoons of the butter over moderately low heat. Add the leeks. Cover and cook, stirring occasionally, until tender but not browned, about 10 minutes. Transfer to a bowl and set aside.

2 In the same skillet, melt the remaining 3 tablespoons of butter with the oil. Add the onions. Cover and cook over moderately low heat, stirring occasionally, for 15 minutes. Uncover, and raise the heat slightly. Add the sugar and cook, stirring, just until the onions are tender and golden, about 15 minutes.

(Continued)

3 Return the leeks to the pan and cook with the onions for about 3 minutes. Reduce the heat slightly. Sprinkle the onions with the flour and cook, stirring constantly, for 2 to 3 minutes. Remove from the heat and set aside to cool slightly.

4 In a large bowl, beat the eggs lightly with the cream. Add the onions and mix well. Stir in the cayenne, nutmeg, and grated cheese. Season to taste with salt and white pepper. (*Cover and refrigerate the flan mixture for 4 to 24 hours before proceeding.*)

5 About 1 hour before serving, preheat the oven to 375 degrees. Butter a 10-inch quiche dish or similar shallow baking dish. Adjust the seasonings of the flan mixture, if necessary, and add the chives. Stir well and pour the mixture into the prepared baking dish.

6 Bake in the middle of the oven until the flan is set and nicely browned, about 40 minutes. Remove from the oven and let stand for 5 to 10 minutes before cutting and serving.

My Mother's Banana Bread

*D*oes the world really need another banana-nut loaf? Yes, if it's as good as this one. This is moister than most and very banana-y, rich enough for dessert but not too sweet for teatime or after school or even breakfast. Before I was "big enough" to bake by myself, I stood on tiptoe to drizzle the melted butter and sprinkle the cinnamon-sugar on my mother's banana bread—and I still like to think those finishing touches are what makes this loaf special. MAKES ONE 9-INCH LOAF

2 cups sifted all-purpose flour
1 teaspoon baking soda
½ teaspoon coarse (kosher) salt
3 large, very ripe bananas
8 tablespoons (1 stick) unsalted butter, at room temperature
1 cup sugar
2 large eggs
⅔ cup chopped walnuts
1 tablespoon unsalted butter, melted
Cinnamon-sugar (see Note)

1 Preheat the oven to 350 degrees. Butter a 9-inch loaf pan. Dust lightly with flour. Invert the pan and tap it to knock out excess flour; set aside. Sift together the already sifted flour, baking soda, and salt. Set aside.

2 Peel the bananas, cut them in 1-inch chunks, and mash them on a big flat plate with a fork; if the bananas are as ripe as they should be, this is easily done and gives a nice texture, thick and creamy with lots of banana bits. (You can also mash the bananas with a potato masher or an electric mixer set on low speed. Do not use a food processor; processed banana puree is too runny for this recipe.) Set aside the bananas.

3 In the large bowl of an electric mixer, cream the butter and sugar together until fluffy. One at a time, beat in the eggs. With the mixer on low speed, gradually add the sifted dry ingredients, scraping down the sides of the bowl occasionally and beating only until blended. Briefly beat in the mashed bananas. Remove the bowl from the mixer and stir in the chopped nuts.

(Continued)

4 Pour the batter into the prepared loaf pan and smooth the surface with a spatula. Bake in the center of the preheated oven for about 1 hour, or until a cake tester inserted in the middle comes out clean. During baking, the top of the loaf will probably crack.

5 Remove the pan to a cake rack and let rest for about 15 minutes. Then, while the loaf is still warm, drizzle it with the melted butter and sprinkle with cinnamon-sugar. Let cool completely before removing from the pan. Wrap the loaf in aluminum foil or plastic wrap and refrigerate for at least 8 hours before slicing and serving.

NOTE To make cinnamon-sugar, combine 1 tablespoon cinnamon and ½ cup granulated sugar; do not use super fine sugar in this mixture—it should be crunchy. Stir until well blended and store in a tightly covered container. When I was growing up, we always had a jar of cinnamon-sugar in the pantry; it was—and is—wonderful on hot buttered toast.

LES BONS TEMPS

▲▲▲▲▲▲▲▲▲▲▲▲▲▲▲▲▲▲▲▲▲▲▲▲▲▲▲▲▲▲▲

*Country Ham Balls with
Hot-and-Sweet Mustard*

▲

Shrimp Étouffée

Steamed Rice

▲

French Bean and Tasso Salad

▲

*Vanilla Lovers' Vanilla Ice Cream
with Hot Buttered Rum Sauce*

▼

Alphonse Picou, clarinetist, born in New Orleans, 1878:

> "Those were happy days, man, happy days. Buy a keg of beer for one dollar and a bag full of food for another and have a *cowein*. These boys don't have fun nowadays. Talking 'bout wild and wooly! There were two thousand registered girls and must have been ten thousand unregistered. And all crazy about clarinet-blowers!"

—SHAPIRO AND HENTOFF,
Hear Me Talkin' to Ya

▲

Country Ham Balls with Hot-and-Sweet Mustard

These tasty little morsels can be prepared well in advance and then just slipped into the oven an hour before serving. I call them "country" ham balls because they're simple to make and have an old-fashioned down-home goodness. But be sure to use plain baked ham here; real country hams, such as Smithfield, are too salty for this recipe.

MAKES 3 TO 4 DOZEN HAM BALLS

½ *pound ground pork butt*
1 *pound boneless baked ham, finely ground*
½ *cup finely chopped onions*
1 *cup soft breadcrumbs, made from day-old homestyle white bread, crusts removed*
1 *large egg*
1½ *tablespoons hot-and-sweet mustard (see Note)*
¼ *teaspoon Quatre-Épices (page 68)*
3 *tablespoons heavy cream*
Pinch of coarse (kosher) salt
Freshly ground black pepper
⅓ *cup dark brown sugar*
1½ *teaspoons dry mustard*
¼ *cup fresh orange juice*
¼ *cup distilled white vinegar*

MUSTARD DIPPING SAUCE

2 *cups hot-and-sweet mustard*
6 to 10 *tablespoons fresh orange juice, approximately*

1 In a large bowl, break up the ground pork, loosening it with your fingers. Scatter the ham, onions, and breadcrumbs over the pork and toss together. Beat the egg lightly with the mustard, Quatre-Épices, cream, salt, and pepper; add to the meat and mix gently but thoroughly. Cover and chill for at least 4 hours; the mixture will become firmer and easier to handle when cold.

(Continued)

2 In a small bowl, mix the brown sugar, dry mustard, orange juice, vinegar, and ¼ cup water, stirring to dissolve the sugar and mustard. Cover and set aside.

3 Form the chilled mixture into 1-inch balls, shaping them firmly so they won't fall apart while baking. Arrange the ham balls on a large baking sheet with a slightly raised rim (such as a jelly-roll pan), leaving a little space between them so they will brown evenly; use 2 baking sheets, if necessary. *(The ham balls can be prepared to this point a day in advance. Cover airtight with a double thickness of aluminum foil and refrigerate. Refrigerate the basting sauce separately. Remove the ham balls and the sauce from the refrigerator about 2 hours before serving, but keep covered until ready to cook.)*

4 One hour before serving, spoon hot-and-sweet mustard into a small serving bowl and gradually whisk in enough orange juice to make a dipping sauce slightly thicker than heavy cream. Cover and set aside at room temperature.

5 Preheat the oven to 350 degrees. Remove the foil covering from the baking sheet. Stir the basting sauce and spoon evenly over the ham balls. Bake, turning and basting occasionally with pan juices, until lightly browned on the outside and cooked through but still moist inside, 30 to 45 minutes. Turn the ham balls in the pan juices and transfer to a serving tray or platter. Serve immediately with dipping sauce.

NOTE Several brands of hot-and-sweet mustard (a/k/a honey mustard and Russian-style mustard) can be found in specialty food stores and some supermarkets.

Shrimp Étouffée

Étouffer, meaning to "smother," is a Cajun cooking technique mostly applied to seafood. Here shrimp are smothered under a blanket of aromatic vegetables and thick, richly seasoned roux-based sauce. That's almost as good as being smothered with love. SERVES 12

4 pounds medium shrimp, in the shell
1 cup peanut or corn oil
1 cup flour
2½ cups finely chopped onions
½ cup thinly sliced scallions, white only
1½ cups finely chopped green bell peppers
1 cup finely chopped celery
2 teaspoons finely chopped garlic
1 teaspoon finely chopped fresh thyme leaves or ¼ teaspoon crumbled dried thyme
½ teaspoon cayenne, or to taste
1 teaspoon freshly ground black pepper
1 tablespoon fresh lemon juice
2 teaspoons Worcestershire sauce
½ cup thinly sliced scallions, tender green only
Salt
¼ cup finely chopped flat-leaf parsley
2 tablespoons unsalted butter, cut into 6 pieces
6 cups Steamed Rice (page 39), for serving

1 Peel and devein the shrimp, reserving the shells. Rinse the shrimp, pat dry, and refrigerate in a covered container. Coarsely chop the shells and put them in a large saucepan with 10 cups cold water. Bring to a boil, then lower the heat and simmer for 20 minutes to make a quick light stock for the étouffée. Strain the stock through several thicknesses of dampened cheesecloth and discard the shells. Return the strained stock to the saucepan and reduce to 5 cups. Keep warm over very low heat while you cook the roux and vegetables.

(Continued)

2 In a heavy large skillet (preferably cast iron), heat the oil over moderate heat until very hot but not smoking. Gradually add the flour, about ⅓ cup at a time, whisking rapidly to blend. Cook, stirring constantly with a long-handled spoon, until golden. Reduce the heat to moderately low. Continue stirring the roux, lowering the heat even further as it darkens, until it gives off a nut-like fragrance and turns a rich medium-brown.

3 Immediately (but carefully, to avoid splattering) add the chopped onions, white of scallions, bell peppers, celery, garlic, thyme, cayenne, and pepper. Stirring constantly, cook for about 15 minutes, until the vegetables are tender. (This is my favorite part because the only thing that smells better than a brown roux is vegetables cooking in a brown roux!) Remove from the heat and set aside for about 3 minutes to cool slightly.

4 Stir the hot shrimp stock. Gradually add 3 cups of the stock to the skillet, stirring rapidly to blend. Transfer the contents of the skillet to a heavy large flameproof casserole. Deglaze the empty skillet with an additional 1 cup hot stock, scraping loose the rich residues in the pan. Pour this deglazing liquid into the casserole and stir to blend. Stir in the lemon juice and the Worcestershire sauce. Bring to a boil, then lower the heat and simmer gently, stirring often, for 15 minutes. (*The recipe can be prepared to this point several hours in advance. Set aside at room temperature. Reheat gently before proceeding.*)

5 The sauce should be thick but flowing; thin with a little more hot shrimp stock, if necessary, and heat until bubbling. Add the shrimp and the scallion greens. Simmer, stirring, just until the shrimp are cooked through and the sauce is piping hot, about 3 minutes. Season with salt to taste and stir in the chopped parsley. Remove from the heat. Quickly tilt the pot so the sauce pools on one side and beat in the butter, 2 or 3 pieces at a time. Turn the shrimp in the sauce to coat evenly. Serve at once, mounding a little freshly cooked rice in the middle of each plate and ladling the étouffée around it.

French Bean and Tasso Salad

*T*asso is spicy Cajun smoked pork, used primarily as a seasoning meat with rice, beans, and eggs. I keep some in the freezer and constantly find new things to do with it—like this spirited salad.

There's no real substitute for tasso, but you can also make this salad with smoked duck or chicken breast or with any good full-flavored smoked ham; the taste will be different (and milder) but still delicious.

SERVES 10 TO 12

2 teaspoons Creole mustard
4 tablespoons red wine vinegar
1/8 teaspoon sugar
3/4 teaspoon coarse (kosher) salt
Freshly ground black pepper
3/4 cup mild extra-virgin olive oil
3 pounds haricots verts or crisp young green beans, tipped
2 ounces tasso, diced (6 to 8 tablespoons)
6 tablespoons thin scallion rounds, white and tender green
3 tablespoons finely chopped flat-leaf parsley
Tomato wedges, for garnish (optional)

1 In a small bowl, combine the mustard, vinegar, sugar, salt, and pepper; whisk to blend. Whisking constantly, gradually add the oil, by droplets at first and then in a thin stream, to make an emulsified vinaigrette. Set aside.

2 Cut the green beans into 2- to 3-inch lengths. Over high heat, bring a large pot of salted water to a vigorous boil. Gradually drop in the beans and boil, uncovered, just until crisp-tender, 2 to 3 minutes for haricots verts and a little longer for green beans. Drain the beans immediately and plunge them into cold water to stop the cooking process and set their color. Drain again and pat dry.

(Continued)

3 Place the blanched beans in a large salad bowl and add the diced tasso and scallion rounds. Mix the dressing again, pour it over the salad, and toss well. Cover and refrigerate for at least 4 hours, or overnight, if desired. Remove from the refrigerator 30 minutes before serving so the salad's lively flavors will not be muted by cold. Just before serving, adjust the seasonings with more salt and pepper if necessary. Sprinkle on the parsley and toss well. Garnish with ripe tomato wedges, if desired.

NOTE Tasso can be ordered from K-Paul's Louisiana Mail Order, 501 Elysian Fields, PO Box 770034, New Orleans, LA 70177-0034; telephone: 1-800-654-6017. Both mild and regular tasso are available, but be fore-warned that these are Cajun definitions; most cooks will find the mild quite hot enough. Tasso can also be ordered from Aidells Sausage Company, 1575 Minnesota Street, San Francisco, CA 94107; telephone: 1-415-285-6660.

Vanilla Lovers' Vanilla Ice Cream

When the good times roll, plain vanilla gets dressed in its sundae best.

People who think vanilla ice cream is too plain tend to overcompensate with too much sugar and cream and eggs while skimping on the flavoring itself. No wonder they don't love vanilla ice cream.

This is for people who do. MAKES ABOUT 1 QUART

2 cups heavy cream
1 cup milk
½ cup sugar
Pinch of salt
3 large egg yolks
1 tablespoon plus 1 teaspoon pure vanilla extract

1 In a heavy medium saucepan, combine the cream, milk, sugar, and salt. Cook over moderate heat, stirring frequently, until the sugar dissolves and the mixture is hot, 6 to 8 minutes.

2 In a large bowl, beat the egg yolks lightly. Gradually whisk in the hot cream in a very thin stream. Return the mixture to the saucepan and cook over moderately low heat, stirring constantly, until the custard thickens enough to lightly coat the back of a metal spoon, 5 to 7 minutes. (Do not let the temperature exceed 180 degrees or you will have scrambled eggs instead of custard.)

3 Pour the custard through a fine-mesh sieve into a metal bowl. Set the bowl in a basin of ice and cold water and let stand, stirring occasionally, until the custard has cooled to room temperature. Stir in the vanilla extract. Cover and refrigerate for at least 4 hours, or until very cold.

4 Pour the chilled custard into an ice-cream maker and freeze according to the manufacturer's instructions. Let the ice cream soften slightly before serving.

Hot Buttered Rum Sauce

MAKES ABOUT 1½ CUPS

8 tablespoons (1 stick) unsalted butter, cut into 8 pieces
1 cup, very firmly packed, dark brown sugar
½ cup heavy cream
Pinch of coarse (kosher) salt
1¼ to 1½ teaspoons fresh lemon juice
2 tablespoons dark rum

1 Put the butter in a heavy saucepan over moderately low heat. When it is about half melted, gradually sprinkle in the brown sugar, stirring constantly with a wooden spoon until the butter and sugar are completely melted together. Slowly add the cream in a thin steady stream, stirring to blend all the ingredients into a smooth sauce. Add the salt. Raise the heat slightly and cook, stirring and scraping down the sides of the pot, until the sauce is very hot but not quite simmering. Remove from the heat and stir in the lemon juice and rum. Set aside for at least 5 minutes to let the rum lose its raw taste and mellow slightly.

2 Over a moderately low flame, reheat, stirring, just until very hot; do not let simmer. Spoon over ice cream and serve immediately. (*This sauce can be made in advance and kept in a covered container in the refrigerator for 1 week or longer. Let come to room temperature, then reheat in a microwave oven on 50% or in a heavy saucepan over a low flame.*)

MY FAVORITE CHINESE SIT-DOWN DINNER

▲▲▲▲▲▲▲▲▲▲▲▲▲▲▲▲▲▲▲▲▲▲▲▲▲▲▲▲▲▲

Cantonese Poached Shrimp with
Chive and Ginger Dipping Sauce

▲

Velvet Corn and Crab Soup

▲

Szechuan Peppercorn Duck Breasts
Eggplant Coins with Many Treasures

▲

Long Life Noodles with
Spicy Meat Sauce

▲

Bittersweet Chocolate Ice Cream

▼

I know people who hate Indian food, Greek food, Mexican food, German food, and/or Spanish food. I have European and American friends who sneer at English food and one Parisian friend who never eats French food.

But nobody doesn't like Chinese food.

And a Chinese menu that includes shrimp, crabmeat, duck, fresh Oriental vegetables, noodles with spicy meat sauce, and homemade ice cream definitely has something festive for everyone. What makes the cook feel festive is knowing that every one of these delicious dishes can be prepared entirely or almost entirely in advance. This is my favorite Chinese sit-down dinner because I get to sit down at it, too.

▲

Cantonese Poached Shrimp

This is a perfect way to poach shrimp for any purpose.
SERVES 8 AS AN APPETIZER OR WITH OTHER CHINESE DISHES

2 pounds large shrimp, in the shell
½ cup dry sherry
3 quarter-size slices ginger, lightly smashed
2 scallions, lightly smashed
1½ tablespoons coarse (kosher) salt
About 1 cup Chive and Ginger Dipping Sauce (recipe follows)

1 Using kitchen shears, cut the legs off the shrimp. Slit each shell open down the back to the last segment and pull out the intestinal vein. Without removing the shells, rinse the shrimp and set aside.

2 In a stockpot or large saucepan, combine 12 cups water with the sherry, ginger, scallions, and salt. Bring to a boil over high heat and boil for 1 minute. Add the shrimp. Let the water come to a second boil, then cover the pot and remove from the heat. Let stand for about 2 minutes, just until the shrimp are bright pink and cooked through. Drain immediately in a colander and rinse under cold running water until cool; pat dry. Cover and refrigerate. (*The shrimp can be prepared up to 1 day ahead.*)

3 To serve, arrange the shrimp on a large, attractively garnished platter and give every 2 guests a small bowl of dipping sauce to share. To eat, peel a shrimp up to its tail section; because the shell was slit open before cooking, it is easily removed now. Holding the shrimp by its tail, dip it in the Chive and Ginger Dipping Sauce. Enjoy.

Chive and Ginger Dipping Sauce

*I*f Marco Polo did, in fact, bring pasta from China to Italy, I am simply and belatedly returning the favor by bringing olive oil to China. A fine extra-virgin olive oil, used sparingly and only as a seasoning, adds depth and richness to this sauce, just as a small amount of Oriental sesame oil can add interest to certain Western salad dressings and marinades.

This is delicious with steamed or grilled fish as well as poached shrimp. And if you feel like crossing yet another culture, you'll find it's also a sublime dipping sauce for sashimi. MAKES ABOUT 1⅓ CUPS

1 cup light soy sauce, preferably low-sodium Japanese soy sauce
2 tablespoons fresh lemon juice
2 tablespoons rich but mild extra-virgin olive oil
1 tablespoon superfine sugar
1½ tablespoons very finely hand-chopped *fresh ginger*
1 tablespoon finely hand-chopped *fresh hot green chilies*
1 tablespoon snipped fresh chives

1 In a small bowl, combine the soy sauce, lemon juice, olive oil, and sugar; stir to dissolve the sugar. Add the ginger and chilies and mix well. *(The sauce can be prepared ahead to this point. Cover and set aside in a cool place for up to 2 hours.)*

2 Shortly before serving, stir in the snipped chives.

Velvet Corn and Crab Soup

I insist that you make this sweet and delicate soup with fresh corn—but only if the corn is locally picked just hours earlier on an August day when you happen to feel like making soup. Otherwise, you are much better off with flash-frozen corn than with out-of-season, out-of-town, supermarket "fresh." And the frozen product is certainly far superior to the canned creamed corn that even acclaimed Chinese restaurants (and acclaimed Chinese cookbooks) settle for in their soup. SERVES 8 TO 12

4 packages (10 ounces each) frozen cream-style corn
1½ teaspoons sugar, preferably superfine
¼ cup dry sherry
2 teaspoons minced fresh ginger
4 tablespoons thin scallion rounds, white and tender green
3 tablespoons peanut or corn oil
1 pound fresh lump crabmeat, picked over to remove any cartilage
6 cups chicken stock
Salt and freshly ground white pepper
2 tablespoons cornstarch dissolved in ¼ cup cold chicken stock
4 large egg whites

1 Cook the frozen corn according to the directions on the package. In a food processor fitted with the steel blade, process the cooked corn in short bursts to break up the kernels; the texture should be that of canned creamed corn (but the taste will be fresher).

2 In a small bowl, dissolve the sugar in the sherry; set aside. In another small bowl, combine the ginger and 2 tablespoons (mostly white) of the scallion rounds; reserve the remaining 2 tablespoons (mostly green) of scallion rounds to add to the finished soup.

3 Set a heavy large saucepan or flameproof casserole over high heat until hot. Add the oil, swirl to coat the bottom of the pan, and heat for a few seconds. Lower the heat to moderate and scatter in the ginger-scallion mixture; stir-fry briskly for about 10 seconds. Add the crabmeat and toss lightly to mix. Splash in the sugar-sherry mixture, give everything a good stir, and immediately add the chicken stock.

(Continued)

4 Increase the heat slightly and stir in the corn, blending well. Bring the soup to a near-boil, stirring constantly, then turn the heat low and simmer gently for 1 minute. Season with salt and white pepper to taste. Mix the cornstarch mixture again and slowly add it to the pot, stirring until the soup is smoothly thickened. Remove from the heat.

5 In a small pitcher or bowl (preferably one with a pouring lip), beat the egg whites lightly with a fork just until frothy. Add to the pot in a thin steady cream and stir gently as lacy egg-threads form in the soup. If the soup cannot be served immediately, cover the pot tightly and keep warm over the lowest possible heat for up to 30 minutes. Just before serving, transfer the soup to a large tureen or serving bowl and sprinkle with the reserved scallion rounds.

NOTE Leftover Corn and Crab Soup makes a lovely lunch or light supper. Let cool, then cover and refrigerate for up to 3 days. Reheat in a microwave oven or in a heavy pot set over low direct heat. Stir well before serving.

Szechuan Peppercorn Duck Breasts

SERVES 6 AS A MAIN COURSE, 8 TO 10 WITH OTHER CHINESE DISHES

4 teaspoons Szechuan peppercorns
3 whole duck breasts, boned and cut in half, with excess fat removed but skin intact
2 teaspoons coarse (kosher) salt
3 tablespoons thinly sliced scallions, white and tender green
1½ tablespoons very finely chopped fresh ginger
¼ teaspoon Chinese five-spice powder
1½ tablespoons dark soy sauce

1 In a heavy small skillet, toast the Szechuan peppercorns over moderately low heat, shaking the pan frequently, until the peppercorns darken and become fragrant, 3 to 4 minutes; it is normal for them to smoke before they darken, but do not let them scorch. Pour the toasted peppercorns out of the skillet immediately, let cool, and then crush very coarsely with a mortar and pestle. *(The peppercorns can be prepared several days in advance; store in a tightly covered container, away from heat and light.)*

2 One day before serving, score the skin of the duck breasts at 1-inch intervals in a deep crisscross pattern, cutting down into the fat without piercing the meat. In a shallow tray or baking pan, mix the Szechuan peppercorns, salt, scallions, and ginger. Roll the duck breasts in the mixture, coating both sides evenly. Arrange the duck breasts, skin side up, in the tray and cover with plastic wrap. Refrigerate for 24 hours, turning the breasts over once.

3 About 90 minutes before serving, rinse most of the seasonings off the duck breasts and pat dry. In a small bowl, dissolve the five-spice powder in the soy sauce; rub the duck breasts all over with this mixture, then cover with plastic wrap and refrigerate until ready to cook.

4 *To serve warm:* About 15 minutes before serving, set the broiler rack about 4 inches from the heat and preheat the broiler. Broil the duck breasts, skin side down, for 1 minute. Turn the breasts over and broil, skin side up, for 3 minutes. Transfer to a carving board and let stand for 1 minute. Remove the skin and fat from the duck breasts and cut the meat crosswise into thin diagonal slices. Fan out the slices on a warmed serving platter, moisten with any juices, and serve at once.

5 *To serve cool:* Up to 2 days before serving, broil the duck breasts on both sides as directed in Step 4; let cool completely, then wrap airtight and refrigerate. No more than 4 hours before serving, remove the skin and all fat from the duck breasts and cut the meat crosswise into thin diagonal slices. Arrange the slices on a serving platter, cover with plastic wrap, and return to the refrigerator until about 30 minutes before serving.

Eggplant Coins with Many Treasures

This is a perfect do-ahead dish for parties or picnics because its complex flavors and textures are best appreciated at room temperature.

SERVES 8 WITH OTHER CHINESE DISHES

SAUCE

1½ tablespoons dark brown sugar

3 tablespoons dark soy sauce

1 tablespoon Szechuan chili sauce

⅛ teaspoon freshly ground black pepper

3 tablespoons dried tree-ear mushrooms

6 water chestnuts, preferably fresh, peeled

1½ teaspoons finely chopped garlic

4 nickel-size slices fresh ginger, peeled and bruised

2 pounds long, narrow eggplants, preferably lavender eggplants
   about 1 inch in diameter

1½ teaspoons coarse (kosher) salt

4 to 6 cups peanut or corn oil, for deep-frying

¼ cup thinly sliced scallions, white and tender green

Sprigs of fresh coriander, for garnish

1 In a small bowl, combine the brown sugar, soy sauce, chili sauce, pepper, and ½ cup water; stir to dissolve the sugar. Cover the sauce and set aside.

2 Soak the mushrooms in very hot water until supple, about 20 minutes (valued primarily as a texture food, they will never become soft). Rinse well, remove any really hard or gristly bits, and cut the mushrooms into penny-size pieces. Rinse the water chestnuts and pat them dry; cut crosswise into ⅛-inch slices, then cut the slices into ⅛-inch slivers. Place the tree ears, water chestnuts, garlic, and ginger together on a plate; cover with plastic wrap and refrigerate. (*The recipe can be prepared to this point several hours before cooking.*)

3 Rinse and dry but do not peel the eggplants. Remove the stem and blossom ends and slice the eggplants crosswise into ½-inch-thick "coins." Sprinkle with the coarse salt and let drain in a colander for 30 minutes. (Salting rids eggplant of juices that are sometimes bitter and reduces the amount of oil it absorbs when fried.) Rinse and pat dry.

4 Line a large tray or baking sheet with paper towels and place it conveniently (but not dangerously) near the stove. Heat a wok over high heat until hot, then add the oil and heat it to 375 degrees. Add to the hot oil as many eggplant slices as will fit without crowding. Fry, turning once, for 3 to 4 minutes, or until tender and lightly browned. With a Chinese mesh spoon or a skimmer, transfer this batch of eggplant "coins" to the towel-lined tray to drain. Wait for the oil to reach 375 degrees again, then add and fry the next batch of eggplant. Repeat until all the eggplant has been fried and drained. Let the oil cool slightly, then remove all but 1 tablespoon from the wok.

5 Heat the tablespoon of oil in the wok until hot, then lower the heat to moderate and tip in the mushrooms, water chestnuts, garlic, and ginger. Stir-fry just until sizzling and fragrant, about 10 seconds; do not let brown. Add the eggplant slices and toss to combine.

6 Add the sauce and stir well, then cover the wok and lower the heat. Simmer slowly, turning the eggplant once or twice, until almost all the sauce has been absorbed, 5 to 10 minutes. Add the scallions, season with salt to taste, and remove to a serving bowl. Let cool completely. (*The cooked and cooled eggplant can be covered and refrigerated for up to 24 hours before serving.*) Serve at room temperature, garnished with sprigs of fresh coriander.

Long Life Noodles
with Spicy Meat Sauce

Next time you go to Chinatown, stop in a Chinese market and pick up a can of bean sauce (also known as "brown bean sauce" and "whole bean sauce"), a can of Szechuan chili sauce, and a couple of pounds of fresh Chinese egg noodles. Buy your pork while you're there, too and, let the Chinese butcher grind it for you; it will be not too lean, not too finely ground, just right for this dish.

Traditionally served on birthdays (which the Chinese celebrate every decade rather than every year), these noodles symbolize longevity and therefore should never be cut. "Zha zhang mein," as the Chinese call it (or "Szechuan spaghetti," as my guests call it), is fabulous food for ten in less than twenty minutes.

SERVES 10 TO 12 WITH OTHER CHINESE DISHES

One: The Noodles

2 pounds Chinese egg noodles or linguine, preferably fresh
1 tablespoon peanut oil
1 teaspoon Oriental sesame oil

1 Over high heat, bring a large pot full of unsalted water to a rolling boil. Gently shake out the noodles, separating the strands. Add to the boiling water gradually, about ¼ pound at a time, stirring after each addition. Cook until tender but still slightly firm, 2 to 3 minutes for fresh Chinese noodles. Drain immediately in a colander, then rinse with cold water until chilled. Drain again, very thoroughly.

2 Stir the peanut oil and sesame oil together. Add to the noodles and gently toss to coat. (*The noodles can be prepared up to 1 day ahead. Cover tightly or seal in a plastic bag and refrigerate.*)

Two: Spicy Meat Sauce

⅔ cup Chinese bean sauce
3 to 4 teaspoons Szechuan chili sauce
2 tablespoons sugar, preferably superfine
2 tablespoons dry sherry
½ cup peanut or corn oil
2 pounds ground pork butt

3 In a small bowl, mix the bean sauce and Szechuan chili sauce; set aside. In another small bowl, stir the sugar and sherry together until the sugar dissolves; set aside.

4 Heat a wok over high heat. Add the oil, swirling it in a wide circle so it coats the wok as it runs down, and heat until hot but not smoking. Loosen the pork with your fingers and add. Stir-fry briskly over high heat, breaking up any lumps, just until the meat is no longer pink; do not let it become dark or crusty.

5 Add the bean sauce/chili sauce mixture and cook with the meat, stirring rapidly, until bubbling hot, 1 to 2 minutes. Splash in the sugared sherry and cook over high heat for about 30 seconds longer. Remove the wok from the heat and turn the meat mixture out into a large bowl. Let cool completely, then cover and refrigerate until ready to use. (*The sauce may be refrigerated for up to 2 days, or frozen for up to 1 month.*) Let come to room temperature before reheating.

Three: Putting It Together

GARNISHES

3 cups very fresh, crisp bean sprouts
2 cups peeled, seeded, and shredded cucumbers, well drained
Chinese hot chili oil

Spicy Meat Sauce
½ cup thinly sliced scallions, white and tender green
Parboiled noodles
Szechuan chili sauce

(Continued)

6 On the day of your dinner, prepare the garnishes. Put the bean sprouts and cucumbers in separate serving dishes; cover tightly and refrigerate until ready to serve.

7 Shortly before serving, reheat the Spicy Meat Sauce over moderately low heat; stir frequently and add a few tablespoons of water if the sauce seems dry. When piping hot, add the scallions and mix well.

8 While the sauce is reheating, reheat the noodles in a covered serving bowl in a large steamer or microwave oven. Pour the meat sauce over the noodles and mix well. Taste; if your spicing seems subdued, stir in a little more Szechuan chili sauce. If necessary, cover and heat the saucy noodles for 1 or 2 minutes longer, until steaming hot.

9 Serve at once, with the three garnishes. Each guest takes some noodles and sauce, stirs in some chili oil if desired, and tops it all off with a sprinkling of bean sprouts and cucumber shreds. Each mouthful is like a kaleidoscope of tastes (sweet, salty, spicy, and bland) and textures (slippery, chewy, soft, and crunchy).

Bittersweet Chocolate Ice Cream

*O*nce upon a time, every Sunday night, people "went out for Chinese." Happy families and unhappy families were all alike, dunking crispy little noodles in duck sauce while waiting for their egg rolls and spareribs and subgum chow mein. Every Sunday night I asked our waiter what was for dessert, and every Sunday night he said, "Ice cream. Vanilla, chocolate, pistachio," and every Sunday night my father said that wasn't worth missing Ed Sullivan for.

This is.

Adapted from a Krön (as in Krön Chocolatiers) family recipe, this is the darkest, densest chocolate ice cream I've ever tasted.

MAKES ABOUT 2½ QUARTS

2 large eggs
5 cups heavy cream
6 ounces bitter baking chocolate
1 cup milk
1 can (14 ounces) condensed milk
8 ounces semisweet chocolate, coarsely chopped or broken

1 In a large bowl, beat the eggs lightly with 3 cups of the cream. Set aside.

2 In a heavy medium saucepan, combine the baking chocolate, the milk, and the remaining 2 cups of cream. Heat gently, stirring, until the chocolate is complete dissolved. Stir in the condensed milk. Remove from the heat.

3 In the top of a double boiler, melt the semisweet chocolate over hot, but not simmering, water. Add the baking chocolate mixture and mix well. Then whisk the chocolate mixture into the beaten eggs and cream, blending thoroughly. Cover and refrigerate for at least 6 hours, or until very cold.

4 Stir the chilled ice-cream base well, then divide it into 2 batches and freeze in an ice-cream maker according to the manufacturer's instructions. Scoop into containers and put in the freezer to "ripen" for at least 6 hours, or overnight if possible. Transfer to the refrigerator to soften slightly before serving.

GUNS AND BUTTER

A Feast of the Mujahedeen

▲▲▲▲▲▲▲▲▲▲▲▲▲▲▲▲▲▲▲▲▲▲▲▲▲▲▲▲

Aushe Keshida

▲

Skewers of Grilled Lamb

*Basmati Rice Palow with
Leeks and Dill*

Spinach Cooked with Sorrel

▲

*Raspberries with
Thick Yogurt Cream
and Orange Blossom Honey*

▼

When my friend Maureen Lambray, an American photographer, told me how she had gone to Afghanistan to cover the Russian invasion for *Time* magazine, and how she had been smuggled across the Pakistani border at Peshawar, and how she had disguised herself as a boy and traveled with the Afghan freedom fighters, I didn't come right back with, "So how was the food?"

But the question would not have seemed trivial to an Afghan, Maureen said later. In war as in peace, hospitality is very important in the Afghan code of honor; the way a host feeds his guests is a moral as well as a social measure of the man. Besides, Afghans are proud of their food. They pay great attention to preparing it, serving it, and enjoying it. Maureen says she often ate with rebel soldiers who put down their Kalashnikovs and AK-47s while they served food on silver platters.

Afghan food is a little Indian, a little Far Eastern, a little Middle Eastern, and more than a little Persian, but different from—and more accessible than—any of these influences. The cuisine uses a wide variety of spices but is not hotly spicy, and features noodles and dumplings reminiscent of the Chinese but also includes a very un-Chinese abundance of raw fresh fruit and raw vegetable salads. Cooks often combine the fragrant basmati rice beloved by both Afghans and Indians with the fresh green herbs beloved by both Afghans and Persians. Yogurt, a staple here as in all the surrounding countries, appears at every meal and sometimes at every course. Tough guys drink tea, as does everyone else in this Muslim country.

But all these tea drinkers and yogurt lovers are also great meat eaters. Pork is eschewed for religious reasons, but lamb is consumed with great gusto, especially when impaled on long, sword-like iron skewers and grilled over an open fire. "If I had to describe Afghan food," says Maureen, "I would say it was both fierce and gentle, just like the Afghans themselves."

▲

Aushe Keshida

GARLIC-BUTTERED NOODLES FROM THE KHYBER PASS

The Khyber Pass is one of the most famous mountain passes in the world, heavily defended for centuries as the essential route between the Indian peninsula and Afghanistan. It is also the name of a storefront restaurant in downtown New York City, where many marvelous dishes are created from a simple Afghan noodle dough. First, appetizers like aushak, delicate steamed scallion dumplings, and boulanee kadu, thin crisp-fried turnovers filled with spiced pumpkin puree. Then the platters of noodles, served with three different toppings: aushe naana, with yogurt and buttermint sauce; aushe gooshti, with yogurt and meat sauce; and my favorite, aushe keshida—a tangle of silky noodles with tart yogurt and a rich drizzling of hot browned butter and garlic.

What makes Afghan pasta special is not the ingredients—egg, flour, water, and salt, the same as any other pasta—but the extraordinary care with which it is crafted. In Khyber Pass's tiny kitchen, Afghan noodle dough is made fresh daily and then hand-rolled and hand-cut as needed. More important, the cut pasta is never allowed to dry out but is cooked while still soft—and cooked not in water but in stock (an Afghan extravagance based on Afghan thrift, since the stock is made from kebab trimmings and bones). The result is a flavorful and exquisitely tender noodle, the best I've ever tasted. Owner Sayed Shah, a former diplomat who fled his homeland after the Communist coup and who welcomes diners to Khyber Pass as if they were guests in his home, was characteristically generous in sharing this recipe.

MAKES 8 SMALL BUT RICH APPETIZER SERVINGS

One: Chakkah Yogurt

2 cups plain whole-milk yogurt

1 At least 2 hours in advance, place the yogurt in a large square of cheesecloth or a fine-mesh sieve. Tie the ends of the cheesecloth together to form a loose bag and hang from a kitchen faucet or place the strainer over a deep bowl.

(Continued)

2 Let the yogurt drain for 1½ to 2 hours, until reduced to about 1 cup. *(This thickened yogurt, known as* chakkah, *can be used immediately or covered and refrigerated for up to 2 days. If refrigerated, let come to room temperature before preparing the Keshida Sauce.)*

Two: Afghan Noodles

1 large egg
1 cup lukewarm water (about 85 degrees)
1 teaspoon salt
3 cups bleached white flour (see Note)

3 Break the egg into a medium-sized bowl and break up with a whisk. Add the water and whisk until frothy. Add the salt and dump in 1 cup of the flour; whisk to blend. Dump in a second cup of flour; using a large spoon, mix well. Add another ½ cup of flour and use the spoon to mix very well, until no flour shows. Mix in the remaining ½ cup flour. In the bowl, knead the dough with your hands for about 1 minute until it is a soft, smooth ball.

4 Sprinkle a work surface with a little flour. Turn the ball of dough out onto the surface. Knead for about 1 minute, sprinkling with a little more flour if necessary, until the dough is like soft bread dough, smooth and not at all sticky. Form into a ball again and return to the bowl. Cover with a clean towel and let rest in a warm, draft-free place for 1 hour. *(After resting, the dough can be used immediately or can be covered airtight and refrigerated for up to 24 hours. If refrigerated, bring to room temperature before proceeding.)*

5 Cut the noodles just before you are ready to cook them, so they don't have a chance to dry out; this is the secret of their silken texture. Sprinkle a large work surface with flour. Divide the ball of dough into 2 pieces. Using a large heavy rolling pin, roll the first piece out into a rectangle about ⅛ inch thick. Slice off and discard about 1 inch of dough from each side of the rectangle (these edges are too thick to make good noodles). Cut the trimmed rectangle into 4 long strips. Stack the strips on top of each other. Cut across the strips to make noodles ¼ to ⅓ inch wide and about 3 inches long. Cover the noodles with plastic wrap and set aside while you roll out the second ball of dough and cut it into noodles.

NOTE For soft Afghan noodles, it is important to use bleached white flour; unbleached flour produces too firm a dough.

Three: Cooking the Noodles

*3 quarts chicken stock, degreased and lightly salted, or 2 quarts chicken stock plus
  1 quart water*
2 teaspoons finely chopped garlic
2 tablespoons chopped onions
Afghan Noodles
2 tablespoons unsalted butter, melted
½ teaspoon coarse (kosher) salt

6 In a large saucepan or stockpot, bring the stock or the mixed stock and water to a boil over high heat. Add the garlic and the onions and boil for 1 or 2 minutes. Over high heat, gradually add the noodles, stirring after each addition. Boil for 5 minutes.

7 Drain well, reserving the stock for some other use, and transfer the noodles to a warmed bowl. Toss with the melted butter and the salt, then cover and keep hot in a low (about 150 degrees) oven.

Four: Keshida Sauce

½ pound (2 sticks) unsalted butter, cut into 16 tablespoons
2 tablespoons finely chopped onions
*2 tablespoons hand-chopped (not minced) garlic, the pieces no smaller than match
  heads*
1 cup Chakkah (pages 243–244), at room temperature
Hot Afghan Noodles
½ teaspoon crumbled dried mint leaves
½ teaspoon Hungarian sweet paprika

8 In a heavy skillet, melt the butter over moderate heat. Add the onions. Cook, stirring, for a couple of minutes, until the onions start to brown. Add the garlic. Adjust the heat and cook slowly, stirring, until the garlic is just starting to brown and is still slightly crunchy. Remove the skillet from the heat immediately and set aside.

9 Spread half the Chakkah in the center of a warmed serving platter and cover it with the hot noodles. Reheat the garlic butter for a few seconds, just until bubbling. Pour the hot butter and the golden brown onions and garlic evenly over the noodles. Top with the remaining Chakkah. Sprinkle with dried mint and paprika and serve at once.

Skewers of Grilled Lamb

When not part of an Afghan menu, these juicy kebabs are perfect partnered with Couscous and Roasted Pepper Salad (pages 107–109) and Eggplant and Minted Yogurt Salad (pages 138–139). SERVES 8 TO 10

1 large onion, peeled and coarsely chopped
3 large cloves garlic, peeled and coarsely chopped
⅓ cup fresh flat-leaf parsley, leaves only
¼ cup fresh coriander leaves
1 tablespoon ground cumin
2 teaspoons Hungarian sweet paprika
½ teaspoon cayenne
½ teaspoon freshly ground black pepper
⅔ cup mild olive oil
4 pounds boneless leg of lamb, cut into 1- to 1½-inch cubes
Coarse (kosher) salt

1 In a food processor fitted with the steel blade, combine the onion, garlic, parsley leaves, coriander leaves, cumin, paprika, cayenne, and pepper. Process on-and-off, scraping down the sides of the processor bowl occasionally, just until the mixture is very finely chopped but not pureed. Transfer to a large mixing bowl and stir in the olive oil.

2 Add the lamb. Turn the meat until evenly coated with the marinade. Cover and refrigerate for 24 hours, stirring 2 or 3 times.

3 Thread the marinated lamb on skewers. Cover and reserve any marinade remaining in the bowl. (*The recipe can be prepared to this point up to 2 hours ahead. Arrange the skewers in a single layer on a large platter or tray and cover with aluminum foil or plastic wrap. Set aside in a cool place but do not refrigerate.*)

4 Prepare a charcoal fire or preheat a gas grill. Season the skewered lamb with salt to taste. Grill, turning once and basting with the reserved marinade, for about 10 minutes if you like your lamb rare or a little longer if you like it authentically Afghan. The skewers can also be cooked indoors under a broiler.

Basmati Rice Palow with Leeks and Dill

A palow is an Afghan pilaf and leeks are a favorite Afghan vegetable.
SERVES 8 AS A SIDE DISH

2 cups basmati rice
2 cups sliced leeks, white parts only
5 tablespoons unsalted butter
¾ teaspoon ground cumin
⅛ teaspoon Garam Masala (page 97)
⅓ cup chopped fresh dill
2⅔ cups chicken stock
1 teaspoon coarse (kosher) salt

1 Pick over the rice to remove any foreign particles and wash it in several changes of cold water until the water no longer turns milky. Put the washed rice in a large bowl, cover with 4 cups fresh cold water, and soak for 30 minutes. Pour the soaked rice into a large strainer and set aside to drain.

2 While the rice is draining, put the butter in a heavy 3- to 4-quart flameproof casserole and let it melt over moderate heat. Add the leeks and stir for a few seconds, then reduce the heat to low. Cover the pot and sweat the leeks in the butter until softened but not browned, about 5 minutes. Raise the heat to moderate, add the well-drained rice, and stir until every grain is well coated with butter, about 2 minutes. Add the ground cumin, Garam Masala, and dill; cook for a few seconds longer, stirring to blend all the ingredients. Add the stock, season with the salt, and bring to a boil. Give the bubbling mixture a gentle stir, cover tightly, and reduce the heat to its lowest level. Cook very slowly, without lifting the lid, for 25 minutes.

3 Turn off the heat under the pot. Lift the lid, quickly stretch a clean kitchen towel over the pot, and immediately replace the lid on the pot over the towel. Pull up the corners of the towel and fold them on top of the pot lid. Let stand, undisturbed, for 10 minutes. (During this time, the

(Continued)

retained heat in the pot will complete the cooking process while the towel absorbs rising steam that would otherwise condense on the underside of the lid and drip back onto the rice, making it wet and sticky.)

4 Remove the lid and the towel. With a large fork, lift and fluff the rice gently. Serve immediately or replace the lid on the pot and keep warm in a low oven for up to 20 minutes.

Spinach Cooked with Sorrel

*I*nfused with spices but not spicy, smoothed with cream but not creamy, this dish of greens has an Afghan elegance that would please even a French *bec fin.* SERVES 8 TO 10

5 pounds fresh spinach, stems removed, or 4 packages (10 ounces each) frozen
    whole leaf spinach, thawed (see Note)
6 tablespoons unsalted butter
2 tablespoons finely chopped shallots
6 tablespoons Sorrel Semi-puree (page 159), at room temperature
1¼ cups heavy cream
3 tablespoons fresh lemon juice
2 teaspoons ground coriander
⅙ teaspoon ground mace
Pinch of cayenne
⅓ teaspoon sugar
Coarse (kosher) salt

1 If using fresh spinach, wash in several changes of cool water, lifting the leaves out each time to leave all sand behind. Blanch in a large quantity of boiling salted water until barely tender, about 3 minutes; refresh under cold running water. Drain in a colander, then squeeze out excess moisture. With a knife, chop into pieces ¼ to ½ long. If using thawed frozen spinach, remove and discard any very thick stems, squeeze out excess moisture, and chop with a knife into ¼- to ½-inch pieces.

2 In a heavy large nonreactive skillet, melt the butter over moderately low heat. Add the shallots and cook slowly, stirring, until softened but not browned, about 2 minutes. Increase the heat to moderate and add the spinach. Turn and stir the spinach in the butter for 1 or 2 minutes, cover tightly, and reduce the heat to moderately low. Cook for 3 minutes, stirring occasionally. Remove from the heat.

3 Add the Sorrel Semi-puree and mix well. Blend in the cream, lemon juice, coriander, mace, cayenne, sugar, and salt to taste. Set over moderate heat and stir until hot. Then cover and turn the heat moderately low. Cook slowly for about 5 minutes, until the spinach has absorbed the cream and is very tender; watch closely, stir frequently, and lower the heat even further, if necessary, to prevent sticking. If the spinach seems dry, add a few more tablespoons of cream but no more than the spinach can absorb. Remove from the heat. *(The recipe can be prepared up to 1 day ahead. Transfer the spinach to a microwaveproof serving dish or to a storage container and let cool completely, cover, and refrigerate. Let come to room temperature before reheating in a microwave oven or over low heat.)* Adjust the seasoning with more salt and/or lemon juice, if necessary, and serve very hot.

NOTE Made with fresh young spinach, this is glorious. Made with frozen leaf spinach, it's damned near as good.

Raspberries with Thick Yogurt Cream and Orange Blossom Honey

This is a personal passion, the only dessert I make even when I'm all alone—though I'm apt to call it dinner then. (It makes a wonderful weekend breakfast too, with nutty whole-grain bread and a bottomless cup of café au lait.)

To serve any number at any time, just put out a bowl of perfect raspberries—don't sugar them, don't even wash them unless you have to—and a bowl of Thick Yogurt Cream (page 142) and a jar of orange blossom honey. Let everyone take some of the cold smooth cream, drizzle honey over it, and scatter tart-sweet berries all around. Taste these things together and you'll know they were born to share a spoon.

O SAUERKRAUT, CREATED IN PARADISE

▲▲▲▲▲▲▲▲▲▲▲▲▲▲▲▲▲▲▲▲▲▲▲▲▲▲▲▲▲▲▲▲▲

*Transylvanian Gulyas of
Sauerkraut and Pork*

Steamed or Boiled Potatoes

*Marinated Cucumbers with
Sour Cream and Dill*

Dark Bread or Rye Rolls

▲

Seckel Pears in Red Wine

▼

This remarkable dish can not only be eaten but also used as a hot water bottle. Housewives usually began preparing it on Saturday morning; toward evening, when it was ready, they wrapped it in a clean cloth and tucked it in at the foot of someone's bed. It served as a remarkable footwarmer throughout the winter months, at the foot of the bed under the goose-down comforter. On Sunday it was eaten and the leftover was tied up in the same manner and again laid in bed. Usually it lasted for quite a few days, both in bed and on the table. It was never boiled, only reheated in the oven. The odd thing about this dish is that it gets better as it ages. As a matter of fact many people prepare it purposely at least the day before, to reheat on the day when they want to serve it.

—GEORGE LANG,
The Cuisine of Hungary

Transylvania is a land of mountains and valleys and forests and, they say, seven hundred and seventy-seven castles; of Hungarians, Rumanians, Armenians, Saxon-Germans, and Jews; of superstition and scholarship, Dracula and Bartok. Long a part of Hungary, the area came under the influence of the Turks, who introduced coffee-drinking and the cultivation of capsicum peppers—including those used for paprika—as well as many more subtle Asian influences to Hungary. Transylvania is now a part of Rumania.

All of this has gone into the pot, and what has come out, for centuries, is simple food with an astonishingly complex flavor, peasant food that inspires odes. One such, by the Transylvanian Saxon poet Sigerius, begins "O Sauerkraut, created in Paradise . . ."

▲

Transylvanian Gulyas of Sauerkraut and Pork

The rich make gulyas with a lot of pork, the poor make it with a little pork, and the Jews (and occasionally others) make it with no pork, but instead with beef or smoked goose breast or chicken pieces or duck. A Transylvanian feinschmecker will tell you that sauerkraut with pheasant is very good but no better than sauerkraut with pig's feet. A Transylvanian housewife will tell you that *hers* is the best of all.

Mine is seasoned with onions, garlic, and paprika, layered with Hungarian sausage and bacon and tender cuts of fresh and smoked pork, and moistened with pork stock, whose natural sweetness perfectly balances the acidity of the kraut. Like most versions of this dish, it can be—and for maximum flavor, should be—made in advance and gently reheated before serving. SERVES 20

3 cloves garlic, crushed through a press
1 teaspoon chopped fresh thyme leaves or ⅓ teaspoon crumbled dried thyme
Coarse (kosher) salt
2 to 2½ pounds meaty country spareribs, cut into 3 or 4 pieces
½ pound slab bacon, preferably double-smoked bacon (see Note)
¾ pound Hungarian smoked sausage (see Note)
8 pounds sauerkraut, preferably "barrel" sauerkraut
4 cups chopped onions
¼ teaspoon sugar
2 teaspoons finely chopped garlic
¼ teaspoon cayenne
3 tablespoons plus 1 to 1½ teaspoons Hungarian sweet paprika
1½ cups dry white wine
1 large bay leaf, broken in half
8 black peppercorns
Freshly ground black pepper
2 smoked pork loin chops, 4 to 6 ounces each (optional)
8 cups Brown Pork Stock (recipe follows)
Rind of a cooked ham, if available (optional)

(Continued)

PARSLEYED SOUR CREAM

3 cups sour cream
3 tablespoons very finely chopped flat-leaf parsley
¼ teaspoon Hungarian sweet paprika
Generous pinch of cayenne
Salt and freshly ground white pepper

Steamed or boiled potatoes, for serving

1 In a small bowl, combine the garlic, thyme, and a pinch of salt; mix well. Rub the spareribs with this mixture. Cover and refrigerate for 24 hours, turning once.

2 Up to 24 hours before cooking, prepare the bacon and sausage. If the bacon has a rind, remove and reserve it; cut the bacon into ¼-inch dice. Cut the sausage into ¼-inch slices. Cover and refrigerate until ready to use.

3 In a very large colander (or in batches), drain the sauerkraut and loosen it with your fingers. Rinse under cool running water, then drain again. Pick up a handful of sauerkraut at a time and squeeze out excess moisture. Cover or bag the rinsed sauerkraut tightly and refrigerate for up to 24 hours, or until ready to cook.

4 In a heavy large skillet, cook the diced bacon slowly until it is golden and lightly crisped. With a slotted spoon, transfer the bacon to a very large mixing bowl. Add the sausage to the skillet and cook slowly, turning once, just until lightly colored; remove and add to the bacon. Add the chopped onions to the fat in skillet and cook slowly until soft and transparent, about 10 minutes. Sprinkle on the sugar. Increase the heat to moderate and cook, stirring, for a few minutes longer, until the onions are golden. Add the garlic and cook for 1 minute. Add the cayenne and 3 tablespoons of the paprika and cook, stirring, for about 30 seconds longer. Remove the skillet from the heat and transfer its contents to the bowl containing the cooked bacon and sausage and their accumulated juices.

5 Rinse the skillet with 1 cup of the wine, stirring and scraping loose any pan deposits; add the wine to the bowl. Add the sauerkraut, bay leaf, and peppercorns to the bowl. Using two large forks and/or your hands, stir and toss the contents of the bowl until everything is well mixed and the sauerkraut is stained and flavored with the juices and spices.

6 Preheat the broiler, placing the broiler rack 4 inches or more from the flame. If the heat is adjustable, turn it moderately low. Lightly oil a shallow pan or rimmed baking sheet just large enough to hold the spareribs without crowding. (Oiling the pan and keeping the heat low are essential to prevent the pan juices from burning while the ribs are browning.) Remove the spareribs from the refrigerator and wipe dry. Sprinkle the pieces lightly with salt and pepper and arrange them 1 or 2 inches apart in the oiled pan. Brown slowly on all sides under the broiler; because the meat was cold, it will not and should not cook through at this time. Remove the pan from the broiler and the meat from the pan. Spoon off and reserve 3 tablespoons of the fatty drippings from the pan; discard the rest. Pour any degreased meat juices into the sauerkraut. Deglaze the broiling pan with the remaining ½ cup of white wine and add to the sauerkraut.

7 Use the reserved 3 tablespoons of drippings to grease the bottom and sides of a 9-quart enameled cast-iron casserole or a similar heavy deep nonreactive pot. Place about a third of the sauerkraut in the bottom of the casserole. Arrange the spareribs in a single layer on top of the sauerkraut and tuck the smoked pork chops in between, standing them bony side up. Cover evenly with the remaining sauerkraut, completely burying the ribs and chops (it's okay if a bone tip sticks out but no meat). Slowly pour on enough hot Brown Pork Stock to come up to the top of the sauerkraut, usually about 5 to 6 cups. Sprinkle 1 teaspoon of the remaining paprika evenly over the gulyas; do not stir.

8 Preheat the oven to 350 degrees. Cut the bacon rind, if available, into 3 or 4 pieces and place them, fatty side down, on top of the gulyas. If the rind of a baked ham is available, cut 3 to 4 ounces of it into large pieces and lay them, fatty side down, on top of the gulyas. If neither bacon rind nor ham rind is available, cut a circle of parchment paper to fit the pot and lay this paper over the gulyas. Set the gulyas over moderate heat and bring to a simmer, then cover tightly and place in the preheated oven. Cook, adding stock as necessary, for 1 to 1½ hours, or just until the meat is tender but not falling apart. Remove from the oven, uncover, and discard the bacon rind and/or ham rind or the parchment paper. Place the pot on a rack to cool as quickly as possible (I hasten the process by doing this near an open window). When the gulyas is completely cool, cover and refrigerate overnight to let the flavors "ripen."

(Continued)

9 The next day, preheat the oven to 300 degrees. Heat the gulyas in the oven just until the spareribs and pork chops are warmed through but not steaming hot. Remove and discard all bones and cut the meat into not-too-dainty bite-size pieces; add to the sauerkraut and mix well. Let the gulyas cool again, transfer it to a covered container, and refrigerate it for up to 2 days or freeze it for up to 2 months. Refrigerate or freeze the remaining pork stock separately. Let stock and gulyas come to room temperature before proceeding.

10 Preheat the oven to 350 degrees. In a small saucepan, bring the pork stock to a boil; remove from the heat. Place the gulyas in the casserole in which it was initially cooked. If the gulyas was frozen, add ½ teaspoon paprika and mix well; if it was not frozen, omit this step. Add enough of the hot pork stock to make the gulyas juicy but do not swamp it. Cover tightly and place in the oven until piping hot throughout.

11 Meanwhile, prepare the Parsleyed Sour Cream. In a small serving bowl, combine the sour cream, parsley, paprika, cayenne, salt, and white pepper; whisk to blend.

12 Using a slotted spoon, serve the gulyas straight from the casserole. Let each guest top his/her portion with Parsleyed Sour Cream. Accompany with very hot small potatoes and cool marinated cucumbers.

NOTE Double-smoked bacon and Hungarian smoked sausage are available at many specialty food stores and large delicatessens and at butcher shops that serve a European clientele. If unavailable, substitute any good-quality slab bacon and Polish sausage.

Brown Pork Stock

▲

MAKES ABOUT 3 QUARTS

6 pounds meaty pork neck bones
¾ pound yellow onions, peeled and quartered
½ pound carrots, washed and cut in chunks
2 large cloves garlic, unpeeled

BOUQUET GARNI

4 sprigs parsley
1 sprig thyme
1 bay leaf
¼ teaspoon coarse (kosher) salt

1 Preheat the oven to 425 degrees. Lightly oil a roasting pan (or 2 pans) large enough to hold all the ingredients. Add the bones and roast them, turning once, for 20 minutes. Scatter the onions and carrots in the pan and roast for 20 minutes longer, stirring once or twice.

2 With a slotted spoon, transfer the browned bones and vegetables to a large stockpot. Pour off and discard the fat from the roasting pan. Add 2 cups water to the pan and deglaze over moderate heat, scraping up any browned particles and caramelized pan deposits that cling to the bottom. Pour this deglazing liquid into the stockpot and add 5 quarts water. Bring to a boil over moderate heat, skimming to remove any scum or foam on the surface. Add the garlic, bouquet garni, and salt. Adjust the heat to maintain a slow steady simmer and cook, partially covered, for 4 hours. Occasionally skim any fat off the surface. (To keep this, or any, stock from becoming cloudy, skim scrupulously and do not stir at any time during cooking or straining.)

3 Line a sieve with several thicknesses of dampened cheesecloth and strain the stock without pressing down on the solids or stirring up the sediment in the pot. Let cool completely, then cover and refrigerate. When the stock has set to a jelly, remove the congealed fat from the surface.

4 Transfer the degreased stock to a clean stockpot or large saucepan. Set the pan half off the heat. Bring to a strong simmer and cook, uncovered, skimming the impurities that rise on the cooler side of the pan, until the stock is reduced to about 3 quarts. Strain and let cool completely. Transfer to covered container(s) and refrigerate. (*The stock may be refrigerated for up to 5 days, or frozen for several months.*)

Marinated Cucumbers with Sour Cream and Dill

6 to 7 pounds long European-style cucumbers, peeled
1½ tablespoons coarse (kosher) salt
1 cup distilled white vinegar
2 tablespoons sugar, preferably superfine
¼ teaspoon freshly ground white pepper
4½ tablespoons finely chopped fresh dill
2 cups sour cream

258
LESLIE
NEWMAN

1 Slice the cucumbers very thin, using the 2-millimeter slicing disk of a food processor or a mandoline. Transfer the cucumber slices to a large bowl, sprinkle with the salt, and toss to mix. Cover with plastic wrap and refrigerate for 1 hour.

2 Pour off the liquid that has accumulated in the bowl and squeeze the juice out of the cucumbers.

3 In a small bowl, whisk the vinegar, sugar, and pepper until the sugar dissolves. Pour this dressing over the cucumbers and turn the slices to coat them evenly. Sprinkle with 3 tablespoons of the chopped dill and toss to mix. Cover and refrigerate for 2 hours, stirring occasionally.

4 Pour the cucumbers into a colander (or divide between 2 colanders or large sieves) and drain well, gently pressing out the marinade. Transfer the cucumbers to a large serving bowl and fold in the sour cream. Add 1 tablespoon chopped dill and season with additional salt to taste. Mix well. Cover and refrigerate for 12 to 24 hours, stirring occasionally. Just before serving, stir again and sprinkle with the remaining ½ tablespoon chopped dill.

Seckel Pears in Red Wine

Vibrantly flavorful but light and refreshing, this is just what's wanted after rich peasant fare like cassoulet or sauerkraut. Seckels are not the only pears I poach, but they are my favorite party pears because they come in individual portions, so to speak, and need not be halved and cored like Bartletts or Boscs. SERVES 20

5 cups young red wine
2 cups sugar
⅓ cup fresh lemon juice
2 teaspoons freshly grated lemon zest
1 teaspoon freshly grated orange zest
1 cinnamon stick, about 3 inches long
20 firm, unblemished seckel pears

1 In a heavy nonreactive 4- to 5-quart casserole, combine the wine, sugar, lemon juice, lemon zest, orange zest, and cinnamon stick. Bring to a simmer, stirring to dissolve the sugar, and simmer gently for 5 minutes to blend and develop the flavors.

2 Peel the pears without removing their stems; shave a thin slice off the rounded bottom of each pear so it will stand upright. Drop each pear in turn into acidulated water to prevent discoloration. When all the fruit has been prepared, drain it well and add it to the poaching liquid. Cook just below a simmer for about 10 minutes, until barely tender. Test by piercing through the bottom with a toothpick or cake tester; when the fruit offers only slight resistance, it is done. Let cool completely, cover, and refrigerate the fruit in the liquid overnight or for up to 2 days. Serve the pears with a generous amount of the delicious wine syrup.

LIKE MOTHER USED TO MAKE

A Pot-and-Pan-Asian Feast

▲▲▲▲▲▲▲▲▲▲▲▲▲▲▲▲▲▲▲▲▲▲▲▲▲▲▲▲▲▲▲

Ants Climbing a Tree

▲

Javanese Spareribs

*Basmati Rice and
Sweet Corn Pilaf*

Thai Cucumber Salad

▲

Toasted Coconut Ice Cream

▼

I am twiced blessed as a mother, but I have never once baked an apple pie.

Or cupcakes. Or brownies. And, although I have two or three terrific cakes in my repertory, I tend to agree with the French that you're either a cook or a baker.

Back when my kids were little, mothers were expected to be both. Every time I turned on the television, June Cleaver had put on her pearls and her apron and knocked off another batch of cookies for the Bake Sale. If nothing said lovin' like something from the oven, Mrs. Newman's babies were in big trouble.

But if I got no Brownie points for my brownies, I could have won all the maternal merit badges for soup-making. Which was not why I did it, of course. I did it because I loved (and still love) soup. And because I could do other things while it cooked, and because, long ago, it was cheap. Back when my firstborn was first born, I made chicken soup every week. For a few dollars, hens who no longer gave eggs would give us beautiful broth and then sandwiches and salads and even baby food for days.

Thirty years later, free-range chickens have driven out stewing hens. Mothers seldom make chicken soup anymore and when they do they call it chicken *stock*.

On balance, though, I think most of the changes we've gone through in the kitchen in the last quarter century have been for the better. Technology has finally really made cooking "Less Work for Mother" while cookbooks, cooking magazines, cooking classes, and cooking shows have made it more interesting and accessible. Supermarkets are selling tofu and masa harina. Today's mother is often a more sophisticated cook than her own mother was, and she is cooking for—and sometimes cooking with—a family of more adventurous eaters.

So what has all this done to our old definitions? Is motherhood still synonymous with apple pie? When my kids called about having dinner on Mother's Day, I decided to ask them. In the last decade of the twentieth century, just what *is* "Mom's home cooking"?

"It's all the things you don't eat at anybody else's house because they're not the same there," my daughter said on a backstage phone in Boston. "Like meat loaf. Or tuna salad. Or applesauce, that's what you always make especially for me."

"Ants Climbing a Tree," my son said in his midtown office. "That's what I think of when I think of you cooking."

Ants Climbing a Tree? Szechuan noodles with spicy minced pork?

"Sure. It's one of my favorite things and I can't get it anywhere else. I always figured that's why you make it a lot when I'm there for dinner."

Applesauce and Ants Climbing a Tree. I thought about it for a while and I realized, they're both absolutely right.

Mom's home cooking is whatever Mom cooks specially for you when you come home.

▲

Ants Climbing a Tree

BEAN THREADS WITH SPICY MINCED PORK

*D*espite the funky, faintly New Wave name, this is a famous old Szechuan dish with terrific texture and taste. It's also cheap and easy and can be made a day or two in advance and then just heated up in a microwave oven or steamer. And you don't *have* to tell anybody that all those little bits of meat in the noodles are supposed to look like ants.

Do not double this recipe; to serve twelve, make the recipe twice.

SERVES 2 TO 3 AS A MAIN COURSE, 6 WITH OTHER CHINESE DISHES

MARINADE

1 teaspoon cornstarch
1 tablespoon dry sherry
1 tablespoon light soy sauce

½ pound ground pork butt
2 bundles (2 ounces each) bean threads (see Note)

SEASONINGS

2 to 3 tablespoons thinly sliced scallions, white part only
2 teaspoons minced garlic
1 teaspoon minced ginger
1 tablespoon Szechuan chili sauce (see Note)
1½ tablespoons ground bean sauce (see Note)

SAUCE

¾ teaspoon sugar, preferably superfine
4 teaspoons light soy sauce
1 cup chicken stock
1 teaspoon sesame oil

3 tablespoons peanut or corn oil
2 to 3 tablespoons thinly sliced scallions, tender green only
Chili oil, for seasoning at table

1 In a medium bowl, combine the cornstarch, sherry, and soy sauce for the marinade; stir to dissolve the cornstarch. Add the ground pork to the marinade and mix lightly but well. Cover tightly, and refrigerate for at least 2 hours, or overnight if possible.

2 In a medium bowl, arrange the bean-thread bundles side by side and add very hot tap water to cover by at least 2 inches. Soak, without stirring, for about 10 minutes, or just until the bundles have become 2 loose skeins of tender noodles. Using kitchen shears, cut through each skein in 4 places to shorten the noodles to an even and manageable length. Drain well. Cover airtight and refrigerate until use, overnight if desired.

3 In a small bowl, combine the sliced white part of scallions, the garlic, ginger, chili sauce, and bean sauce for seasoning. In a second small bowl, combine the sugar, soy sauce, stock, and sesame oil for sauce, stir to dissolve the sugar. Cover both bowls with plastic wrap and set aside for up to 2 hours, or refrigerate overnight until use. *(All these preparations for cooking can be made in advance; let refrigerated ingredients come to room temperature before proceeding.)*

4 When ready to cook, uncover all the containers and line them up beside the stove in order of use: place the oil nearest you, then the seasonings, marinated pork, soaked and drained bean-thread noodles, sauce, and thinly sliced scallion greens.

5 Heat a wok over a high flame. Add the oil, swirling it in a wide circle so it coats the wok as it runs down; heat the oil until very hot. Add the seasonings and stir-fry over high heat for about 10 seconds, until fragrant. Add the pork and stir-fry briskly, breaking it up with a spatula and tossing it with the seasonings just until it changes color.

6 Push the pork to the side of the wok and add the bean-thread noodles. Turn and toss over high heat until stained and flavored, about 30 seconds. (Add a little more oil down the side of the wok if the noodles begin to stick.) Then toss-fry the meat and noodles together for a few seconds, until well mixed.

(Continued)

7 Add the sauce, swirling it around and down the inside of the wok so that it is already bubbling hot when it reaches the bottom. Stir the contents of the wok well. Reduce the heat and simmer very gently, uncovered, until most of the sauce has been absorbed or has evaporated, about 3 minutes. Give the mixture one last good stir, then immediately remove from the heat and transfer to a warmed serving bowl. *(The recipe can be made up to 2 days ahead. Let cool completely, then cover tightly and refrigerate. Just before serving, reheat in a covered bowl set in a microwave oven or large steamer.)*

8 Toss the noodles with the thinly sliced scallion greens and serve at once. Put a jar of chili oil on the table for those who like it extra hot.

NOTE Bean threads (transparent noodles), Szechuan chili sauce, and ground bean sauce are available in Oriental markets and specialty food stores.

▼▼▼

Javanese Spareribs

▲▲▲

These saucy little ribs are easy to make and hard to stop eating. They are wonderful as part of a festive Asian meal or simply served with freshly cooked rice and a crisp green vegetable.

SERVES 10 TO 12 WITH OTHER ASIAN DISHES

2 racks lean meaty spareribs, 2½ to 3 pounds each
1½ cups finely chopped onions
1½ teaspoons very finely chopped garlic
2 teaspoons ground ginger
⅓ teaspoon freshly ground black pepper
1½ to 2 teaspoons sambal oelek, to taste (page 109)
¾ cup ketjap manis (see Note)
2 teaspoons fresh lemon sauce
Coarse (kosher) salt

1 Do not separate the ribs, but have the butcher cut each rack *crosswise* into thirds; you will then have 6 long strips or "belts" (rather like rifle-men's bandoleros), each 2 to 3 inches wide. Cut these long strips into sections of 6 to 8 ribs. Trim away gristle and excess fat and discard any meatless bones.

2 In a large bowl, make a marinade by combining the onions, garlic, ginger, pepper, sambal oelek, ketjap manis, and lemon juice. Add the sparerib sections, turning to coat them thoroughly and evenly with the mixture. Cover and refrigerate for 24 hours, turning the ribs occasionally.

3 About 90 minutes before serving, preheat the oven to 350 degrees. Lightly oil a baking or roasting pan 2 to 3 inches deep (in a shallower pan, juices will evaporate too quickly and then scorch) and large enough to hold all the meat in a single snug but not overlapping layer; use 2 pans if necessary. Drain but do not dry the spareribs. Reserve the marinade remaining in the bowl. Arrange the ribs meaty-side up in the pan and season lightly with coarse salt. Roast for 30 minutes.

4 Without turning the ribs, spoon the reserved marinade evenly over them and cook for 15 minutes longer. Remove from the oven. (But be sure to close the oven door and leave the oven heat turned on.)

5 Lay the sparerib strips on a chopping board. Working swiftly and steadily, cut the ribs apart with a cleaver or heavy sharp knife. Return the ribs to the pan or pans; stir and toss to coat them evenly with the pan juices and sauce. Cover the pan tightly with aluminum foil and bake for 15 minutes.

6 Turn off the oven. Without uncovering the pan, loosen the foil on all sides to let steam escape. Let stand for 15 to 20 minutes in the turned-off oven with the door ajar.

7 Remove the foil cover, turn the ribs in their now thickened sauce, and season with a little more salt and/or lemon juice if necessary. Transfer to a heated platter and serve at once. (*Leftovers can be covered and reheated in a microwave oven or a 325-degree conventional oven.*)

NOTE Ketjap manis is sweet soy sauce, a dark syrupy seasoning essential to Indonesian cooking and especially interesting in marinades for grilled meats and poultry. It can be found in many specialty food stores or mail-ordered from Maison Glass, 111 East 58th Street, New York, NY 10012. If stored in a cool, dark place, it will keep indefinitely.

Basmati Rice and Sweet Corn Pilaf

SERVES 10 TO 12

2 cups basmati rice
6 tablespoons unsalted butter
1 cup finely chopped onions
2 fresh hot green chilies, seeded and finely chopped
4 cups fresh or thawed frozen corn kernels
⅓ teaspoon sugar
1½ teaspoons coarse (kosher) salt
½ teaspoon ground roasted cumin (page 96)
¾ teaspoon Garam Masala (page 97)

1 Pick over the rice to remove any foreign matter and wash it in several changes of cold water until the water is almost clear. Put the rice in a large bowl, cover with fresh cold water, and soak for 30 minutes. While the rice is soaking, bring 6 to 8 quarts of unsalted water to a boil in a deep pot.

2 Meanwhile, about 10 minutes before the rice has finished soaking, prepare the other ingredients for the pilaf. Cut 2 tablespoons of the butter into pieces and set aside at room temperature to soften. In a heavy large flameproof casserole, melt the remaining 4 tablespoons butter over moderately low heat. Add the onions and chilies and cook, stirring, until tender but not browned, about 5 minutes. Add the corn. Sprinkle with the sugar and ½ teaspoon of the salt. Turn the corn in the butter for a minute, then cover and cook gently, stirring once or twice, while you prepare the rice.

3 Drain the soaked rice. Dribble it into the boiling water and stir briefly to keep it from sticking to the bottom of the pot. Boil rapidly, uncovered, for 4 minutes. Drain in a large colander, shaking off excess water.

4 Add the hot rice to the corn in the casserole. Sprinkle with the remaining 1 teaspoon salt. Stir the rice and corn together, mixing well; if the rice seems very dry, add 2 to 3 tablespoons water. Cover tightly, turn the heat very low, and cook for 10 minutes, stirring once or twice. Remove from the heat and let rest, covered and undisturbed, for 5 minutes.

5 Uncover and fluff the pilaf with a fork. Dot with the reserved softened butter and sprinkle with the cumin and Garam Masala. Season with additional salt, if necessary, and toss gently to mix. Serve at once or cover tightly and keep warm for up to 15 minutes in a warm oven with the door ajar. *(Leftovers can be reheated in a covered bowl in a microwave oven or large steamer, but may need perking up with an pinch of spices and/or salt.)*

▼▼

Thai Cucumber Salad

▲▲▲

SERVES 10 TO 12

¾ cup distilled white vinegar
⅓ cup sugar, preferably superfine
½ to 1 teaspoon hot-red-pepper flakes, to taste
¼ teaspoon coarse (kosher) salt
2¼ to 2½ pounds long European-style cucumbers, washed and dried but not peeled
¼ cup finely chopped red onions
¼ cup chopped salted roasted peanuts

1 In a large bowl, combine the vinegar, sugar, hot-red-pepper flakes, and salt. Stir until the sugar is dissolved. Set aside.

2 Score the cucumbers with a fork and then cut them into ¼-inch slices. Stack the slices and cut into quarters. Add the cucumbers and chopped red onions to the bowl of salad dressing and toss well. Cover and refrigerate for 1 to 4 hours, stirring occasionally.

3 Just before serving, add the chopped peanuts. Toss the salad once more and serve in small individual bowls.

Toasted Coconut Ice Cream

There's coconut ice cream and there's toasted almond ice cream," my husband said, one summer day. "So how come there's no toasted coconut ice cream?" There is now. I like to top it with extra toasted coconut and, on some enchanted evenings, to serve it with skewers of grilled pineapple and papaya. MAKES ABOUT 1 QUART

1 cup sweetened shredded or flaked coconut
1½ cups heavy cream
1½ cups milk
2 tablespoons sugar
Pinch of coarse (kosher) salt
3 large egg yolks
½ teaspoon vanilla extract
½ cup sweetened cream of coconut (see Note)

1 Preheat the oven to 325 degrees. Spread the coconut in a thin layer on a baking sheet and toast in the middle of the oven, stirring frequently, for 10 minutes or until golden. Set aside to cool.

2 In a heavy medium saucepan, combine the cream, milk, sugar, and salt. Cook over moderate heat, stirring frequently, until the sugar dissolves and the mixture is hot, 6 to 8 minutes.

3 In a large bowl, beat the egg yolks lightly. Gradually whisk in the hot cream mixture in a thin stream. Return to the saucepan and cook over moderately low heat, stirring constantly, until the custard thickens enough to coat the back of a spoon lightly, 5 to 7 minutes. (Do not let the temperature exceed 180 degrees.)

4 Strain the custard through a fine-mesh sieve into a metal bowl. Set the bowl in a basin of cold water and ice and let stand, stirring occasionally, until cooled to room temperature. Stir in the vanilla extract, the cream of coconut, and the toasted coconut. Mix well. Cover and refrigerate for at least 6 hours, or overnight if possible, to allow the flavor to develop fully.

5 Stir the custard well, then pour into an ice-cream maker and freeze according to the manufacturer's instructions. Let the ice cream soften slightly before serving.

NOTE Sweetened cream of coconut is widely available in cans in supermarkets and specialty stores.

I N D E X

▲